D1130477

JOURNAL FOR THE STUDY OF THE OLD TESTAMENT
SUPPLEMENT SERIES

54

JSOT Press
Sheffield

From Repentance to Redemption

Jeremiah's Thought in Transition

Jeremiah Unterman

Journal for the Study of the Old Testament
Supplement Series 54

Published by JSOT Press
JSOT Press is an imprint of
Sheffield Academic Press Ltd
The University of Sheffield
343 Fulwood Road
Sheffield S10 3BP
England

Typeset by Sheffield Academic Press
and
printed in Great Britain
by Billing & Sons Ltd
Worcester

British Library Cataloguing in Publication Data

Unterman, Jeremiah
From repentance to redemption : Jeremiah's thought in transition.— (Journal for the study of the Old Testament supplement series, ISSN 0309-0787; 54).
1. Bible. O.T. Jeremiah—Criticism, interpretation, etc.
I. Title II. Series
224′.206 BS1525.2

ISBN 1-85075-110-2
ISBN 1-85075-109-9 Pbk

CONTENTS

Acknowledgments 8
Abbreviations 9
Introduction 11

Chapter 1
PROPHECIES OF REDEMPTION TO EPHRAIM DURING THE REIGN OF JOSIAH 23
A. Jer. 3.6-13; 3.19–4.2 23
B. Jer. 31.2-9, 15-22 38
C. The Relationship of Jer. 3.6-13; 3.19–4.2 to 31.2-9, 15-22 53

Chapter 2
PROPHECIES OF REDEMPTION TO THE JUDEANS EXILED WITH JEHOIACHIN 55
A. Jer. 24.4-7; 29.10-14: Authentic Jeremiah or Deuteronomistic? 55
B. Structure, Meaning, and Related Issues 75
C. Summary and Conclusions 86

Chapter 3
PROPHECIES OF REDEMPTION TO JUDAH AND EPHRAIM ON THE NIGHT OF DESTRUCTION 89
A. Jer. 31.27-37 89
B. Jer. 32.36-44 110
C. Conclusions 116

Chapter 4
MISCELLANEOUS PROPHECIES OF REDEMPTION 119
A. Introduction 117
B. Jer. 3.14-18 118
C. Jer. 30.1-17 132
D. Jer. 33.1-26 139
E. Jer. 42.9-12 145
F. Jer. 50–51 146
G. Conclusion 150

Excursus I
AMOS AND HOSEA 153
A. Amos 151
B. Hosea 154
C. Conclusions 164
D. Hosea and Jeremiah 165

Excursus II
THE INFLUENCE OF JEREMIAH UPON EZEKIEL 169

Excursus III
JEREMIAH AND ISAIAH (34–35) 40–66 173

Conclusions 178
Notes 183
Bibliography 203
Index of Biblical References 211
Index of Authors 221

Dedication

לאשתי ,רחל אסתר

'בטח בה לב בעלה'

משלי לא ,יא

To my wife, Reneé,

'The heart of her husband trusts in her'

Prov. 31.11

ACKNOWLEDGMENTS

It would be remiss of me not to acknowledge the debt of gratitude that I owe to those who provided me with support and succor during the research and writing of this treatise.

The wisdom of my doctoral dissertation director, Professor Jacob Milgrom, was of precious benefit. Of no less benefit were the warmth, encouragement, and many kindnesses that he and his wife, Jo, extended to me.

Thanks are also due to Professor Denise Carmody, then chairperson of the Department of Religion at Wichita State University, for her unflagging support evidenced in many ways. Thanks go also to Wichita State University for a summer grant to do research in Israel, and to its Department of Religion for granting the funds for the typing of this study (admirably and patiently done by Ms. Karla Kraft).

Of the other friends and teachers who have stood by me throughout the years, particular recognition goes to Professors Leon Feldman, Howard Lenhoff, Meir Weiss, and Ziony Zevit for their steadfast encouragement. In this regard I must make special mention of the incomparable friendship of Yair Zakovitch.

My mother, Roslyn Eisen Unterman, deserves exceptional acknowledgment here, for, through love and caring, she provided a Jewish atmosphere for my childhood. Finally, to my wife, Reneé, the mother of our children, Efrayim Shmuel and Tiferet Geula, whose faith, love, and devotion sustain me throughout my darkest hours and brighten all my days, this book is humbly dedicated.

Jeremiah Unterman
North Miami Beach, Florida
ערב פסח·תשמז

ABBREVIATIONS

Abbreviations of Modern Scholarly Publications

AB	Anchor Bible
ATD	Das Alte Testament Deutsch
BASOR	*Bulletin of the American Schools of Oriental Research*
BDB	F. Brown, S.R. Driver, and C.A. Briggs, *Hebrew and English Lexicon of the Old Testament*
BZ	*Biblische Zeitschrift*
BZAW	Beihefte zur Zeitschrift für die alttestamentliche Wissenschaft
BWANT	Beiträge zur Wissenschaft vom Alten und Neuen Testament
CBQ	*Catholic Biblical Quarterly*
CBSC	Cambridge Bible for Schools and Colleges
EJ	*Encyclopedia Judaica*
HAT	Handbuch zum Alten Testament
HThR	*Harvard Theological Review*
HUCA	*Hebrew Union College Annual*
IB	*Interpreter's Bible*
ICC	International Critical Commentary
IDB	*Interpreter's Dictionary of the Bible*
IDBS	*Interpreter's Dictionary of the Bible Supplementary Volume*
IEJ	*Israel Exploration Journal*
JBL	*Journal of Biblical Literature*
JNES	*Journal of Near Eastern Studies*
JSOT	*Journal for the Study of the Old Testament*
KAT	Kommentar zum Alten Testament
KHAT	Kurzer Hand-Commentar zum Alten Testament
OTL	Old Testament Library
SBL	Society of Biblical Literature (Seminar Papers/ Dissertation Series)
SVT	Supplements to Vetus Testamentum

TDOT	*Theological Dictionary of the Old Testament*
ThLZ	*Theologische Literaturzeitung*
VT	*Vetus Testamentum*
ZAW	*Zeitschrift für die alttestamentliche Wissenschaft*
ZThK	*Zeitschrift für Theologie und Kirche*

General Reference Works

Neilson *et al.*, 1954	W.A. Neilson, J.A. Knott, P.W. Cachart (eds.), *Webster's New International Dictionary on the English Language*, 2nd edn; Springfield, Mass.: G. & C. Merriam, 1954.
Kittel, 1968	R. Kittel (ed.), *Biblia Hebraica*, 7th edn; Stuttgart: Wurttembergische Bibelanstalt, repr. 1968.
May, 1973	H.G. May and Bruce M. Metzger (eds.), *The New Oxford Annotated Bible: Revised Standard Version*. New York: Oxford University Press, 1973.
NEB, 1970	*The New English Bible*. Oxford, Cambridge: Oxford University Press, Cambridge University Press, 1970.

INTRODUCTION

A. *Definition of Terms*

'Repentance' is not used in this study in the sense of *Webster's* definition (Neilson *et al.* 1954:2112, under 'repent') 'to feel regret, contrition, a compunction for; to be dissatisfied or regretful about'.[1] Rather, 'repentance' translates the prophetic use of the root שוב as a spiritual 'return' (termed 'convenantal' by Holladay 1958:116-157). In its fullest sense, prophetic 'return' encapsulates three sequential steps as are implicit in the call to return in Jer. 3.12-13: (1) acknowledgment of sin (at least inwardly, if not an outward expression), i.e. that Israel has disobeyed God; (2) cessation of sin; (3) the return of the people to the path of obedience and faithfulness.[2] Whether שוב in this classical prophetic meaning can lack step (3) is doubtful. Whatever is less than 'return' cannot truly be called 'return'. It may then take another name, such as 'confession' (√ידה, as in Lev. 26.40),[3] 'seeking' (√דרש, √בקש), or 'contrition' (√נחם, as in Jer. 31.19).[4] The texts in which these terms, and others, appear must be investigated to determine whether or not complete repentance is indicated.

'Redemption' is the spiritual act of God's mercy in reaccepting Israel, which is accompanied by the physical acts of God—restoration of Israel to the land, increase of agriculture and population, reinstitution of the Davidic monarchy, reunification of the people, etc. Similarly, repentence is the spiritual act of the people's will in reaccepting God's authority and manifested by obedient behavior.

B. *Statement of the Problem*

It is an axiom of biblical thought that, in order for Israel to attain a secure and prosperous life in its land, it must be obedient to the commands of God. Once Israel has sinned, and while the people dwell in a divinely ordained state in the land of Israel, they must repent in order to avoid destruction and/or exile.

However, what if the hoped-for repentance is not realized and destruction and/or exile become inevitable? How then is the positive relationship between God and Israel to be renewed? Is repentance a condition of the redemptive process, or not? What role does divine mercy play? On these important religious questions there is a multitude of biblical perspectives. In the priestly literature, confession and contrition are the sum of human activity necessary as a precondition for redemption in exile (Lev. 26.40-41). On the other hand, in Deuteronomy (4.29-31; 30.1-10) and the deuteronomistic (hereafter, dtr.) historiography (1 Kgs 8.44-53) the people must 'return' to God in order to be redeemed. The prophetic literature discloses an ambiguous and diverse picture. In Amos (9.8-15), no human activity is required for restoration. In Hosea, repentance is required in two passages (3.1-5; 14.2-9), but not in two others (2.4-25; 11.1-11). It is strange that in Ezekiel, which is closely related to P, repentance is required for individual physical salvation, but outside of the description of cessation of idolatry (14.1-11; 18.30-32; 20.30ff.), there is no hint that human activity is needed to effect restoration to the land. Indeed, in contrast to Leviticus 26, contrition and remorse take place after redemption (Ezek. 16.54, 63; 20.43; 36.31; 39.26).

The confusion depicted above is compounded, rather than clarified, by the contradictory results of modern scholarship, which are dependent upon the individual scholar and the school of thought to which he belongs. Are Leviticus 26; Deut. 4.30; 1 Kings 8 pre-exilic, exilic, or post-exilic? Is Amos 9.8-15 authentic or not? Is Hosea 1–3 pre-Hosea or not? Is Hos. 3.4-5 dtr. or not? Is the order of verses in Hosea 2 correct or not? Is the order of chapters in Hosea chronological or not? For each of the options listed, there is a scholarly perspective (and the list is only exemplary, not exhaustive).

This confusion is heightened in the book of Jeremiah. In the biblical work which speaks most of repentance,[5] Jer. 3; 31.15-22; 24.4-7; 29.10-14 all mention repentance as a precondition of redemption, but in varying degrees and language. Yet 23.1-8; 30; 31.31-34; 32.36-44; 33 are all passages on restoration which do not allude to repentance. How is one to explain this situation? The obscurity is intensified when one considers that the dominant trend in scholarship is to deny the authenticity of most of the above passages to Jeremiah and to attribute them to exilic or post-exilic editors, such as the deuteronomists. This approach of redaction criticism is more pronounced in Jeremiah than in any other prophetic book.

To investigate the question of the relationship of repentance to redemption in the Bible as a whole, or even in the totality of prophetic literature, if meticulously done, would require a decade. Since all the problems described exist, and are even magnified, in the book of Jeremiah and the scholarship thereon, and since Jeremiah has become a focal point of scholarship, that book has been chosen as the subject for this study.

C. *General Review of Literature*

This book seeks to correct a deficiency in Jeremiah scholarship. Until now no work has been written which investigates in a systematic and in-depth fashion the relationship of repentance to redemption in Jeremiah. Of a certainty, many studies of a general or theological nature have occasionally dealt with this issue. However, they have touched upon the subject only superficially or incidentally. Introductions to the Hebrew Bible, encyclopedia articles, and books on the religion of ancient Israel suggest to the researcher certain lines of thought, but are unable to provide a clear and exact picture of the matter at hand. Often they obscure rather than brighten the path of the researcher. A few representative examples (among an abundance of available ones) will illustrate this confusion:

1. Eichrodt (1967:468-69), in reference to two crucial Jeremiah passages, 24.7 and 31.31ff., comments that[6]

> *the deepest mystery of true conversion* is revealed in the fact that it is *solely the work of God*, who makes the new heart in which inward obstinacy is overcome by obedient receptiveness [Jer. 24.7; in 31.31ff the word *šûb* does not occur, but the substance is identical], just as the prophet has experienced within himself, and continually requests for himself [Jer. 15.19; 17.14].

Is there, indeed, no difference between 24.7 and 31.31ff.? Is it of no importance than 'in 31.31ff. the word *šûb* does not occur'? Are 24.7 and 31.31ff. truly similar to 15.19 and 17.13? Although Eichrodt answers in the affirmative,[7] his opinions are based upon dubious assumptions. He appears to want to harmonize diverse texts where attention to detail is required.

2. In contradistinction to Eichrodt, Kaufmann (vol. 3, 1967:470-71) states,[8]

> The turning-point to redemption will be *repentance*. Jeremiah stirs up the exiles to return to their God and to seek him with all their heart . . . then . . . He shall restore their fortunes (24.7; 29.10-14) . . . after *repentance* will come not only territorial and political salvation, but *spiritual salvation* also . . . God will give Israel 'one heart and one way' to fear the Lord all the days . . . (32.39) . . . The new covenant will not only be freedom from evil, but a cleaving to the good . . . (31.30-33 [31-34]). Jeremiah . . . looks forward . . . to the redemption of man from sin . . . The Israelite earmark of this vision is the idea of *repentance*: even the Divine salvation of the purification of the heart will not come about without *human* repentance . . .

Kaufmann also connects 24.7 with 31.31-34, but he arrives at the reverse of Eichrodt's conclusion. According to Kaufmann, the spiritual return is not God's act upon the people, but is the people's act *prior* to God's redemption. The conflicting views of Eichrodt and Kaufmann require resolution.

3. The new covenant passage has aroused discrepant interpretations in another direction. According to von Rad (vol. II, 1965:213) the new covenant will consist of the same law as the one given at Sinai, only it will be mediated differently. Yet, Fohrer (1972:265, 283) envisions no place for the Sinaitic law within the new covenant. Which is the case? This issue, too, demands investigation.

Here and there monographs and articles have appeared on one aspect or another of the stated topic, but they are, at the best, of limited assistance. Philological commentaries, as detailed as they may be, only infrequently deal comprehensively with ideological problems, even in their lengthy introductions. The more well-known and/or significant works of scholarship will be presented here, although it should be noted that each study must be judged on its specifics—thus, all relevant material will be commented upon in the body of this treatise.

Several studies have been produced on the subject of repentance:

1. Dietrich's work (1936) on repentance in the Old Testament and Judaism attempts an ideological understanding of the occurrences of the concept for each prophet, but without benefit of literary analysis.

2. In an article on the theme of repentance in the OT prophets, Wolff (1951) attempts to define the concept, to differentiate among

the prophets, and even to put repentance in a chronological persepctive. However, this essay suffers from superficiality. In a later publication, Wolff (1978) does discuss the relevant passages on repentance and redemption in Deuteronomy and the dtr. history. That article will be reviewed in Chapter 2, below.

3. A milestone in research upon the root שוב was reached with the appearance of Holladay's book on that subject in 1958. That treatise is a systematic, comprehensive discussion of the root and the passages in which it appears. He isolates and comments upon each occurrence, and refers to the relevant literature. As such, his work is a valuable tool. He does not, however, question the conclusions of scholarship on the authenticity of the texts under discussion (although in later works he does—Holladay 1960; 1962; 1975; 1976).[9]

4. Milgrom analyzed repentance in Amos and Isaiah in 1964 (with a footnote on repentance in Isaiah in the 'post-purge reformation'). Later, Milgrom brought a whole new perspective to the investigation of repentance with his studies on the priesthood and the sacrificial system (1975; 1976a; 1976b). These placed prophetic repentance against the background of Israelite ritual.

A few works have dealt with the relationship of repentance to redemption in particular:

1. Fohrer (1967) published an article on this topic in Hosea which will be reviewed in Excursus I, below.

2. Levinger (1962) wrote an essay on repentance in Jeremiah in which he includes a few pages on eschatological repentance in the book. Unfortunately, he brings together diverse passages without attempting to investigate each against its own historical background.

3. In 1972, Martens produced a dissertation entitled *Motivations for the Promise of Israel's Restoration to the Land in Jeremiah and Ezekiel*, which comes close to the present topic. However, certain key passages, such as the new covenant one, are not considered. Additionally, there is a surprising admission that there will be no attempt to set up an exact, chronological analysis 'because of the disputability of dates for many texts, due partly to uncertainty in identifying secondary texts' (1972:36). This unwillingness to investigate anew the provenience of the relative texts greatly limits the value of Martens's analysis and conclusions. Nonetheless, Martens's remarks are frequently interesting and there is no excuse for the virtual ignorance of his study in subsequent scholarship. Such will not be the case here.

4. In 1976, Böhmer published a treatise entitled *Heimkehr und neuer Bund: Studien zu Jeremia 30–31*. Planting himself firmly within the ranks of those scholars who adhere to the theory of the dtr. edition of Jeremiah, Böhmer engages in a criticism of most of the passages discussed below. He diverges but little from the works of Thiel (1973) and Hermann (1965), and thus does not provide a fresh approach to the text. Inexplicably, he does not show awareness of the work of Bright (1951; 1965; 1966). Böhmer's views will be reviewed in detail in the chapters below.

5. By far the most significant work for the purposes of the present study has been that done by Raitt. His book, *A Theology of Exile: Judgment/Deliverance in Jeremiah and Ezekiel* (1977), is a truly original contribution to the examination of the thought of those two prophets.[10] The key chapters in Raitt's book are entitled 'The Shift from Doom to Salvation', 'The Prophetic Oracle of Deliverance', and 'The Content of the Deliverance Message'. This is a well-structured and highly systematic work in which many key passages are investigated anew. The most serious criticism of this book is its failure to re-examine passages which 'are generally attributed to later stages in the development of the prophetic book' (1977:121). Raitt's treatment concerning particular texts will be referred to repeatedly in the course of this study and will be the subject of detailed comment.

6. Milgrom has made some of his unpublished observations on eschatological repentance available to the present author. These thought-provoking views have helped provide direction for this study.

D. *Attendant Problems*

No analysis of a topic in Jeremiah can be complete without reference to the questions of date, authenticity, and historical background of the relevant passages. These questions are complicated by two factors: (a) the popular scholarly theory of a widespread exilic or post-exilic redaction by the dtr. school, and (b) the shorter version in the Septuagint.

It is not necessary to recapitulate here the development of the theory of the dtr. redaction from the time of Duhm (1901) and Mowinckel (1914). Surveys of that nature may be found in recent commentaries and monographs (e.g. Nicholson, 1970; Böhmer, 1976; Thompson, 1980). It should, however, be pointed out that this theory has been reaffirmed and accentuated with increasing regularity and certainty in the last decade and a half, as evidenced specifically by the writings of Nicholson, Thiel, Böhmer, and Carroll (1981) (all of whom owe a particular debt to Hyatt 1942; 1951; 1956). The last of these works, that by Carroll, brings one full-cycle back to the contention of Duhm that only a minute number of verses in the book, those in poetry, are attributable to the prophet himself. As implied, this view and the attendant one of the dtr. edition rely on the suppositions that (a) one can define categorically between prose and poetry, and (b), in any case, Jeremiah could not have been the author of both (Carroll 1981:8-28; McKane 1981:260). These suppositions have been radically challenged in the ground-breaking study by Kugel on parallelism, who proves (1981:77-84) that parallelism is present in the so-called 'prose' of Jeremiah.[11] Thus, the lines of distinction between the two rhetorical styles in Jeremiah are blurred.

To re-examine the theory of the dtr. edition of Jeremiah in its entirety is beyond the scope of this study. Nonetheless, each time that it appears as a scholarly position concerning a passage under discussion, it will be dealt with in detail. In this connection, for example, Chapter 2 will contain a lengthy critique of the theory of the second, exilic edition of the dtr. history.

Similarly, when the LXX version of Jeremiah differs from the Masoretic Text in a relevant passage, it will be analyzed and pertinent scholarship will be cited.[12]

E. *Methodology*

If the analysis herein accomplished and the results gained diverge from the dominant trends of Jeremianic scholarship, this is due solely to the methodology employed, for meaning and method are interrelated. Too often the methods used in the examination of passages in Jeremiah are arbitrary. For example, the dependence of Jer. 24.1-10 and 29.10-14 upon Deuteronomy is set on the basis of linguistic similarities alone, without an attempt to determine whether or not the ideological content and the structure are similar. Or, in a different vein, previous research is often contradicted without consideration of the arguments involved.[13] In this regard, it is astonishing that most American and European non-Jewish scholars are still unable to read the wealth of material available either in modern Hebrew or the medieval Rabbinic commentaries.[14] Their ignorance of these works of scholarship makes their own studies obviously suspect.

Another common methodological flaw is found in assumptions based upon pre-conceived notions, such as the prose-poetry issue mentioned above. Time and again one reads in Jeremianic scholarship such presumptions and presumptive statements as:

> It is not at all probable that Jeremiah would have had an interest in the continuation of the Levitical priesthood in such strong terms as occur here (Hyatt, in his commentary on 33.14-26).

> 31.35-37 employs an argument from nature to history utterly unlike and contradictory to Jeremiah elsewhere. I would add to the post-Jeremianic material 30.16-17 and probably 31.15-22: the former because like mid-exilic pieces, it is very Zion-oriented and vindictive against Judah's enemies, the latter because it is a very broken genre not readily compared with any of the deliverance passages to be considered below (Raitt 1977:251).

> The climate of the salvation oracles would suffocate a Jeremiah, or send him into paroxysms of rage against such smug relief in the perfectibility of human society. Although sophisticated theological arguments may be advanced to show how only a Jeremiah could have authorized such hopes, and how the catastrophe of the exile radically altered his thinking on the matter, I suspect that the Jeremiah of the early oracles would have been appalled at the chauvinistic optimism of the salvation oracles (Carroll 1981:200).

Indeed, the prophets are, regularly, not perceived by modern scholars to have the characteristics attributable to every thinking, reflective individual—the traits of complexity and growth, and the very human nature of not being completely and consistently logical.

It behooves the scholar to be always conscious of the inability both to dissipate totally the mists that obscure the past and to loose entirely the mental fetters placed upon the self by life-experiences. Narrow-mindedness in scholarship is often evinced by the consistent use of only *some* critical approaches while eschewing others. The true scholar must be *holistic* in research. This term is defined in an illuminating article on methodology by Greenberg (1980:145) as 'emphasizing the organic or functional relation between parts and wholes'. The tendency in scholarship is to explain away textual difficulties and incongruencies as corruptions (copyists' misspellings, misplacement of verses, illogical order of passages, faulty dates, etc.), intrusive additions, or editorial insertions. Mistakes, of course, occur, but one should have recourse to them only after every other available means of analysis has been applied, tested, and found wanting. Anything and everything that can serve as a tool to understand the received text better should be used.

What Greenberg calls 'holistic', Weiss (1984)[15] terms 'total-interpretation'—a method based upon the developments of 'New Criticism' and the technique of 'close-reading'.[16] In Weiss's words (1984:26-27), it is a

> methodological imperative to pay close attention to the text, to every word, to the word-order and syntax, to synonyms and metaphors, to unusual syntactical phenomena, to the structure of every sentence and to the structure of the work as a whole. All this must not be done from a statistical perspective, by classifying and counting, not by enquiring into separate elements as such but by examining the function of each linquistic and structural element within the whole work, by answering the question of how all the individual parts are welded to make up the formal unity of the whole . . .
>
> . . . interpretation does not mean the explanation of every detail in the work by itself but rather the explanation of every detail in the light of the whole creation and the explanation of the whole creation on the basis of all its details.

Greenberg (1980:146) has conveniently listed the appropriate questions with which the interpreter must arm himself when approaching a passage:

> Is the unit which is delimited formally (by, say, opening and closing formulas) shown to be a unit through its structure (a recognized pattern?), its content, its figures or its verbal devices?
> How much interrelation and reference occurs among its parts?
> How much repetition (if with variations, are they significant)?
> How much irregularity occurs (in grammar, in length of lines, etc.), and how much regularity?
> In the event of non-sequentiality, is another ground of collocation evident (e.g., thematic, or verbal association)?
> Are effective elements present besides the plain sense of sentences, such as alliteration, punning, or chiasm?
> To what do they call attention?
> How much ambiguity is present; what are its causes and effects?
> Are elements which seem opaque illuminated by considering their placement (significance through juxtaposition)?
> To what extent are themes, peculiarities or difficulties recurrent elsewhere? In identical or variant form? If not in the Bible, then outside it?

> How far is one's perception of the main message of a unit corroborated by later readers (postbiblical literature, medieval commentaries); if there is a difference, why?

Greenberg (1980:148-49) creates a telling analogy when he relates the holistic interpreter to the ideal reader:

> Our holistic interpretation seeks to reconstitute the perception of the text by an ideal reader living at a time when it had reached its present disposition. 'Ideal reader' is a personified realization of the possibilities inherent in the text at that moment . . . the context of densest significance for that ideal reader will have been the canonical book . . . Our ideal reader will have been sensible of resonances, echoes and illusions, and the holistic interpreter will attempt to reproduce his sensibilities. The ideal reader will have also been familiar with the literary, the historical, and the environmental allusions in the book; the exegete must resort to the rest of biblical literature (preferably, but not exclusively, to works that might have been known to the prophet), and, where relevant, to extrabiblical literature for such information. The ideal reader treats the book as full of significance (it offers a key to his people's destiny in the past and future); the interpreter will strain to discover this significance through the battery of questions listed above . . . he will use the early witnesses to the Hebrew, conscious of the limitations of such use. Evident compositeness of a literary unit will be duly noted, but not taken to release the interpreter from the obligation to see the interrelation of the components; for all he knows such interrelation as he may discover was already in the mind of whoever collocated these components, perhaps the prophet himself . . .
>
> . . . Ultimately, the holistic interpreter is animated by a respect for his cultural heritage that takes the form of a prejudice in favor of the ancient biblical author-editors and their transmitters. He requires more than a theoretical cause before discounting and disintegrating their products.

The present author owes much to the works of his teachers, Weiss, Greenberg,[17] and Milgrom (whose methodology is illustrated by his meticulous analyses). If this study is of value, it is due to their 'torah'.

F. *Plan*

Each chapter will include a review and critique of the relevant scholarship on the passages in question, an analysis of the structure and meaning of those passages, the analysis of any pertinent extra-Jeremianic texts, a summary and conclusions. The first three chapters will be presented in the chronological order of the texts under examination. This logical order will be justified by the analysis within each chapter. Chapter 1 will investigate the prophecies of redemption to Ephraim during the reign of Josiah; Chapter 2, those addressed to the Judeans exiled with Jehoiachin; and Chapter 3, those concerning Judah and Ephraim at the time of the destruction of Jerusalem by the Babylonians. Chapter 4 will scrutinize miscellaneous prophecies of redemption from various times in the life of the prophet. The conclusions of this treatise will be preceded by excursuses on the prophets Amos, Hosea, Ezekiel, and II Isaiah. The purpose of these excursuses is to place Jeremiah's thought in historical perspective.

It will be demonstrated, through exacting textual and ideological analysis of the prophecies of redemption in Jeremiah, that the dominant trend of scholarship is methodologically flawed and biased. It will be shown that the texts under consideration represent concepts and vocabulary which:

(a) influence or logically precede Ezekiel and II Isaiah:
(b) fit the historical background of the late seventh and early sixth centuries BCE;
(c) relate to, but are essentially different from, the literature and ideology of Deuteronomy and Kings.

In short, a rigorous investigation of the text via objective methods will result in a rational explanation of the development of Jeremiah's thought on the relationship of repentance to redemption based upon the historical and ideological background of the prophet himself.

The book of Jeremiah often resembles a complex maze. The reader should take note that, as this study progresses, the careful conclusions reached concerning each examined passage become the building blocks for future understandings until, by the end of the book, the maze has been transformed into a multi-level house with clearly delineated stairs, rooms, and floors. However, if one does not begin at the beginning but rather enters at some middle point, then confusion and not comprehension is apt to be the result.

Chapter 1

PROPHECIES OF REDEMPTION TO EPHRAIM DURING THE REIGN OF JOSIAH

A. 3.6-13, 19–4.2

6 וַיֹּאמֶר יְהוָה אֵלַי בִּימֵי
יֹאשִׁיָּהוּ הַמֶּלֶךְ הֲרָאִיתָ אֲשֶׁר עָשְׂתָה מְשֻׁבָה יִשְׂרָאֵל
הֹלְכָה הִיא עַל־כָּל־הַר גָּבֹהַּ וְאֶל־תַּחַת כָּל־עֵץ רַעֲנָן וַתִּזְנִי־
7 שָׁם׃ וָאֹמַר אַחֲרֵי עֲשׂוֹתָהּ אֶת־כָּל־אֵלֶּה אֵלַי תָּשׁוּב וְלֹא־
8 שָׁבָה וַתִּרְאֶה בָּגוֹדָה אֲחוֹתָהּ יְהוּדָה׃ וָאֵרֶא כִּי עַל־כָּל־
אֹדוֹת אֲשֶׁר נִאֲפָה מְשֻׁבָה יִשְׂרָאֵל שִׁלַּחְתִּיהָ וָאֶתֵּן אֶת־
סֵפֶר כְּרִיתֻתֶיהָ אֵלֶיהָ וְלֹא יָרְאָה בֹּגֵדָה יְהוּדָה אֲחוֹתָהּ
9 וַתֵּלֶךְ וַתִּזֶן גַּם־הִיא׃ וְהָיָה מִקֹּל זְנוּתָהּ וַתֶּחֱנַף אֶת־הָאָרֶץ
י וַתִּנְאַף אֶת־הָאֶבֶן וְאֶת־הָעֵץ׃ וְגַם־בְּכָל־זֹאת לֹא־שָׁבָה אֵלַי
בָּגוֹדָה אֲחוֹתָהּ יְהוּדָה בְּכָל־לִבָּהּ כִּי אִם־בְּשֶׁקֶר נְאֻם־
11 יְהוָה׃ וַיֹּאמֶר יְהוָה אֵלַי צִדְּקָה נַפְשָׁהּ מְשֻׁבָה
12 יִשְׂרָאֵל מִבֹּגֵדָה יְהוּדָה׃ הָלֹךְ וְקָרָאתָ אֶת־הַדְּבָרִים הָאֵלֶּה
צָפוֹנָה וְאָמַרְתָּ שׁוּבָה מְשֻׁבָה יִשְׂרָאֵל נְאֻם־יְהוָה לוֹא־אַפִּיל
13 פָּנַי בָּכֶם כִּי־חָסִיד אֲנִי נְאֻם־יְהוָה לֹא אֶטּוֹר לְעוֹלָם׃ אַךְ
דְּעִי עֲוֹנֵךְ כִּי בַּיהוָה אֱלֹהַיִךְ פָּשָׁעַתְּ וַתְּפַזְּרִי אֶת־דְּרָכַיִךְ
לַזָּרִים תַּחַת כָּל־עֵץ רַעֲנָן וּבְקוֹלִי לֹא־שְׁמַעְתֶּם נְאֻם־יְהוָה׃

19 וְאָנֹכִי אָמַרְתִּי אֵיךְ אֲשִׁיתֵךְ בַּבָּנִים וְאֶתֶּן־לָךְ
אֶרֶץ חֶמְדָּה נַחֲלַת צְבִי צִבְאוֹת גּוֹיִם וָאֹמַר אָבִי תִּקְרְאוּ־
כ לִי וּמֵאַחֲרַי לֹא תָשׁוּבוּ׃ אָכֵן בָּגְדָה אִשָּׁה מֵרֵעָהּ כֵּן בְּגַדְתֶּם
21 בִּי בֵּית יִשְׂרָאֵל נְאֻם־יְהוָה׃ קוֹל עַל־שְׁפָיִים נִשְׁמָע בְּכִי
תַּחֲנוּנֵי בְּנֵי יִשְׂרָאֵל כִּי הֶעֱווּ אֶת־דַּרְכָּם שָׁכְחוּ אֶת־יְהוָה
22 אֱלֹהֵיהֶם׃ שׁוּבוּ בָּנִים שׁוֹבָבִים אֶרְפָּה מְשׁוּבֹתֵיכֶם הִנְנוּ
23 אָתָנוּ לָךְ כִּי אַתָּה יְהוָה אֱלֹהֵינוּ׃ אָכֵן לַשֶּׁקֶר מִגְּבָעוֹת
הָמוֹן הָרִים אָכֵן בַּיהוָה אֱלֹהֵינוּ תְּשׁוּעַת יִשְׂרָאֵל׃
24 וְהַבֹּשֶׁת אָכְלָה אֶת־יְגִיעַ אֲבוֹתֵינוּ מִנְּעוּרֵינוּ אֶת־צֹאנָם

וְאֶת־בְּקָרָם אֶת־בְּנֵיהֶם וְאֶת־בְּנוֹתֵיהֶם׃ נִשְׁכְּבָה בְּבָשְׁתֵּנוּ כה
וּתְכַסֵּנוּ כְּלִמָּתֵנוּ כִּי לַיהוָה אֱלֹהֵינוּ חָטָאנוּ אֲנַחְנוּ
וַאֲבוֹתֵינוּ מִנְּעוּרֵינוּ וְעַד־הַיּוֹם הַזֶּה וְלֹא שָׁמַעְנוּ בְּקוֹל
יְהוָה אֱלֹהֵינוּ׃

ד

אִם־תָּשׁוּב יִשְׂרָאֵל ׀ נְאֻם־יְהוָה אֵלַי תָּשׁוּב וְאִם־תָּסִיר א
שִׁקּוּצֶיךָ מִפָּנַי וְלֹא תָנוּד׃ וְנִשְׁבַּעְתָּ חַי־יְהוָה בֶּאֱמֶת 2
בְּמִשְׁפָּט וּבִצְדָקָה וְהִתְבָּרְכוּ בוֹ גּוֹיִם וּבוֹ יִתְהַלָּלוּ׃

6 The Lord said to me in the days of King Josiah: 'Have you seen what she did, that faithless one, Israel, how she went up on every high hill and under every green tree, and there played the harlot? 7And I thought, "After she has done all this she will return to me"; but she did not return, and her false sister Judah saw it. 8She saw that for all the adulteries of that faithless one, Israel, I had sent her away with a decree of divorce; yet her false sister Judah did not fear, but she too went and played the harlot. 9Because harlotry was so light to her, she polluted the land, committing adultery with stone and tree. 10 Yet for all this her false sister Judah did not return to me with her whole heart, but in pretense, says the Lord.'

11 And the Lord said to me, 'Faithless Israel has shown herself less guilty than false Judah. 12Go, and proclaim these words toward the north, and say,

"Return, faithless Israel,
says the Lord.
I will not look on you in anger,
for I am merciful,
says the Lord;
I will not be angry for ever.
13Only acknowledge your guilt,
that you rebelled against the Lord your God
and scattered your favors among strangers under every green tree,
and that you have not obeyed my voice,
says the Lord.

19' "I thought
how I would set you among my sons,
and give you a pleasant land,
a heritage most beauteous of all nations.
And I thought you would call me,
My Father,
and would not turn from following me.
20Surely, as a faithless wife leaves her husband,

so have you been faithless to me,
O house of Israel,
says the Lord."'
21 A voice on the bare heights is heard,
the weeping and pleading of Israel's sons,
because they have perverted their way,
they have forgotten the Lord their God.
22 'Return, O faithless sons,
I will heal your faithlessness.'
Behold, we come to thee;
for thou art the Lord our God.
23 Truly the hills are a delusion,
the orgies on the mountains.
Truly in the Lord our God is the salvation of Israel.

24 'But from our youth the shameful thing has devoured all for which
our fathers labored, their flocks and their herds, their sons and their
daughters.
25 Let us lie down in our shame, and let our dishonor cover
us; for we have sinned against the Lord our God, we and our fathers,
from our youth even to this day; and we have not obeyed the voice of
the Lord our God.'

4 'If you return, O Israel,
says the Lord,
to me you should return.
If you remove your abominations from my presence,
and do not waver,
2 and if you swear, "As the Lord Lives",
in truth, in justice and in uprightness,
then nations shall bless themselves in him,
and in him shall they glory.'

1. *Review of Scholarship*[1]

Modern Bible critics are extremely divided on the questions of the structure and composition of ch. 3, particularly in terms of the authenticity of these verses, the extent of the literary units, and the addressee (Judah or Ephraim). Their opinions will be presented as they relate to each specific set of verses.

a. *3.6-13*
Many scholars view vv. 6-12a (prose) as derived from a dtr. redactor:

(1) Duhm (1901) and Skinner (1922:82) believe that the similarities to Ezek. 16.44-63 and 23 testify to an editorial hand. Additionally, Skinner remarks that the style of these verses and the character of the parable are foreign to Jeremiah;

(2) May (1945:226) calls 3.6ff. 'one of the most palpably non-Jeremianic sections of the book', but without detailing his objection;

(3) Mowinckel (1946:63) opines that the source of 3.6-12a is in the 'Deuteronomistic circle of tradition';[2]

(4) Hyatt (1942:166), among other arguments, claims that the date in v. 6 is imaginary and was added by a dtr. editor in order to claim that the beginning of Jeremiah's prophecy predated the deuteronomic reforms.[3] In his opinion, v. 8 was added to instruct the reader that Jeremiah adhered to the laws of Deuteronomy (cp. Deut. 24.1-4);

(5) Holladay (1958:133) saw three of Hyatt's arguments in favor of a deuteronomistic redaction as decisive:[4] 1. the style is repetitive; 2. 'Israel' here refers to the Northern Kingdom, not to the whole people; 3. the Northern Kingdom is represented as superior to the Southern;

(6) Thiel (1973:87-91) adds that Jer. 3.6-11 is parallel to 2 Kgs 17.7-23 and that these verses, along with v. 12a, were composed as an interpretation to the genuine words of Jeremiah in vv. 12b-13;[5]

(7) The existence of dtr. phrases in this section, as listed by Weinfeld (1972:359, 361), has cast doubt on its authenticity;

(8) Holladay (1976:48) and Jobling (1978:52) assert that vv. 6-12a are a *prose* interruption to a surrounding Jeremianic poem.[6]

Even some of those scholars who accept the authenticity of vv. 6-11, such as Volz (1928), Driver (1967:251), and Welch (1928:78), view these verses as having been introduced by a compiler into this chapter.

The following arguments are brought in refutation of the above claims:

(1) Bright (1951:21-22), followed by Miller (1955:35-36, 90-91), has shown that, contra Skinner, the material in Ezekiel has not influenced the composition of vv. 6-11, but, rather, has been expanded on the basis of these verses. Furthermore, Bright has pointed to significant differences in language between the dtr. literature and these verses. In reality, Skinner (1922:251) contradicts himself when he accepts the authenticity of the parable of the figs in Jer. 24.1-10. In both 24.1-10 and 3.6-11 two portions of the people are compared and the favored one is in exile;

(2) There is no reason to posit with Hyatt [(4) above] that the words 'in the days of Josiah the king' are the work of an editor. No particular year is mentioned, and, therefore, there is no indication that Jeremiah prophesied this prophecy before the deuteronomic reforms. In any case, why would the deuteronomist wish to claim that Jeremiah began prophesying before these reforms? Additionally, there is no reason to assume that 3.8 was added by a deuteronomist to show that Jeremiah was familiar with the laws of Deuteronomy when 3.1, an unquestioned poetic piece, makes this clear;[7]

(3) Holladay's and Hyatt's arguments [(5) above] are refutable:

1. That the style of 3.6-11 is repetitive is no proof of a dtr. redaction. In a literary section which emphasizes the similarities between two 'sisters', it is natural that their characteristics will be stated in

similar terms. It is not surprising that the prophet would repeat the sisters' names, for in the words '*Backsliding*[8] Israel' and '*Betraying* Judah' one senses the accusation of guilt which serves one of the main purposes of this section—to convince Judah to return to YHWH. Repetitions of this type are abundant in ch. 2,[9] but, because of its assumed poetic form, no one questions its authenticity;

2. The claim that 'Israel' here refers to the Northern Kingdom alone, and not to both halves of the nation together or to Judah alone (the normal usages of 'Israel' in Jeremiah), and therefore testifies to the editorial hand, ignores other appearances of the word in Jeremiah 'poetry': in 5.11 and 31.2, 4, 7, 9 'Israel' refers only to the Northern Kingdom (Skinner, 1922:83, n. 1)
3. Holladay's and Hyatt's third claim is that the superiority of the North over the South in 3.6-11 does not reflect Jeremianic concepts but rather indicates a borrowing by a dtr. redactor based upon Ezekiel (16.44-63 and 23). However, the dtr. passage of 2 Kgs 17.7-40 denigrates the North, proving that the superiority of the North could not possibly be a dtr. idea. Furthermore, this contention of Holladay and Hyatt is based upon a misunderstanding of the text: there is no attempt to depict the North as *absolutely* superior to the South. Rather, the superiority spoken of is only *comparative* in reference to a particular time and situation. This one-time comparison is also the subject in Ezekiel. By rights, Holladay should have also questioned the phrase in 31.9, 'Ephraim is my first-born son', but the authenticity of that 'poetic' verse is not questioned by scholars;

(4) As indicated in the previous paragraph, there are significant differences between 3.6-11 and 2 Kgs 17.7-23 [contra Thiel in (6) above]. Additionally, 2 Kgs 17.15 quotes Jer. 2.5, pointing to a line of influence from the Jeremiah literature to 2 Kgs 17, and not vice versa;

(5) The existence of specific phrases as supporting dtr. authorship of this section [see (8) above] has been admirably attacked by Bright (1951:21, 35), who has proven that the language of 3.6-11 is characteristic of Jeremiah. Even if we were to assume that an editor added some of his own phrases to this section, there are no ideological inconsistencies with the thought of Jeremiah. In other words, if there are editorial glosses in this section, they were done by someone faithful to Jeremiah's concepts.

3.12-13 are considered by most scholars as authentic to Jeremiah, whether they contend that these verses were inserted here by an editor (Volz, 1928; Bright, 1965), or are a nucleus around which an editor placed vv. 6-12a and 14-18 (like Mowinckel, 1946).[10] The majority of critics assert that these verses are addressed to Ephraim, as exemplified by Streane (1913), Volz, Rudolph (1958), and Bright (1965), and with the exception of Duhm and Skinner (1922:83-84). The latter claim that 'Israel' here refers to the entire nation, and therefore they allege that v. 12a is an editorial edition.

Despite the foregoing objections, there are solid lines of connection between vv. 12-13 and 6-11. The expression 'Backsliding Israel' appears only in vv. 6, 8, 11 and 12, and that of 'under every green tree' in v. 13 repeats v. 6 (Bright, 1951:35).[11] Additionally, the prophet's call to Ephraim is most appropriate for those days when Josiah wished to extend the cultic practices of his kingdom over the territory of the northern tribes (2 Kgs 23.15-20). Thus, vv. 12-13 properly fit the 'days of Josiah' mentioned in v. 6.[12]

b. *3.19–4.2*

3.14–18 will be discussed fully in Chapter 4. The reasons for their separation from the surrounding verses are: (1) vv. 12-13, 19-20 refer to the nation in 2nd pers. sing. fem. and 2nd pers. plu. masc., while in vv. 14–18 the nation is referred to either in 2nd pers. plu. masc. or 3rd pers. plu. masc.—never 2nd pers. sing. fem. It should be noted that in v. 13 the Septuagint reads fem. sing. for masc. plu. 'you did not hear', apparently out of a tendency to unify the text. The same tendency is found in the *qere* of v. 19 which replaces the masc. plu. of the *kethib* with fem. sing. for 'call . . . turn back'; (2) v. 18 refers to both the 'house of Judah' and the 'house of Israel' as in exile—a surprising statement since until this point there has been no hint whatsoever of a Judean exile concurrent with that of Israel; (3) vv. 14–18 are concerned with the near or distant future, whereas the entire focus of vv. 6–13,19ff. is the present.

There are two reasons for the insertion of vv. 14–18 here—both on associative grounds: (1) the phrase שובו בנים שובבים 'return backsliding children' (v. 14) is repeated in v. 22 and also is reminiscent of שובה משבה 'return backsliding . . .' in v. 12; (2) הארץ אשר הנחלתי 'the land which I gave for a heritage' of v. 18 echoes ארץ חמדה נחלת צבי 'a pleasant land, the most beautiful heritage . . .' in v. 19.

1. *3.19-20*. The majority of scholars believe that these verses are addressed to Judah or to the entire nation, and that they are a direct continuation of vv. 1-5 (Driver, 1967:250; Volz, 1928; Calkins, 1930:69; Rudolph, 1958; Bright, 1965; Berridge, 1970:77; Thiel, 1973; Brueggemann, 1974;154; Jobling, 1978:45ff). Their arguments rest on the following points: (1) that 3.6–18 have been inserted from elsewhere; (2) the image of the unfaithful wife in vv. 1-5 and 19-20; (3) the similarity between 'you called me "Father"' in v. 4 and 'call me "Father"' in v. 19; (4) the interpretation of the ו of ואנכי in 19 as the oppositive ו whose purpose is to contrast God with the people mentioned in v. 5. Additionally, Duhm holds that vv. 19ff. are addressed to Judah alone (and, therefore, he removes 'the house of Israel' from v. 20 as a later expansion), but he ties them to vv. 12-13. Welch (1928:57) and Hertzberg (1952:94–95) on the other hand, contend that v. 5 is continued in v. 19, but that all these verses refer to the Northern Kingdom. Jobling's

construction of the poem is unique: 3.1-5, 19-20, 12b-13, 21–4.2. He theorizes (1978:52), along with Rudolph, that 'the renewed indictment in vv. 19-20 reads poorly *after* vv. 12-13', but if the order is reversed, then 'Israel' in 3.12b follows well on 'Israel' at the end of v. 20. Additionally, the use of משבה in vs. 12 appropriately follows the negative use of √שוב in v. 19 (1978:50). Why, then, do vv. 19-20 appear *after* the prose section surrounding vv. 12b-13?

> The only plausible reason we can discern for the later dislocation of vv. 19-20 is the similarity of v. 19 to the second prose section, (vv. 14-18; 'land' [vv. 16-18], 'nations' v. 17), and especially 'heritage' (v. 18), are all found in v. 19. We suggest, therefore, that along with the insertion of vv. 14-18 into the Deuteronomic sermon, or afterwards, . . . iii 19-20 . . . was moved from its proper place after v. 5 to its present unnatural setting (1978:53).

Contrary to the above perspective, Giesebrecht (1894), Pfeiffer (1941:282), Holladay (1976:47), Böhmer (1976:24, 27),[13] and Carroll (1981) view vv. 19-20 as a continuation of v. 13, and as addressed to the northern tribes. In contrast to point (4) above, Giesebrecht understands 'But I have said' of v. 19 as representing opposition to the sins of Israel mentioned in v. 13. Holladay (1976:35-54) writes of a 'Harlotry Cycle' of poetic sections arranged possibly by Jeremiah: 2.5-37; 3.1-5. 12b-14a, 19-25. He feels that the four sections denote an A—B—A′—B′ structure (1976:49-52),[14] and that the usages of the root שוב in v. 22 are in chiastic relationship to those of vv. 12b and 14a (1976:50). Only Böhmer (1976:22), who otherwise normally follows Hermann and Thiel, accepts vv. 6-12a as belonging to the greater composition of 3.1–4.2 (minus vv. 14-18).

One last view should be noted. Martens (1972:38), following Weiser's acceptance of vv. 14-18 as early material, claims vv. 11-20 as a Jeremianic unit dating from the Josianic period.

In defense of the position that vv. 19-20 succeed vv. 12-13, it may be argued, against point (2) above, that the image of the faithless wife is present in vv. 12-13 ('you scattered your ways to the strangers'—cp. 2.23, 25). Furthermore, Jobling's analysis of the reversal of vv. 12-13 and 19-20 is sheer conjecture. It seems far more plausible that vv. 14-18 were inserted between vv. 12-13 and 19-20 than that an editor added vv. 14-18 to 12-13 and then plucked vv. 19-20 from after v. 5 to place them before v. 21. But, then, Jobling misreads the text when he sees in vv. 19-20 a harsh indictment as opposed to the gentle mercies of vv. 12-13. In reality, vv. 12-13 are structurally and ideologically parallel to vv. 19-20:[15] (a) each section begins by mentioning God's mercies—v. 12: 'I will not look on you in anger for I am merciful . . . I will not be angry forever'; v. 19: 'I said, "how shall I set you up among the sons and give you a pleasant land, the most beautiful heritage of the nations'";[16] (b) the prophet then passes on to God's demand—v. 13: 'Only acknowledge your transgression'; v. 19: 'I said, "Call me 'father', and don't turn away from following me"'; (c) finally, there is a repetition of the description of the sin found in 3.6-11—the faithlessness of the nation is compared to that of an adulterous woman—v. 13: 'for you have rebelled against YHWH and scattered your ways to the strangers under every green tree and have not obeyed my voice, the speech of YHWH'; v. 20: 'Surely, as a wife faithless[17] to her husband, so you have been faithless to me, house of Israel, the speech of YHWH'.

One more argument may be brought to support the continuity of vv. 12-13, 19-20. In both these sections, Israel is referred to in 2nd pers. fem. sing. and masc. plu., while in vv. 1-5 only the fem. sing. is used (as in 2.33-37).

Thus it appears most reasonable that vv. 19-20 are the logical continuation of vv. 12-13.

2. *3.21-25*. The vast majority of scholars (Giesebrecht, 1894; Volz, 1928; Calkins, 1930:77; Rudolph, 1958; Leslie, 1954:36-38; Bright, 1965) accept vv. 21-25 as the direct continuation of vv. 19-20. Exceptions are Skinner (1922:84-85) and, more recently, Jobling (1978:45ff). Skinner, who is of the opinion that vv. 19-20 are isolated fragments, views vv. 21-25 as an isolated poem placed after vv. 12-13 by a redactor.[18] Jobling, according to his scheme outlined above, attaches vv. 21-25 to vv. 12b-13 on the basis that the penitence expressed in the former makes sense following the mercies of God mentioned in the latter. He (1978:46-47, 51) also sees a 'catchword link' between vv. 13 and 21—the roots קול and שמע occur in both places.

Jobling, however, ignores the connection between vv. 22 and 19. Verse 22a continues the call by God to His *sons* to return to Him, which appears in v. 19b (following the *kethib*). Verse 22b is the sons' positive response: v. 19b—ואמר אבי תקראו לי ומאחרי לא תשובו 'and I said "Call me my Father and don't turn back from following me"'; verse 22—שובו בנים שובבים ... הננו אתנו לך ... 'Return backsliding sons ... Behold we are coming to you'. Thus, vv. 21-25 properly succeed vv. 19-20.

3. *4.1-2*. Mowinckel's assertion that 4.3 begins a new unit, since 4.1-2 represent God's answer to the people's prayer in 3.21-25, is most appealing. 4.3, he claims (1946:39), concerns itself with a new matter, 'Break up your fallow ground', which does not mesh ideologically or stylistically with the previous verses. Furthermore, 4.3 commences with an opening formula—'For thus says YHWH to the people of Judah and Jerusalem'. Additional evidence for the division between 4.2 and 4.3 is the mention of Judah and Jerusalem in the latter. Henderson (1851), Welch (1928:40), Hertzberg (1952:96), and Weinfeld (1976:33, n.59) all point to 'Israel' in 4.1 as referring to Ephraim while 4.3-4 is undoubtedly directed to the Southern Kingdom.[19] Giesebrecht, who also contends that 4.1-2 is addressed to Ephraim, maintains that these verses assume that the divine punishment has already been executed, while 4.3-4 precedes judgment —'lest my wrath go forth like fire and burn with none to quench it' (4.4).

These arguments appear to be sufficient to counteract the views of Streane, Volz, Torrey, (1937:206-208), Rudolph, and Holladay (1976:55ff.) that 4.1-4 is a literary unit addressed to Israel in general and Judah in particular. Holladay's analysis is particularly ingenious. He takes 4.1-4 to be the '*prelude* . . . to the foe cycle' of oracles found in 4.5–6.30, the 'postlude' of which is found in 8.4-10a, 13. The 'prelude' and the 'postlude' thus form 'an "envelope" around the material on the foe from the north'. Holladay's arguments are (pp. 55-56):

(a) The inclusio of *ne'ûrim* in 3.4 and 24 suggests that 3.25 rounds off that material.

(b) The closest analogue for the double use of verbal forms of *šwb* in 4.1 (*'im-tašûb yiśra'el . . . 'elay tašûb*) is not in ch. 3 but in 8.4: *'im-yašûb welo' yašûb*, a parallel that then suggests an inclusio around the total foe cycle.

(c) Both 4.1–2 and 8.4–5 echo material within the foe cycle proper, *and adjoining verses respectively of that material.* Specifically, following the double occurrence of *šwb* in 4.1, we have, in v. 2: *wenišba'ta ḥay-yhwh be'emet*, and (if) you swear "as Yahweh lives in truth"', a parallel to *we'im ḥay-yhwh yo'merû, laken laššeqer yiššabe'û*, 'and if they say "as Yahweh lives"', then they swear falsely', in 5.2. And following the double occurrence of *šwb* in 8.4, we have, in v. 5: *heḥezîqû battarmit meanû lašûb*, a parallel to *ḥizzeqû penêhem missela' meanû lašûb* in 5.3. This is the only occurrence of *šwb* in the foe cycle proper . . . That is to say, 4.1–2 and 8.4–5 not only point to each other, but both point toward 5.2–3.

Holladay goes on to say that 4.3-4 echo Hos. 10.12 and Deut. 10.16; 30.6. He then admits (pp. 56-57) that:[20]

> There is both unity and disunity between vv. 1-2 and 3-4. There is unity, in that v. 2b also is a reminiscence of pre-Jeremianic material (the promises of God to Abraham in Genesis, most closely in Gen. 22.18), and in that *hasirû* in v. 4 and *tasîr* in v. 1 form an inclusio. On the other hand, there is disunity as well between vv. 1-2 and 3-4: the second-person-singular forms in vv. 1-2 give way to plural forms in vv. 3-4, . . . There is a possibility . . . that 4.1-2 was the original form or the prelude, and that vv. 3-4 were added here . . .

Jobling (1978:55, n. 33) has already stated concerning Holladay's point (a) that the inclusio suggested 'is implausible, since v. 4 is so far from the beginning of the poem'. It may be added that vv. 21-25 refer to Israel only in the masc. plu. while vv. 1-5 speak only in the fem. sing. It will be shown later that vv. 21-25 are a response to vv. 12-13, 19-20. Jobling (p. 55) also notes that point (b) assumes a purposeful pun. Furthermore, משבה appears only in 3.6, 8, 11, 12 besides 8.5—Holladay may just as well claim that 4.1-2, by his own logic, belong with the previous verses. Holladay's point (c) focuses on

חי יהוה in 4.2 and 5.2 as well as לכן לשקר in the latter verse. There, too, לכן לשקר has its closest duplicate in 3.23 אכן לשקר. One is forced not only to agree with Jobling that Holladay's remarks are inconclusive, but that Holladay may be actually, against his will, pointing to a connection between 4.1-2 and the previous verses!

Concerning Holladay's comments on the relationship of 4.1-2 to vv. 3-4, that there are echoes in both sections of pre-Jeremianic material proves nothing. Long ago Gros (1930) illustrated that Hosea's influence on Jeremiah is pervasive. Indeed, is it not a given that Jeremiah consciously inherits Israelite religious tradition? Furthermore, תסיר שקוציך 'remove your abominations' and הסרו ערלות לבבכם 'remove the foreskins of your heart' form no inclusio—the former is externally directed, the latter internally.

The weight of the evidence indicates that 4.1-2 is the logical successor of the preceding verses and not the succeeding ones.

2. *Structure and Meaning*

a. *3.6-11*. Verse 6 begins a new literary unit as indicated by its opening words which are written in typical prelude form—'YHWH said to me in the days of Josiah the King'. Verses 6-11 present God's historical survey of the idolatry of Israel and Judah with a particular indictment of Judah by way of comparison.[21] The two kingdoms are portrayed as unfaithful sister-wives משבה ישראל and בגודה/בגדה יהודה. The first was punished by 'divorce', i.e. exile, for her 'adultery', while the second did not learn from the mistakes of the first and brazenly 'went and whored also' (v. 8). Moreover, she has pretended to repent—'(she) has not returned to me . . . with all her heart but with a lie . . .' (v. 10).[22] Thus, it is due to Judah's more negative behavior that Israel is preferred by God (v. 11).[23]

b. *3.12-13*. After this introduction, the stage is set for the call to Israel to repent, which follows logically upon the preference for Israel stated in v. 11. Verses 12-13 emphasize the mercies of God which are extended to the exiles of Ephraim ('Go and cry out these words *north*-wards').[24] God's preparedness to accept those who return to Him[25] is expressed by His promise—'I will not be angry forever' (v. 12). The three components of repentance are alluded to in v. 13: (1) recognition of sin—דעי עונך. The root ידע is used in this sense in 2.19, 23; 14.20; 31.19; (2) cessation of sin—here, idolatry, a conclusion required by the accusation 'you've scattered your favors to the strangers under every green tree' (similarly, cp. 2.25—מנעי); (3)

obedience to God—the denotation of the expression ובקולי לא שמעתם (cp., for example, 7.23; 9.12).

c. *3.19-20*. As pointed out above, vv. 19-20 are structurally and ideologically parallel to vv. 12-13.

d. *3.21-25*. The metaphor of the adulterous woman ends in v. 20, and the prophet abandons the fem. sing. in favor of the masc. plu. for Ephraim as he describes the people's contrition in vv. 21-25. In v.21 the prophet interjects his voice to depict the scene of Israel's supplication (cp. 31.15). The words of v. 22a, שובו בנים שובבים ארפה משובתיכם 'return backsliding sons, I will heal your backslidings', are an ideological reiteration of v. 12, שובה משבה ישראל לא אפיל פני בכם כי חסיד אני . . . לא אטור לעולם 'return backsliding Israel . . . I will not look upon you in anger for I am merciful . . . I will not be angry forever'; once again the call to Israel to return to YHWH is heard, and once again the assurance of God's mercies is mentioned.

Jeremiah then places in the people's mouths a response to this call and to God's demands (vv. 13, 19) by way of a confession in vv. 22b-25. The confession contains 3 components: (1) acknowledgment of YHWH as God and savior—'Behold, we are coming to you, for you are YHWH our God . . . indeed, in YHWH our God is the salvation of Israel (vv. 22b, 23b); (2) rejection of idolatry—'Indeed, (swearing) falsely is from the hills,[26] the multitude[27] of mountains . . . shame[28] has devoured the toil of our forefathers from our youth . . .' (vv. 23a, 24a); (3) contrition composed of confession of sin and acknowledgment of refusal to obey YHWH—'Let us lie down in our shame and let our disgrace cover us, for we have sinned against YHWH our God, we, and our forefathers, from our youth until this day, and we have not obeyed the voice of YHWH our God' (v. 25). Thus, the three components of the confession complement the three of repentance in v. 13 (pp. 29-30 above). The relationship of vv. 21-25 to vv. 12-13, 19-20 is further attested by repetitions of language: v. 12 משבה and v. 22 משובתיכם; v. 13 ביהוה אלהיך and v. 21 יהוה אלהיכם; v. 22 יהוה אלהינו and v. 25 ליהוה אלהינו; v. 13 דרכיך 'your way' and v. 21 דרכך 'your way'; v. 13 ובקולי לא שמעתם and v. 25 ולא שמענו בקול; v. 19 תשובו and v. 22 שובו בנים שבבים.

e. *4.1-2*. The prophecy ends in 4.1-2 with God's response to the people's confession. Now the people are addressed in the 2nd pers. masc. sing. and, in v. 2b, in the 3rd (!) pers. masc. sing. A similar usage of 2nd and 3rd pers. masc. sing. in one verse takes place in Jer. 30.8:

> אשבר עלו מעל צוארך ומוסרותיך אנתק ולא יעבדו בו עוד זרים
> 'I will break his yoke from off your neck, and I will burst your bonds, and strangers shall no longer enslave *him*'.

It appears that the use of the masc. sing., particularly, testifies to YHWH's affection for His people, cp. Jer. 30.10-11; 31.20; Hos. 11.1, 8-9; 13.4-5; 14.6-9.

4.1 is a conditional promise stated through a parallelism, the meaning of which is not obviously clear. The verse may be translated (1) 'If you return Israel, the speech of YHWH, to me, (then) you shall dwell[29] / if you remove your abominations from before my face, then you shall not wander'; or (2) 'If you return, the speech of YHWH, return to me . . .'; or (3) 'If you return . . . (then) you shall return to me . . .' The first choice of 'dwell' for the second תשוב in the verse is improbable when one considers such verses as 3.7; 8.4; 15.19; 31.18 where the second appearance of the root שוב always refers to spiritual return. The second choice is also objectionable since it demands an imperative where there should be an apodosis, just as its parallel member, ולא תנוד, is a consequence of the condition.[30] Only the third choice, therefore, is reasonable.[31] However, this alternative, too, is problematic, for what does it mean to say 'If you return, then you shall return to me'? The solution derives from 15.19—'If you return, then I shall return you to me'—and 31.18—'Cause me to return that I may return'. In other words, if the people repent, God will take them back—the positive relationship between YHWH and His people will be renewed.[32] Since the return of the people to God implies, for the Northern exiles, a return to the land,[33] ולא תנוד is a consequence of אלי תשוב, i.e. Ephraim will no longer 'wander' off his land. According to Jeremiah, exile is a symbol of the deterioration of Israel's relationship with its God. The ideal relationship can only be established with an ingathering of exiles to the land as a result of divine redemption.

God's response to the people's contrition, then, is that if they will indeed repent and abandon their idolatrous ways, then God will accept them and bring them back from exile. Furthermore, Ephraim's faith in YHWH, as expressed by the oath חי יהוה (4.2), will cause a radical transformation of the people's condition, so that it will become a paragon after which the nations will desire to model themselves—והתברכו בו גוים ובו יתהללו 'then nations shall bless themselves in him, and in him they shall glory'. Consequently, Ephraim will fulfill the promise of God to Abraham in Gen. 12.2-3.

> and I will make you a great nation and will bless you and magnify your name so that you will be blessed and I will bless those who bless you and those who curse you I will curse, and all the families of the earth shall bless themselves by you (ונברכו בך; cp. Gen. 18.18; 22.18; 26.4; 28.14).

f. *Hosea 14.2-9*. Support for the claim of the unity of 3.12-13, 19–4.2 may be brought from Hos. 14.2-9—a shorter literary unit, but, nonetheless, one of similar structure and language. This passage from Hosea is also a prophecy of redemption to Ephraim. A comparison follows:[34] (1) both passages commence with a call to repentance which reminds Israel of its sins (Hos. 14.2 שובה ישראל עד יהוה אלהיך כי כשלת בעונך 'Return Israel to YHWH your God for you have stumbled in your iniquity' and Jer. 3.12-13 שובה משבה ישראל... אך דעי עונך כי ביהוה אלהיך פשעת 'return backsliding Israel... only acknowledge your iniquity for you have rebelled against YHWH your God'; Hos. 14.3 ושובו אל יהוה and Jer. 3.22a שובו בנים שובבים); (2) following the call, both prophets insert words of contrition into the mouths of the people (Hos. 14.3b-4 and Jer. 3.22b-25; the root ישע is used in both Hos. 14.4 and Jer. 3.23); (3) the words of contrition result in God's pledge of blessing and security on the land (in *Jeremiah* these favors are conditional upon the completion of the process of repentance, Hos. 14.5-9; Jer. 4.1-2).

Additionally, only in Hos. 14.5, ארפה משובתם, and Jer. 3.22 ארפה משובתיכם is a form of משובה coupled with the root רפא.

The affinities of structure and language between Hos. 14.2-9 and Jer. 3.12-13, 2–4.2 are sure testimony to the influence of Hosea on Jeremiah here[35] and to the unity of the later passage.

3. *Summary and Conclusions*

Jer. 3.6-13, 19–4.2 is a literary unit and an authentic prophecy of Jeremiah dating from the days of Josiah. It consists of four sections arranged in logical order:

(1) 3.6-11—God's historical survey of the idolatrous behavior of Israel and Judah. The result is an indictment of Judah and, in reflection of that indictment, a justification of Israel;

(2) 3.12–13, 19-20—The judgment of Israel as less reprehensible

than Judah evokes God's merciful response—a call for repentance with an assurance that God's anger is not permanent (v. 12), and a reminder that God wishes to give Israel of His bounty (v. 19). Repentance has three stages: a. recognition of sin; b. abandonment of idolatry: c. obedience to YHWH (which assumes acceptance of His divinity);

(3) 3.21-25—Ephraim responds with weeping and supplication which illlustrate its preparedness to repent (v. 21). After a further call to repent by God (3.22a), Ephraim confesses (vv. 22b-25). The confession contains three components which complement those of repentance: a. acknowledgment of YHWH as God and savior; b. rejection of idolatry; c. acknowledgment of sin and refusal to obey YHWH;

(4) 4.1-2—God responds favorably, but since confession is not in itself repentance, the divine promise of redemption is put in conditional form—it is contingent upon the people actually carrying out in action that which it has confessed verbally. When the people's repentance is fulfilled then God's promises will be fulfilled—ingathering of exiles, security upon the land, and blessings that will cause Ephraim's name to be glorified among the nations

One more question of structure and meaning must be addressed: what is the relationship, if any, of this prophecy of redemption to Ephraim to the surrounding literary units? An examination of the encircling material shows that 3.6-13, 19–4.2 is the middle section of five blocks of material[36] which appear to succeed one another in logical order:

(1) 2.4-37—Addressed to 'the House of Jacob and all the families of the House of Israel' (v. 4), this section accuses the people again and again of ungrateful faithlessness and obstinate idolatry (exceptions are the reference to brutality against the innocent poor in v. 34 and political disloyalty in v. 36). The people's response is either rejection of YHWH (vv. 20, 25, 29) or denial of guilt (vv. 23, 35);

(2) 3.1-5—continued accusation of idolatry, but for the first time in the book there is a call to 'return' to God, ושוב אלי (3.1).[37] The people do repent, but falsely (vv. 4-5, another element that appears here for the first time). Nonetheless, even this false repentance marks a progression from the people's attitude in 2.4-37. *The ties of 3.1-5 to the previous*

verses (the motif of the adulterous wife, the particular description of whoredom on the wayside in 3.1-3 and 2.20, 23-25, 33, the pollution of the land in 3.1-2 and 2.7, 20, and the usage of the root רעה in 3.2, 5 and 2.13, 19, 27, 28, 33) *and to the succeeding ones* (aside from the motifs of the adulterous wife, whoredom, and pollution of the land—v. 9, the usage of the root שוב throughout, רעים in v. 1 and רעה in v. 20 in the sense of 'lover', על שפי(י)ם in vv. 2 and 21, the root כלם in vv. 3 and 25, קראת לי אבי in v. 4 and אבי תקראי לי in v. 19, and הינטר לעולם in v. 5 and לא אטור לעולם in v. 12) *indicates that 3.1-5 is a transition passage between 2.4-37 and 3.6ff*. Also, the position here of false repentance inbetween the denial of guilt in ch. 2 and the true repentance of 3.21-25 designates this passage as transitional;

(3) 3.6-13, 19–4.2;

(4) 4.3-4—like 3.1-5, a transition passage between 3.6-13, 19–4.2 and 4.5ff. 4.3-4a are a call for repentance, reminiscent of the main theme of the previous passage, and 4.4b is a threat of punishment, the main subject of the succeeding verses. Furthermore, this section is addressed to Judah and Jerusalem, the addressees of the following unit;

(5) 4.5ff.[38]—the coming punishment (which assumes a refusal of the people to repent, and may have as its purpose to convince the people to repent in order to avoid catastrophe).

The arrangement outlined above has all the earmarks of intentionality. All the material in it is not only Jeremianic, but, excluding 3.14-18, from his early prophecies. Thus, there is no reason to assume that Jeremiah himself was not the arranger.[39] Indeed, if the scroll story of ch. 36 is reliable,[40] then it is probable that these five blocks made up a good portion of it.

If the above reasoning is correct, then a new insight into the significance of the prophecy of redemption to Ephraim may have been revealed. When Jeremiah is told in 3.12 'Go and call out these words *northward*', there is no indication that the intention is for him to go to the north of Israel, but rather to face north and speak from where he stands. If this be the case, then it is most probable that his audience are Judeans, specifically Jerusalemites. In other words, the prophecy is ultimately directed towards Judah, not Israel. The message, then, by implication, is that if Judah wishes to escape exile and be a recipient of God's mercies, it must repent. If not, then

Ephraim will be the favored one *alone*, for Judah will be exiled. Evidence for this interpretation comes from the fact that this prophecy is immediately succeeded by 4.3-4, 5ff., which promise terrible destruction upon Judah and Jerusalem if they fail to repent. How this prophecy of redemption to Ephraim must have shocked the Judeans who thought that it was their tribe who were now the sole heirs to the role of God's people (cp. 2 Kgs 17.18)!

This is not to say that Jeremiah did not believe that Ephraim would ever return. He, certainly, must have wished with all his being for the repentance of Ephraim and its return from exile. However, his audience is Judean and his words are directed to them no less than to Ephraim.

One last conclusion: 3.6-13, 19–4.2 contains two preconditions for redemption for the exiled Ephraim, one not less essential than the other—YHWH's mercies and Ephraim's repentance. Repentance has been discussed thoroughly above. YHWH's mercies are manifest in several ways: (1) He initiates the reconciliation by calling to the people to return: (2) the message itself, which reveals YHWH's favorable intentions—'I will not be angry forever . . . Now shall I place you among my children and give you a pleasant land, the most beautiful possession of all the nations' (3.12,[41] 19); (3) the images of husband and wife, father and son, which imply more than a temporary relationship.

B. 31.2-9, 15-22

כֹּה אָמַר יְהוָה מָצָא חֵן בַּמִּדְבָּר עַם שְׂרִידֵי חָרֶב הָלוֹךְ א
לְהַרְגִּיעוֹ יִשְׂרָאֵל׃ מֵרָחוֹק יְהוָה נִרְאָה לִי וְאַהֲבַת עוֹלָם 2
אֲהַבְתִּיךְ עַל־כֵּן מְשַׁכְתִּיךְ חָסֶד׃ עוֹד אֶבְנֵךְ וְנִבְנֵית 3
בְּתוּלַת יִשְׂרָאֵל עוֹד תַּעְדִּי תֻפַּיִךְ וְיָצָאת בִּמְחוֹל מְשַׂחֲקִים׃
עוֹד תִּטְּעִי כְרָמִים בְּהָרֵי שֹׁמְרוֹן נָטְעוּ נֹטְעִים וְחִלֵּלוּ׃ 4
כִּי יֶשׁ־יוֹם קָרְאוּ נֹצְרִים בְּהַר אֶפְרָיִם קוּמוּ וְנַעֲלֶה צִיּוֹן ה
אֶל־יְהוָה אֱלֹהֵינוּ׃ כִּי־כֹה ׀ אָמַר יְהוָה רָנּוּ לְיַעֲקֹב 6
שִׂמְחָה וְצַהֲלוּ בְּרֹאשׁ הַגּוֹיִם הַשְׁמִיעוּ הַלְלוּ וְאִמְרוּ הוֹשַׁע
יְהוָה אֶת־עַמְּךָ אֵת שְׁאֵרִית יִשְׂרָאֵל׃ הִנְנִי מֵבִיא אוֹתָם 7
מֵאֶרֶץ צָפוֹן וְקִבַּצְתִּים מִיַּרְכְּתֵי־אָרֶץ בָּם עִוֵּר וּפִסֵּחַ הָרָה
וְיֹלֶדֶת יַחְדָּו קָהָל גָּדוֹל יָשׁוּבוּ הֵנָּה׃ בִּבְכִי יָבֹאוּ וּבְתַחֲנוּנִים 8
אוֹבִילֵם אוֹלִיכֵם אֶל־נַחֲלֵי מַיִם בְּדֶרֶךְ יָשָׁר לֹא יִכָּשְׁלוּ
בָּהּ כִּי־הָיִיתִי לְיִשְׂרָאֵל לְאָב וְאֶפְרַיִם בְּכֹרִי הוּא׃

14 כֹּה ׀ אָמַר יְהוָה קוֹל בְּרָמָה נִשְׁמָע נְהִי בְּכִי
תַמְרוּרִים רָחֵל מְבַכָּה עַל־בָּנֶיהָ מֵאֲנָה לְהִנָּחֵם עַל־בָּנֶיהָ
טו כִּי אֵינֶנּוּ׃ כֹּה ׀ אָמַר יְהוָה מִנְעִי קוֹלֵךְ מִבֶּכִי וְעֵינַיִךְ
מִדִּמְעָה כִּי יֵשׁ שָׂכָר לִפְעֻלָּתֵךְ נְאֻם־יְהוָה וְשָׁבוּ מֵאֶרֶץ
16 אוֹיֵב׃ וְיֵשׁ־תִּקְוָה לְאַחֲרִיתֵךְ נְאֻם־יְהוָה וְשָׁבוּ בָנִים
17 לִגְבוּלָם׃ שָׁמוֹעַ שָׁמַעְתִּי אֶפְרַיִם מִתְנוֹדֵד יִסַּרְתַּנִי וָאִוָּסֵר
כְּעֵגֶל לֹא לֻמָּד הֲשִׁבֵנִי וְאָשׁוּבָה כִּי אַתָּה יְהוָה אֱלֹהָי׃
18 כִּי־אַחֲרֵי שׁוּבִי נִחַמְתִּי וְאַחֲרֵי הִוָּדְעִי סָפַקְתִּי עַל־יָרֵךְ
19 בֹּשְׁתִּי וְגַם־נִכְלַמְתִּי כִּי נָשָׂאתִי חֶרְפַּת נְעוּרָי׃ הֲבֵן יַקִּיר
לִי אֶפְרַיִם אִם יֶלֶד שַׁעֲשׁוּעִים כִּי־מִדֵּי דַבְּרִי בּוֹ זָכֹר
אֶזְכְּרֶנּוּ עוֹד עַל־כֵּן הָמוּ מֵעַי לוֹ רַחֵם אֲרַחֲמֶנּוּ נְאֻם־
כ יְהוָה׃ הַצִּיבִי לָךְ צִיֻּנִים שִׂמִי לָךְ תַּמְרוּרִים שִׁתִי
לִבֵּךְ לַמְסִלָּה דֶּרֶךְ הָלָכְתִּי שׁוּבִי בְּתוּלַת יִשְׂרָאֵל שֻׁבִי
21 אֶל־עָרַיִךְ אֵלֶּה׃ עַד־מָתַי תִּתְחַמָּקִין הַבַּת הַשּׁוֹבֵבָה כִּי־
בָרָא יְהוָה חֲדָשָׁה בָּאָרֶץ נְקֵבָה תְּסוֹבֵב גָּבֶר׃

2 Thus says the LORD:
'The people who survived the sword found grace in the wilderness;
when Israel sought for rest,
3 the LORD appeared to him from afar.
I have loved you with an everlasting love;
therefore I have continued my faithfulness to you.
4 Again I will build you, and you shall be built,
O virgin Israel!
Again you shall adorn yourself with timbrels,
and shall go forth in the dance of the merrymakers.
5 Again you shall plant vineyards
upon the mountains of Samaria;
the planters shall plant,
and shall enjoy the fruit.
6 For there shall be a day when watchmen will call in the hill country of Ephraim:
"Arise, and let us go up to Zion,
to the LORD our God"'.
7 For thus says the LORD:
'Sing aloud with gladness for Jacob,
and raise shouts for the chief of the nations:
proclaim, give praise, and say,
"The LORD has saved his people,
the remnant of Israel".
8 Behold, I will bring them from the north country,

and gather them from the farthest parts of the earth,
among them the blind and the lame,
the woman with child and her who is in travail, together;
a great company, they shall return here.
9With weeping they shall come,
and with consolations I will lead them back,
I will make them walk by brooks of water,
in a straight path in which they shall not stumble;
for I am a father to Israel,
and Ephraim is my first born.

15Thus says the LORD:
'A voice is heard in Ramah,
lamentation and bitter weeping.
Rachel is weeping for her children;
she refuses to be comforted for her children,
because they are not.'
16Thus says the LORD:
'Keep your voice from weeping,
and your eyes from tears:
for your work shall be rewarded says the LORD,
and they shall come back from the land of the enemy.
17There is hope for your future says the LORD,
and your children shall come back to their own country.
18I have heard Ephraim bemoaning,
'Thou hast chastened me, and I was chastened.
like an untrained calf;
bring me back that I may be restored
for thou art the LORD my God.
19For after I had turned away I repented;
and after I was instructed, I smote upon my thigh;
I was ashamed, and I was confounded,
because I bore the disgrace of my youth'.
20Is Ephraim my dear son?
Is he my darling child?
For as often as I speak against him,
I do remember him still.
Therefore my heart yearns for him
I will surely have mercy on him, says the LORD.
21'Set up waymarks for yourself,
make yourself guideposts;
consider well the highway,
the road by which you went.
Return, O virgin Israel,
return to these your cities.

[22]How long will you waver,
O faithless daughter?
For the LORD has created a new thing on the earth:
a woman protects a man.'

1. *Review of Scholarship*

Chapters 30–31 received their classic differentiation from the rest of the book by Mowinckel (1914:45-48), who labelled them 'D'. These chapters are commonly known (along with chs. 32–33) as the 'Book of Consolation' due to their common theme of redemption (cf. Rudolph, 1958; Bright, 1965). Concerning the verses under discussion, there is a diversity of scholarly views relating to dating, authenticity, identity of addressee, and extent of literary units (these perspectives will be recorded when appropriate).

a. *31.2-6, 15-22*

The general tendency of scholarship is to see 31.2-6, 15-20 (or 22) as authentic early prophecies of Jeremiah addressed to the Northern tribes. This position is held by (among others) Duhm, Skinner (1922:300-302), Rudolph (except that he understands vv. 21-22 to be directed towards the entire people), Böhmer (1976:51-55, 70-71; although he deems vv. 21-22 to be exilic), and Carroll (1981:200; who admits his dependence on Böhmer). Goldman's opinion (1952:109) that these verses are earlier than Jeremiah has not been accepted.

All of the scholars mentioned above consider 31.2-6 to be an isolated prophecy, as is 31.15-22 (with the exceptions of Skinner, Böhmer, and Carroll). Hyatt (1956), followed by Lindars (1979:47), dates this material to the fall of Jerusalem. Lindars argues that since 31:2-6 contains no word of repentance, it does not fit into the time of the Josianic reforms. Therefore, it must have been composed after 31.15-22 'as a response to the people when their repentance is an accomplished fact' (1979:52), i.e. 'when the city fell' (p. 55). Thus, the mention of Ephraim in vv. 18 and 20 refers to Judah, who is 'in a position comparable to that of Ephraim long before' (p. 54). Like Skinner (1922:301-302, 305-306), Lindars (1979:52-55) divides vv. 15-22 into three units: vv. 15-17, 18-20, and 21-22. Lindars's view will be challenged in section 2 below.

b. *31.7-9, 10-14*

Most scholars doubt the authenticity of vv. 7-9, 10-14. Duhm, Bright (1965), Carroll (1981:209-210) and others all believe these verses to be late-exilic at the earliest due to their (seeming) dependence upon the style and content of Deutero-Isaiah. Lindars (1979:52) suggests that vv. 7-9, 10-14 were added by the Deuteronomic editor on the basis of v. 20 (cf. v. 9). The opposite view, that these verses are authentic to Jeremiah and that Deutero-Isaiah was influenced by them, has been championed by Cassuto (1973:150-152) and Paul (1969:105-108). Unfortunately, neither one substantiates their claims, other than that the theme of redemption fits just as easily into the prophecies of Jeremiah as it does into those of Deutero-Isaiah (Cassuto, 1973:152).

Martens stands alone in asserting that 31.2-14 is a literary unit comprised of three salvation oracles: vv. 2-6, 7-9, 10-14:

> The first . . . portrays a future situation of normalcy in the Land, finding its epitome in the worship of Yahweh in Zion . . . the second . . . concentrates on the exodus from the exile which will make the portrayal of the good life in the Land possible. The third . . . depicts the material well-being of Israel, . . . is not mindful of the worship aspects . . . looks beyond the return to prosperity; and in describing the good things of Yahweh, it presents the setting in which the cult will be performed (1972:76-77).

The relationship of 31.7-9, 10-14 to Deutero-Isaiah will best be explained by an analysis of the literary connection of vv. 7-9 to 10-14 and by a comparison of vv. 7-14 to Isa. 35.3-10.[42] First, the comparison (points of contact will be indicated by roman letters and underlinings):

Jer. 31.7-14

כי כה אמר ה׳ (e) רנו ליעקב שמחה
וצהלו בראש גוים השמיעו הללו
(a) ואמרו (b) הושע ה׳ את עמך
את שארית ישראל הנני מביא אותם
מארץ צפון וקבצתים מירכתי ארץ בם
(c) עור (d) ופסח הרה וילדת יחדו
קהל גדול (k) ישובו הנה בבכי
יבאו ובתחנונים אובילם אוליכם אל
(f)נחלי מים (g) בדרך ישר
(h) לא יכשלו בה . . . כי (j) פדה
ה׳ את יעקב (i) וגאלו מיד חזק
ממנו (l) ובאו ורננו במרום ציון
. . . אז (m) תשמח בתולה . . . והפכתי
אבלם (n) לששון ונחמתים
(m) ושמחתים (o) מיגונם

Isa. 35.3-10

חזקו ידים רפות וברכים כשלות אמצו
(a) אמרו לנמהרי לב חזקו אל תיראו הנה
אלהיכם נקם יבוא גמול אלהים הוא יבוא
(b) וישעכם אז תפקחנה עיני (c) עורים
ואזני חרשים תפתחנה אז ידלג כאיל (d)
פסח (e) ותרון לשון אלם כי נבקעו במדבר
(f) מים ונחלים בערבה והיה השרב לאגם
וצמאון (f) למבועי מים בנוה תנים רבצה
חציר לקנה וגמא והיה שם מסלול
(g) ודרך ודרך הקדש יקרא לה לא יעברנו
טמא והוא למו הלך (g) דרך ואוילים
(h) לא יתעו לא יהיה שם אריה ופריץ
חיות בל יעלנה לא תמצא שם והלכו (i)
גאולים (j) ופדויי ה׳ (k) ישבון (l)
ובאו ציון ברנה (m) ושמחת עולם על
ראשם (n) ששון (m) ושמחה ישיגו ונסו
(o) יגון ואנחה

7For thus says the LORD:
'Sing aloud with gladness
for Jacob,
and raise shouts for
the chief of the
nations:
proclaim, give praise, and
say,

3Strengthen the weak
hands,
and make firm the
feeble knees.
4Say to those who are of a
fearful heart,
'Be strong, fear not!
Behold, your God will

'The LORD has saved
his people,
the remnant of Israel'.
8Behold, I will bring them
from the north
country,
and gather them from the
farthest parts of
the earth,
among them the blind and
the lame,
the woman with child
and her who is in
travail, together;
a great company, they
shall return here.
9With weeping they shall
come,
and with consolations
I will lead them back,
I will make them walk by
brooks of water,
in a straight path in
which they shall
not stumble;
for I am a father to Israel,
and Ephraim is my
first-born.
10 Hear the word of the
LORD, O nations,
and declare it in the
coastlands afar
off;
say, "He who scattered
Israel will gather
him.
and will keep him as a
shepherd keeps
his flock".
11For the LORD has ran-
somed Jacob,
and has redeemed
him from hands
too strong for
him.

come with
vengeance,
with the recompense
of God.
He will come and save
you'.
5Then the eyes of the blind
shall be opened,
and the ears of the
deaf unstopped;
6then shall the lame man
leap like a hart,
and the tongue of the
dumb sing for
joy.
For waters shall break
forth in the
wilderness,
and streams in the
desert;
7the burning sand shall
become a pool,
and thirsty ground
springs of water;
the haunt of jackals shall
become a
swamp,
the grass shall become
reeds and rushes.
8And a highway shall be
there,
and it shall be called
the Holy Way;
the unclean shall not pass
over it,
and fools shall not err
therein.
9No lion shall be there,
nor shall any ravenous
beast come up on
it;
they shall not be found
there,
but the redeemed shall
walk there.

[12]They shall come and sing
aloud on the
height of Zion,
and they shall be radiant
over the
goodness of the
LORD,
over the grain, the wine,
and the oil,
and over the young of
the flock and the
herd;
their life shall be like a
watered garden,
and they shall languish
no more.
[13]Then shall the maidens
rejoice in the
dance,
and the young men
and the old shall
be merry.
I will turn their mourning
into joy,
I will comfort them,
and give them
gladness for
sorrow.
[14]I will feast the soul of the
priests with
abundance,
and my people shall
be satisfied with
my goodness,
says the LORD'.

[10]And the ransomed of the
LORD shall
return,
and come to Zion with
singing;
everlasting joy shall be
upon their heads;
they shall obtain joy and
gladness,
and sorrow and sighing
shall flee away.

The texts on p. 42 above show at least fifteen similar usages of language, and in near-identical order. In fact, the root רנן which appears in Jer. 31.7 appears in Isa. 35.2 as well as 35.6, so that the order is broken only by 'k' and the reversal of 'i' and 'j' in Jer. 31. The only possible rational conclusion can be that one passage must be dependent upon the other.

Yet the question remains, 'Who is the borrower and who the lender?' In order to provide an answer, the literary connection between Jer. 31.7-9 and 10-14 must be analyzed. And, lo and behold, while Isaiah 35 *is* a literary unit, Jer. 31.7-9 and 10-14 are *not* organically related. For one thing, the phrase 'Hear the word of YHWH', which begins v. 10, is a typical opening formula of Jeremiah's prophecies—cp. 2.4; 7.2; 17.20; 19.3; 21.11; 42.15; 44.24. Second, in vv. 10-14 the prophet describes the return to *Zion* and to the material abundance which there awaits (v. 12), and then refers to the portion of the priests in this prosperity (v. 14).[43] At the time of the utterance of these words, then, there are no priests officiating at the Temple in Jerusalem, but rather, they are in exile with the rest of the people (vv. 10, 12). Unquestionably, the reference in v. 14 cannot be to the priests of Ephraim, for these Jeremiah, an Aaronide, would have considered disqualified. The prophecy in vv. 10-14, therefore, assumes the exile of Judah and the destruction of the Temple. This assumption is absent from the previous verses. Verse 6, in which the ascent of Ephraim to Zion is portrayed, takes for granted that Judah is dwelling upon its own territory, for if Judah had also been exiled, the prophet would have announced the return of the entire people to Zion, and not just that of Ephraim. It must be concluded that vv. 10-14 are concerned with Judah and are unconnected to vv. 2-9 which are directed to the Northern tribes. Furthermore, 31.23-25, which are addressed to Judah, have an obvious likeness to vv. 10-14: cp. 'the height of Zion' (v. 12) with 'holy hill' (v. 23); 'over the grain, the wine the oil and the young of the flock' (v. 12) with 'the farmers and those who wander with their flock' (v. 24); נפשם כגן רוה 'their soul shall be like a watered garden' (v. 12) and ורויתי נפש 'I will satisfy the soul' (v. 14) with הרויתי נפש 'I will satisfy the soul' (v. 25); דאבה 'languish' (v. 12) with דאבה 'languished (v. 25); יחדו 'together' (v. 13) with יחדו 'together' (v. 24). The root דאב appears only in these verses in Jeremiah, and rarely elsewhere (Lev. 26.16; Deut. 28.65; Ps. 88.10; Job 41.14). רוה נפש appears in the Bible only in these verses. It is clear that vv. 10-14 and 23-25 speak to the same people in the same situation—Judah in exile. Verses 7-9 and 10-14, then, are independent of one another.

If vv. 10-14 are not in their organic setting, how did they come to be placed after vv. 2-9? Ostensibly, the ordering was motivated by associative considerations—the common theme of redemption from exile and similar vocabulary: cp. v. 10, שמעו . . . גוים . . . אמרו 'hear . . . nations . . . and say' with v. 7, הגוים השמיעו . . . אמרו 'nations, hear . . . say'; v. 10, ממרחק 'from a distance' with v. 2, מרחוק 'from a distance'; v. 11, את יעקב 'Jacob' with v. 7, ליעקב 'to Jacob'; v. 12 with v. 6, ציון

'Zion'; v. 12, ורננו 'and sing' with v. 7, רנו 'sing'; v. 13, תשמח בתולה במחול 'a virgin shall rejoice in a dance' with v. 4, בתולת ישראל... במחול משחקים 'the virgin of Israel in the dance of the joyous ones'; v. 13, ושמחתים 'I will make them joyous' with v. 7, שמחה 'joy'.[44] Additionally, vv. 13 and 16 depict the turning of sorrow into happiness.

Evidently, vv. 7-9 and 10-14 had already been placed next to each other before the anonymous prophet of Isaiah 35 made use of them for his own composition. This deduction appears to be far more reasonable than the possibility that vv. 10-14 were attached to vv. 7-9 on the basis of the single prophecy in Isaiah 35. The closeness of the relationship between Jer. 31.7-9, 10-14 and Isaiah 35 also militates against Lipinski's claim (1972:1354) that 'Stylistic similarities to Deutero-Isaiah in Jeremiah... 31.6-8 can be explained on the supposition that both prophets made use of the same conventional form of priestly oracles'. Furthermore, Isaiah 35 looks like an expansion of Jer. 31.7-9, 10-14: cp. Jer. 31.8 'the blind and the lame' with Isa. 35.5-6, 'then the eyes of the blind shall be opened and the ears of the deaf unstopped; then the lame man shall leap like a heart and the tongue of the dumb sing for joy'; Jer. 31.9, 'I will make them walk by brooks of water, in a straight path in which they shall not stumble', with Isa. 35.6b-9 in their entirety; Jer. 31.13, 'from their sorrow', with Isa. 35.10, 'and sorrow and sighing shall flee away'. The result of the above analysis is inescapable—Jer. 31.7-9 and 10-14 were written and coupled together previously to the composition of Deutero-Isaiah in Isaiah 35.[45] This conclusion, also, testifies against those scholars mentioned above who would doubt the authenticity of Jer. 31.7-9, 10-14.

c. *The Meaning of 31.22* נקבה תשובב גבר

The meaning of the last three words of 31.22 has been a crux for scholarship. The problem is already reflected in the LXX which translates the second half of the verse. ὅτι ἔκτισε κύριος σωτηρίαν εἰς καταφύτευσιν καινὴν, ἐν ᾗ σωτηρίᾳ περιελεύσονται ἄνθρωποι. Tov (1981:68) remarks on the difficult syntax of the LXX and the unclear meaning of καταφύτευσιν and περιελεύσονται. The Targum interprets ועמא בית ישראל יתנהון לאוריתא which is in a similar vein to Rashi, 'that the female shall go back after the male to ask him to marry her', who cites Cant. 3.2, ואסובבה בעיר... אבקשה 'I will go about the city... I will seek him'. In like fashion, Kara and Kimḥi understand these words to mean that Israel will return to God. Abarbanel offers three explanations: (1) that Israel will no longer be subject to the nations, but rather that Israel will subjugate them (in this he is followed by Altschuler's *Meẓudat David*); (2) that Rachel's prayer causes God to be merciful to her children; (3) that Israel's return to God causes God to benefit them.

Similarly to Abarbanel's first explanation, Luzzatto interprets that a woman will guard a man, i.e. there will be no war; Orelli states that a woman will shield a man, i.e. the people will guard the land even though they are defenseless; Rudolph comments that security in the land will be so great that a woman will be able to defend a man; Holladay (1971-72:219), citing 30.5-7, says 'Your warriors have become female? Look—God's new creation: the female will surmount the warrior! Take heart; come home';[46] Lundbom (1975:32-33) sees 30.5-6 and 31.22b as constituting an inclusio, in which the words under discussion are translated 'the *female* protects the *soldier*'. Most of these scholars refer to the use of the root סבב in Deut. 32.10, which seems to indicate protection.

Recent suggestions have included those of: Trible (1976-77:280), that 'Female surrounds man' is 'the denoument of an aesthetic object . . . the poem describes itself . . . it resists extrinsic formulations and requires imaginative interpretation'; Jacob (1977:182-84), who opts for the traditional interpretation of Israel's return to God; Anderson (1978:468, 478), who, basing himself on Weiser's proposal that these problematic words refer to 'the renewal of the creation-blessing of fertility . . . from which the people will arise anew', believes that 'the woman will enfold a man' means 'that the bereaved Virgin Israel will have a son, a posterity, and therefore a future in the land promised to Israel's ancestors'.

Many scholars, including Bright, Nicholson, Lindars (1979:32-33), and Carroll (1981:212), appear more impressed by the obscurity of the language than by any particular interpretation. Zeiner (1957:282-83) has attempted to erase the words by conceiving them as a corrupt dittography.

The phrase under discussion will be examined in section 2 below.

2. *Meaning and Ultimate Structure*

a. *31.2-6*. In words reminiscent of the exodus from Egypt,[47] vv. 2-3 emphasize YHWH's love[48] and goodwill towards His downcast people, Israel (i.e. Ephraim—cp. vv. 5-6). This encouraging beginning is succeeded in vv. 4-5 by God's promise to 'Virgin Israel' that she will return from exile, be rebuilt in her land,[49] and will enjoy agricultural fruitfulness and security.[50] This section concludes with v. 6 which alludes to a new unification of Ephraim and Judah in terms of the worship of YHWH, when Jerusalem will once again fulfill her role as the religious center of the entire nation.[51]

b. *31.7-9*. Following the image of lover and virgin in the previous verses, vv. 7-9 describes the relationship of YHWH to Israel in terms of father and son (v. 9).

In v. 7, God commands an anonymous audience[52] to rejoice for the sake of Jacob and to 'shout for joy for the head of the nations'. The language used to indicate the objects of this clause is, admittedly, ambiguous.[53] Nonetheless, the verbs are clear—joy is to be acclaimed. This being the case, הושע cannot be possibly understood as the imperative 'Save!', for if the salvation of Israel is in doubt, then what reason is there to be happy? Additionally, the verb הללו reveals that the verse is not concerned with an entreaty to God, but rather with praise, thanksgiving, and proclamation of YHWH's beneficial deeds, e.g. Jer. 20.13: הללו יהוה for *He has delivered* the life of the needy from the hand of the evildoers'.[54] Therefore, it is preferable to accept the translation of the Septuagint and Targum 'saved', i.e. הוֹשִׁעַ. If so, then the MT must be understood as God commanding the audience to say to Jacob the patriarch, 'YHWH has saved *your* people,[55] the remnant of Israel'.

God's promise to gather in the exiles of Ephraim is the subject of v. 8, while v. 9 is His description of this return accompanied by the people's 'crying . . . and supplications' as an expression of their contrition (cp. 3.21).[56] The passage ends with YHWH's declaration 'Ephraim, he is my firstborn'. It seems that, in vv. 7-9, God's fatherhood of Israel is the motivation for welling up of the divine mercies and the decision to restore Ephraim to his homeland.

c. *31.15-20.* After the comforting words to the patriarch, God now turns to the matriarch, Rachel, and urges her to dry up her tears for 'her children', the exiles of Ephraim, are coming back to their land (vv. 15-17). The grounds for the restoration are stated in vv. 18-20. God hears Ephraim's confession which expresses his desire to return to God, as well as his call to God to help in this process (vv. 18-19).[57] That this call to help is forthcoming is apparent in v. 20—Ephraim's confession stirs up God's feelings of parenthood and, hence, its mercies.

d. *The Relationship between 31.7-9 and 15-20.* In several ways, vv. 7-9 and 15-20 are complementary passages in regards to both structure and meaning:

1. God's words, addressed to an anonymous audience, which serve as a prelude. In v. 15 Rachel's despair is described, while in v. 7 Jacob's despair is alluded to (else why proclaim joy?).

2. God comforts both of Ephraim's ancestors with a promise that the exiles shall return (vv. 7b-9a, 16-17).
3. Ephraim shows signs of contrition (vv. 9a, 18-19).
4. God proclaims His parenthood of Ephraim as motivation for His merciful actions (vv. 9b, 20).

There are also certain linguistic similarities: מארץ צפון 'from the land of the North' in v. 8 and מארץ אויב 'from the land of the enemy' in v. 16; בבכי... ובתחנונים 'with crying and weeping' in v. 9 and בכי תמרורים 'with bitter crying' in v. 15; ישובו הנה 'they will return here' in v. 8 and ושבו 'and they will return' in vv. 16, 17 (in the latter verse, לגבולם 'to their border').

An enlightening element of the complementary aspect of these two passages is the way in which God expressed his parenthood. To Jacob, the father, God depicts his fatherhood, כי הייתי לישראל לאב ואפרים בכרי הוא 'for I am a father to Israel and Ephraim is my firstborn' (v. 9, cp. 2 Sam. 7.14 אני אהיה לו לאב והוא יהיה לי לבן 'I will be to him a father and he will be to me a son'; also, Exod. 4.22; Pss. 2.7; 89.27-28). But to Rachel, the mother, God depicts his motherhood! This interpretation may be defended by the following points: (1) v. 20 contains no language that indicates specifically fatherhood; (2) the parallel phrases המו מעי לו רחם ארחמנו suggest the womb image. Although מעים can denote the inward parts of either a male or female body, it means womb in Gen. 25.23; Isa. 49.1; Ps. 71.6; Ruth 1.11. Note particularly the almost identical expression in Cant. 5.4 ומעי המו עליו. Furthermore, the root רחם most probably always alludes to 'motherly compassion' in the verb form, since the noun form means 'womb';[58] (3) the root שעשע is used in Isa. 66.12 in the context of a metaphor of a child played with on its *mother's* knee, and the following verse explicitly mentions the motherhood image of God כאיש אשר אמו תנחמנו כן אנכי אנחמכם 'as one whom his mother comforts, so I will comfort you'; cp. Isa. 49.14-15.[59] In other words, God is usurping the caring roles of both father and mother (cp. Isa. 63.16; Ps. 27.10).

It thus seems incontrovertible that 3.7-9 and 10-15 are organically related.

e. *31.21-22 and its Relationship to 31.2-6*. The parent-child image of vv. 7-9, 15-20 is dropped and the lover-virgin image of vv. 2-6 is picked up in vv. 21-22. In v. 21 God calls Virgin Israel (cp. v. 4) to return to her land (the double use of שובי echoes the double ושבו in

vv. 16-17; למסלה 'to the path' and דרך may point back to the בדרך of v. 9).[60] In order to understand the complete sense of v. 22, it behooves us to review the love image of vv. 2-6. The words of vv. 2-3, מצא חן במדבר...ואהבת עולם אהבתיך על כן משכתיך חסד 'found grace in the wilderness... I have loved you with an everlasting love, therefore I have drawn you with faithfulness' are reminiscent of 2.2, זכרתי לך חסד נעוריך אהבת כלולתיך לכתך אחרי במדבר 'I remember the faithfulness of your youth, your bride's love, how you followed me in the wilderness', and, also, Hos. 2.16, 21, הנה אנכי מפתיה הולכתיה המדבר . . . וארשתיך לי לעולם 'Behold I will allure her and will bring her into the wilderness... and I will betroth you to me forever', וארשתיך לי בצדק ובמשפט ובחסד וברחמים 'I will betroth you to me in righteousness, and in justice, and in faithfulness, and in mercy'. ועוד תטעי כרמים 'again you shall plant vineyards' in v. 5 may very well echo Hos. 2.17, נתתי לה את כרמיה 'I will give her her vineyards'. However, the vineyard is well known as a place where lovers meet (Judg. 21.19-23, note the reference to the girls dancing; Cant. 7.13), as well as symbolizing love and the lover (Isa. 5.1-2; Cant. 1.6, 14; 2.15; 8.11-12).

The dancing of the virgin in v. 4 brings to mind Cant. 1.7 שובי שובי השולמית שובי שובי ונחזה בך מה תחזו בשולמית כמחלת המחנים 'Turn, turn O Shulammite, turn, turn that we may look upon you. Why should you look upon the Shulammite as upon a dance of Mahanaim'; here the dancer is turning as she dances, so that שובי means סבי Similarly, in Cant. 2.17, סב דמה לך דודי לצבי 'turn, my beloved like a gazelle', the Septuagint and Peshitta read סב as if שוב were written.

The description of the love dance is relevant to Jer. 31.22, as is the love poetry of the Song of Songs. The root חמק which appears in v. 22 occurs elsewhere in the Bible only in Cant. 5.6 and 7.2. Of the two, only the first is significant—'I opened to my beloved but my beloved חמק, passed on, my soul left when he spoke', בקשאתיהש ולא מצאתיהו קראתיו 'I sought him but didn't find him, I called him but he didn't answer me'; the lover has 'gone away', 'distanced himself' from the woman. This is how Jer. 31.22 must be understood, but here it is the girl who has distanced herself from her lover. The man—God—no longer will allow the virgin—Ephraim—to continue to remain at a distance. Note, too, that Cant. 5.6 uses language to describe the woman searching for the man which elsewhere can refer to the people seeking after God, as in Jer. 29.12-13, וקראתם אתי . . . ובקשתם אתי ומצאתם (cp. Deut. 4.29; Hos. 5.6, 15), so it is easy to see in עד מתי תתחמקין 'how long will you distance yourself' the intimation of repentance.

Therefore, God creates something new. It will be the reverse of that acknowledged wonder 'the way of a גבר man with a young woman' (Prov. 30.19). Rather, the virgin will now relate to the man in a new way, נקבה תסובב גבר, she will dance around him in a dance of love. In other words, God will cause His people to return to Him, a return which has never occurred before (תסובב is a pun on השובבה).

Verse 22, then, is God's response to Ephraim's plea in v. 18, 'cause me to return (to you) and I shall return'. The conclusion of the above analysis is that vv. 2-6 and 21-22 form an inclusio around vv. 7-9, 15-20. In vv. 2-6 God promises that Israel will be redeemed and in vv. 21-22 He tells how—He will cause the people to return to Him.

f. *31.2-9, 15-22: General Structure* The general structure of the literary unit 31.2-9, 15-22 is that of an A, B, B′, A′ pattern:

A. Verses 2-6: the love of YHWH for Virgin Israel and the promise of return from exile (vv. 2-5); return to YHWH (v. 6).

B. Verses 7-9: the promise to an ancestor of return from exile (v. 8); signs of Ephraim's contrition (v. 9a); declaration of God's parenthood of Ephraim (v. 9b).

B′. Verses 15-20: the promise to an ancestor of return from exile (vv. 16-17); signs of Ephraim's contrition (vv. 18-19); declaration of God's parenthood of Ephraim (v. 20).

A′. Verses 21-22: the love of YHWH for Virgin Israel and the promise of return from exile (vv. 21-22); the return to YHWH (v. 22).

3. *Summary and Conclusions*

In light of the above discussions, Jer. 31.2-9, 15-22 has been shown to be a literary unit comprising a prophecy of redemption by Jeremiah to the exiled Northern tribes. Verse 6, with its reference to a call to the inhabitants of Ephraim to worship in Jerusalem, can best be comprehended against the background of the period in which Josiah sought to extend Judean cultic practices northwards (2 Kgs 23.15-20).[62]

This prophecy emphasizes two catalysts needed for crystallization of redemption—YHWH's mercies and Ephraim's repentance. The transition from exile to restoration takes place via a three-step process:

1. YHWH hears Ephraim's contrition and confession which expresses his readiness to return to his God (vv. 18-19; cp. v. 9a);
2. This confession stirs up YHWH's mercies (v. 20; cp. v. 9b), which YHWH extends to Ephraim (vv. 2-3) and promises to restore him to his land in security and prosperity (vv. 4-9, 16-17);
3. However, the return to YHWH has not yet materialized—Ephraim cannot go it alone, 'cause me to return and I shall return' (v. 18). YHWH demands of the people a dual return—to Him and to the land (vv. 21-22a), with the latter dependent upon the former. Then YHWH, in His mercies, promises Ephraim that He will cause the people to return to Him (v. 22b), which also implies restoration to the land. Return to YHWH and return to the land, though interwoven with one another, are not identical. Rather, they should be seen as two elements of a single process, which, at its completion (after the return to YHWH brings about restoration to the land) results in the creation of the ideal relationship between YHWH and His people—a mutual relationship cemented in love and faithfulness.

There is no way to determine with any degree of certainty whether Israel's contrition precedes God's mercies or not. The contrition of Ephraim has been placed as the first step in the process here because God is depicted as having *heard* it, a fact which accounts for the ensuing arousal of YHWH's mercies (v. 20). Nevertheless, the possibility that YHWH's mercies were moved because of the harshness of their physical condition cannot be disregarded, 'the people who are left of the sword have found favor in the desert' (v. 2). It is even possible that YHWH's declaration of His merciful intentions in vv. 2-9 was the motivating force behind Ephraim's confession.

In 31.2-9, 15-22 the divine mercies are expressed through YHWH's desire and intentions; the images of His love in terms of parenthood, compassion, and the love of a man for a young woman; His promise to effect his people's repentance. One senses that, although redemption is conditional upon Israel's repentance, YHWH's mercies are the more significant factor.

C. The Relationship of 3.6-13, 19–4.2 to 31.2-9, 15-22

There are many points of contact between the two prophecies analyzed in this chapter:

1. God extends His Mercies to Ephraim (3.11-12; 31.2-3; note the occurrence of the root חסד in both prophecies);
2. God calls His people to repentance (3.12; 31.22);
3. Ephraim's crying and supplications (3.21; 31.9);
4. Ephraim confesses (3.22; 31.18; note the nearly identical 'for you are YHWH our/my God'; 3.23-25; 31.19);[63]
5. God's parenthood of Ephraim (3.19, 22; 31.9, 20);
6. Settlement in the land of Israel (4.1; 31.5);
7. The exalted status of the nation vis-à-vis the rest of the peoples (4.2; 31.7);
8. Both prophecies conclude with a reference to the condition of repentance (4.1; 31.22);
9. The phrase 'a voice . . . is heard' (3.20; 31.15).

The plethora of affinities between the two prophecies is further testimony for the claim that they were written in the same period. It should be noted however, that, even though both prophecies envision the necessity of repentance as a precondition to redemption, 31.2-9, 15-22 appear to emphasize more the aspect of YHWH's mercies. This may be an indication that Jeremiah has begun to shift his view, to doubt that the people can realize repentance without divine assistance. Thus, 31.2-9, 15-22 may have been written at a somewhat later date than 3.6-13, 19–4.2.

Chapter 2

PROPHECIES OF REDEMPTION TO THE JUDEANS EXILED WITH JEHOIACHIN

The most common and most serious scholarly argument against the authenticity of both Jer. 24.4-7 and 29.10-14, the passages to be examined in this chapter, has been that these verses underwent a thoroughgoing dtr. redaction. This claim hinges on the relationship of Jer. 24.4-7 to Deut. 30.1-10 and of Jer. 29.10-14 to Deut. 4.29-31. In current scholarship, both these passages in Deuteronomy are viewed as belonging to a late, second edition of Deuteronomy done in the period of the Babylonian exile. Before an exposition of the Jeremiah material can be attempted, the arguments for dtr. authorship must be examined. This chapter, then will take the following order: a review of scholarship concerning the dtr. edition of Jer. 24.4-7 and 29.10-14; the comparison of these passages with Deut. 30.1-10 and 4.29-31, respectively; the theory of the late, second edition of Deuteronomy as it relates to these passages in Deuteronomy; other issues of structure and meaning in Jer. 24.4-7 and 29.10-14.

A. Jer. 24.4-7 and 29.10-14: Authentic Jeremiah or Deuteronomistic?

1. *Review of Scholarship*

a. *Jer. 24.4-7*

4 ה וַיְהִי דְבַר־יְהוָה אֵלַי לֵאמֹר׃ כֹּה־אָמַר
יְהוָה אֱלֹהֵי יִשְׂרָאֵל כַּתְּאֵנִים הַטֹּבוֹת הָאֵלֶּה כֵּן אַכִּיר אֶת־
גָּלוּת יְהוּדָה אֲשֶׁר שִׁלַּחְתִּי מִן־הַמָּקוֹם הַזֶּה אֶרֶץ כַּשְׂדִּים
6 לְטוֹבָה׃ וְשַׂמְתִּי עֵינִי עֲלֵיהֶם לְטוֹבָה וַהֲשִׁבֹתִים עַל־
הָאָרֶץ הַזֹּאת וּבְנִיתִים וְלֹא אֶהֱרֹס וּנְטַעְתִּים וְלֹא אֶתּוֹשׁ׃
7 וְנָתַתִּי לָהֶם לֵב לָדַעַת אֹתִי כִּי אֲנִי יְהוָה וְהָיוּ־לִי לְעָם
וְאָנֹכִי אֶהְיֶה לָהֶם לֵאלֹהִים כִּי־יָשֻׁבוּ אֵלַי בְּכָל־לִבָּם׃

> 4 Then the word of the LORD came to me: [5]'Thus says the LORD, the God of Israel: Like these good figs, so I will regard as good the exiles from Judah, whom I have sent away from this place to the land of Chaldeans. [6]I will set my eyes upon them for good, and I will bring them back to this land. I will build them up, and not tear them down; I will plant them, and not uproot them. [7]I will give them a heart to know that I am the LORD; and they shall be my people and I will be their God, for they shall return to me with their whole heart'.

The claims for dtr. redaction in Jer. 24.4-7:

1. May (1942:154; 1945:218) contends that ch. 24 comes from the pen of Jeremiah's biographer, a scribe who lived between 500 and 450 BCE and used many stereotypical deuteronomic expressions,[1] such as מעל האדמה אשר נתתי להם ולאבותיהם 'from the land which I gave to them and their fathers' (v. 10);

2. Hyatt (1951:84-85), whose views are echoed but not cited by Nicholson (1973) and Carroll (see below), argues with reference to ch. 24 that

> The attitude expressed here about the exiles accords well with the attitude of later times which saw in the Jews who had gone into Babylonian exile and later returned the true Israelites, and with the view of those who considered the exiled Jehoiachin as the legitimate king and opposed the claims of Zedekiah. It does not accord with Jeremiah's ideas expressed elsewhere, and is filled with D phraseology, most noticeably in verses 6, 7, 9 and 10. It is difficult to believe that Jeremiah thought God's favor depended on whether one were exiled or not, rather than upon repentance and obedience. In chapter 5 he expressed the opinion that all classes in Jerusalem were sinful. The viewpoint of chapter 24 is not consonant with Jeremiah's viewpoint in the letter to the exiles in chapter 29, nor with his general attitude toward Zedekiah. That king was friendly to the prophet and apparently wished to follow his counsel, but was weak and unwilling to risk the disfavor of the pro-Egyptian party among his officials... Whether D freely composed this chapter or rewrote some material which he found, we do not know; but in its present form it is his product and not Jeremiah's.

3. Holladay (1958:136) compares ch. 24 with the parables in Jeremiah 13 and 18:

> In each case there is a statement of the parable which is free of Deuteronomistic phraseology (xiii 1-8, xviii 1-4, xxiv 1-3) followed by an interpretation of the parable which is heavy with Deuteronomistic phrases (xiii 9-11, xviii 5-12, xxiv 4-10)... The passage is plainly Dtst.

4. According to Nicholson, (1970:80-81) 24.4-7 and 29.10-14 reflect the same 'Deuteronomistic kerygma according to which Israel's "turning again" to Yahweh and her obedience to his Law would guarantee her renewed existence as his people'. Nicholson continues,

> however, a considerable advance has been made upon xviii. 7-10, for whilst it is still Israel's 'turning again' which will secure forgiveness and restoration, such a 'turning again' is now assured by Yahweh himself who now takes the initiative so that Israel *will* 'turn again' (xxiv. 7; cf. xxix. 12). That is to say, the conditional 'if' has now receded and the element of promise has come to the forefront of the kerygma.

Is there any textual evidence from either Deuteronomy or the dtr. history which reflects or parallels the 'considerable advance' that Nicholson sees in Jer. 24 and 29? Nicholson presents none, and for a very good reason: there is none. Furthermore, although Nicholson posits Jer. 18.7-12 as dtr. he does not explain the cause for the ideological development from Jeremiah 18 to Jeremiah 24 and 29, nor does he explain why the same ideology is not present in all three passages.

Elsewhere, Nicholson (1973:205) states that Jeremiah 24 and 29 are dtr. redactions which reflect the ideology of Deut. 30.1-10. Additionally, he (1973:207) compares 24.7, 'I will give them a heart to know me' (and the similar promise in 31.33 and 32.38-39), with the circumcision of hearts mentioned in Deut. 30.6.

In his summary on the dtr. provenience of ch. 24, Nicholson concludes (1970:110) that

> In its present form this passage clearly belongs to the Jeremianic prose tradition the language and style of which are well in evidence throughout. At the same time the striking imagery which it employs indicates that it is based upon an authentic saying of the prophet himself. The fact, however, that it owes its present form to the prose traditionalists means once again that any interpretation of it solely in terms of Jeremiah's teaching is inadequate. We have here yet another example of the phenomenon . . . in which an oracle or saying originally uttered by the prophet himself has subsequently been developed and applied by those who transmitted it to meet a particular need or provide instruction on a problem which was of concern or relevance to them in the situation in which they lived. Viewed from this point of view the reason why the original prophetic saying concerning the good and bad figs has been subjected to further development and expansion becomes clear, for in drawing a sharp distinction between those who had undergone judgment and were in exile after 597 B.C. and those who had been untouched by that judgement and remained in Judah, it would have continued to be of relevance for those in exile throughout the exilic period and who regarded themselves as the 'good figs' through whom alone renewal would come as against those who remained in Judah. That this is so is evidenced by the inclusion amongst the 'bad figs' of those who fled to Egypt (Jer. xxiv. 8), which very clearly presupposes the situation brought about after 586 B.C. and the murder of Gedaliah and the flight of the Judean community to Egypt. This means that the composition of chapters xxiv and xxix was motivated primarily by a specifically theological and polemical intention, for they seek to assert the claims of the Babylonian diaspora to be the true remnant of Israel through whom alone renewal and

> restoration would be wrought by Yahweh as against those who either remained in Judah or lived in Egypt during the exilic period.

Particularly confusing in Nicholson's presentation is the absence of a delineation of the original saying of the prophet. Certainly, there must have been *some* prophecy connected to v. 3. Furthermore, it is inconceivable that ch. 24 could have been of comfort to those who were exiled with Zedekiah, for vv. 8-10 apply to them a horrid curse, with no word of redemption. In order for Jeremiah 24 to read as Nicholson would have it, the historical reference in v. 1, the reference to Zedekiah and his contemporaries in v. 8, and the references to the kingdoms and places of exile in v. 9 would all have had to be deleted;

5. Thiel (1973:255-56) views Jer. 24 and 29 as not just parallels, but counterparts with linguistic correspondence, both written by a deuteronomist. He compares the phrase 'to return with the whole heart' in 24.7 with 1 Sam. 7.3; Deut. 30.2, 10; and 1 Kgs 8.48;

6. Although Böhmer (1976:32) accepts 24.5 as authentic, he judges vv. 6-7 to be late because of dtr. motifs and formulas;

7. Pohlmann (1978:29-30, 192), citing similar arguments to those of Nicholson, Thiel, and Böhmer, also posits that Jeremiah 24 is the work of a redactor, but does not label him as dtr., rather as exile-oriented;

8. Carroll (1981:202), also, claims that Jeremiah 24 has been redacted and is 'designed to replace the Jerusalem community associated with Zedekiah in Yahweh's affections with the exiles associated with Jeconiah, so it clearly emanates from that group'. Rather than support this blatantly cynical statement, he (1981:325, n. 6) notes, 'Whether the sections supporting the Babylonian exiles are to be derived from a Babylonian or a Palestinian source and whether during or after the exile are issues undetermined by the data available in the tradition'.

In support of the authenticity of Jer. 24.4-7:

1. Skinner (1922:324) understands the phrases 'they shall be to me a people, and I will be a God to them' (Jer. 24.7) and 'from the land which I gave to them and their fathers' (v. 10) not as dtr., but as expressions natural to the ideological world of the covenant—a central concept in Jeremiah's spiritual environment. These expressions, then, are hardly the sole property of the deuteronomist. Skinner's omission of a discussion on the phrases 'I shall give you a heart to know me' and 'for they will return to me with all their heart' (v. 7) weakens his argument;

2. Welch (1928:160-65) asserts that ch. 24 fits the historical background of Jehoiachin's exile. Those who remain upon the land believe in their security; the exile has passed them by and they are still dwelling in the shadow of the Temple under the assumption that, in the eyes of God, they are better than their exiled brethren. According to Welch, in ch. 24 Jeremiah wishes to prove to those who remain that God's beneficent promise for the future is directed

towards the exiles. Those already taken captive will learn that God is with them even in Babylon and that His presence is not circumscribed by the borders of Israel and Judah. If, then, the exiles repent, they will enjoy His mercies. Those who remained on the land did not grasp the concept of God's omnipresence, and, therefore, are mistaken in thinking that they are closer to Him than the exiles. Consequently, exile shall now be the fate of those who have remained in order that they, too, shall learn the lesson of God's omnipresence. Welch rejects the idea that the purpose of the prophecy is limited to the declaration of punishment upon those who pride themselves unjustly on their superiority, for if that was the purpose then there would be no reason for Jeremiah's favorable attitude towards the exiles.

Welch's speculation concerning the theological lesson which God wants to teach those who remained after Jehoiachin's exile has no support in the text. Furthermore, Welch ignores the reference to 'those who dwell in the land of Egypt' (v. 8)—words which slam the door on his argument. Why are the Judeans who dwell in Egypt included among those who must learn of God's presence in the lands of exile? Do those in Egypt believe that they are closer to God than those in Babylon? To these questions Welch does not provide an answer;

3. Rudolph argues for the authenticity of ch. 24 on the basis of comparisons with Jer. 1.44ff.; 3.6ff.; and 13.1ff. (the relationship of ch. 24 to 3.6ff. will be examined later);

4. Precisely that terminology in *Jeremiah* which has been identified by modern scholarship as dtr. is apprehended by Kaufmann (1967:432-39) as a patented sign of Jeremianic composition of ch. 24. While Kaufmann notes the correspondence between Jer. 24.7 and Deut. 29.3 and 30.1-6, he envisions Deuteronomy as having been an essential part of Jeremiah's educational upbringing. In his (1967:440) words, 'there is no doubt that Jeremiah learned the Book of Deuteronomy from his youth and inculcated its language and images . . he was the prophet of the book'.

Although Kaufmann's outlook is very seductive, it seems too simplistic for he does not give the prophet credit for an independent thought process. In other words, Kaufmann conceives of Jeremiah as a mimic of Deuteronomy, and does not grant the possibility of understanding the prophecy of ch. 24 in terms of the prophet's own historical background. The significance of this element will be discussed further;

5. In an adaptation of Mowinckel's theory of the sources of *Jeremiah*, Bright (1966:19-28) has labeled ch. 24 as belonging to a wider source—A′. This literary type includes Jer. 1.4-19; 13.1-11; 18.1-12; 19.1-13; 27; 32.6-15, 17-25; and 35. Similar prophecies external to *Jeremiah* are found in Isa. 6.1–8.18; Amos 7.1-9.4; and 1 Kings 22. Chapter 24 particularly resembles the visions of Amos. The aim of this literary type is to prove that the prophet is the messenger of YHWH. Chapter 24, like the other appearances of this literary type in Jeremiah, is, according to Bright (1966:28), of the prophet's own prophecies. Previously, Bright (1951:15-35) attempted to prove that the

prose passages in Jeremiah were consistent with the prophet's words, even if they had undergone some redaction. These passages were written down no later than ten years after the destruction of the Temple (1951:22, 25, 27-28).

Concerning the claim that the reference to those dwelling in Egypt (v. 8) reflects the flight of Judeans after 586 BCE, Bright (1965) notes

> This does not require us to date the passage after 587 . . . Undoubtedly Jews of the pro-Egyptian party, who had favored resistance to Babylon, had fled there when Jehoiakim became Nebuchadnezzar's vassal (ca. 603), or when Nebuchadnezzar invaded Judah in 598/7.

Indeed, that Judeans sought refuge in Egypt before 587 is attested by the tragic story of Uriah ben Shemaiah (Jer. 26.20-23);

6. Berridge (1970:63-65) points to ch. 24 as the pure form of the literary-prophetic type of a vision and its explanation. For him (1970:66), the consecutive expressions ויהי דבר יהוה אלי 'the word of YHWH came to me' and כה אמר יהוה 'thus says YHWH' (vv. 4-5) are a hallmark of the prophet's style. As evidence, Berridge cites the same combination in 2.1-2;

7. The most sophisticated published treatment to date of the prophecies of redemption in Jeremiah (and Ezekiel) is that of Raitt (1977). Raitt (1977:112) numbers six prose passages as derived from Jeremiah 'with his own first circle of faithful disciples' and which 'represent the mind of Jeremiah as concerns Judah's future *after it has gone into exile*': 24.4-7; 29.4-7, 10-14; 32.6-15, 42-44; 31.31-34; 32.36-41; 33.6-9 ('a sequence approximating the degree of certainty which we can have that the words and ideas are authentically Jeremianic'). Of these, Raitt believes that 24.4-7 is the 'earliest and paradigmatic passage'. By comparing the use of 'good' in Jer. 24.6 with Jer. 8.15; Mic. 1.12; Amos 9.4, Raitt (1977:114-15) concludes that 'good' in v. 6 designates 'an action of deliverance instead of . . . God's blessing'. In Deuteronomy and dtr. texts, 'good' never refers to deliverance, but is commonly used in reference to God's blessing of fertility, such as in Deut. 30.5 and 9 (1977:253, n. 17).[2]

Raitt (1977:115-17) collates the six passages mentioned above and finds that they have most of the following elements in common: (1) they are adressed to exiled Judeans; (2) 'There is a remembrance of a time of judgment, so that the promised deliverance exists in a residual tension with the judgment without that recognition's diminishing or qualifying the dimensions of salvation in the new era'; (3) YHWH gives the people 'a new capacity to respond to him', most frequently a 'heart'; (4) a form of the formula 'I will be your God and you will be my people'; (5) 'Knowing God, or obeying God, is specified as another goal of the divine intervention'; (6) 'God restores their fortunes, or returns them to their land, by use of the imagery of *šûb*, often doubled'; (7) repentance is not a prerequisite but a consequence of God's saving act; (8) 'The proclamation of God's initiative, his "I will", comes prior to the mention of any human initiative'; (9) 'This "I will" initiative may have a goal or intended result (changed conditions, changed relationship, changed people), but it does not have an explanation in a "ground", "basis", or "motivation" like the Accusation section of an Oracle of Judgment'. To Raitt (1977:119), the commonality of these elements implies that these six passages 'belong in their first formulation to within less than a decade of one another, and speak to the same constellation of concerns from the same basic theological perspective'.

Raitt (1977:120) then compares the six passages in Jeremiah with the three 'Deuteronomistic promises of a good future which envision or presuppose a time of exile . . . Deut. 4.26-31; 30.1-10; and 1 Kgs 8.46-53'. Raitt notes three major differences between the two groups: (1) in the dtr. passages deliverance is conditional upon repentance (Deut. 4.29, 30; 30.2, 10; 1 Kgs 8.47, 48), while in Jeremiah 'God's gracious initiative is unconditional, is usually stated first, and dominates the tone of the entire promise';[3] (2) As opposed to Jeremiah, in the 'Deuteronomistic promises the restoration is performed with some consideration given to God's prior commitment to "the fathers" of the present . . . generation (Deut. 4.31; 30.5, 9; 1 Kgs 8.53)'; (3) Unlike the Jeremiah oracles, 'The three Deuteronomistic passages all make explicit that God's response involves . . . an expression of unconditional and womblike love (. . . the . . . image *raham*: Deut. 4.31; 30.3; 1 Kgs 8.50)'.

In the above discussion, differences (2) and (3) appear questionable as to their decisiveness. A reference to the 'fathers' appears in Jer. 24.10, which Raitt (1977:113) indicates that he accepts as part of the organic whole of the prophecy, and, as has been shown in the previous chapter, Jer. 31.20, which contains the root רחם, is authentic. Furthermore, in a later chapter it shall be demonstrated that 33.26, which names the Patriarchs as well as containing the root רחם, is authentic. Nonetheless, Raitt's difference (1) is decisive, as was independently arrived at and demonstrated by the present author (Unterman, 1975:32-33, 44-45). As stated at the beginning of this chapter, the relationship between Jer. 24.4-7 and Deut. 30.1-10 will be examined in detail after a discussion of the authenticity of Jer. 29.10-14. It will also be established that Jer. 24.4-7 and 29.10-14 cannot be equated with the other four Jeremiah oracles mentioned by Raitt.

b. *Jer. 29.10-14*

כִּי־כֹה אָמַר יְהוָה כִּי לְפִי
מְלֹאת לְבָבֶל שִׁבְעִים שָׁנָה אֶפְקֹד אֶתְכֶם וַהֲקִמֹתִי עֲלֵיכֶם
אֶת־דְּבָרִי הַטּוֹב לְהָשִׁיב אֶתְכֶם אֶל־הַמָּקוֹם הַזֶּה׃ כִּי 11
אָנֹכִי יָדַעְתִּי אֶת־הַמַּחֲשָׁבֹת אֲשֶׁר אָנֹכִי חֹשֵׁב עֲלֵיכֶם נְאֻם־
יְהוָה מַחְשְׁבוֹת שָׁלוֹם וְלֹא לְרָעָה לָתֵת לָכֶם אַחֲרִית
וְתִקְוָה׃ וּקְרָאתֶם אֹתִי וַהֲלַכְתֶּם וְהִתְפַּלַּלְתֶּם אֵלָי וְשָׁמַעְתִּי 12
אֲלֵיכֶם׃ וּבִקַּשְׁתֶּם אֹתִי וּמְצָאתֶם כִּי תִדְרְשֻׁנִי בְּכָל־ 13

לְבַבְכֶם׃ וְנִמְצֵאתִי לָכֶם נְאֻם־יְהוָה וְשַׁבְתִּי אֶת־שְׁבִיתְכֶם 14
וְקִבַּצְתִּי אֶתְכֶם מִכָּל־הַגּוֹיִם וּמִכָּל־הַמְּקוֹמוֹת אֲשֶׁר הִדַּחְתִּי
אֶתְכֶם שָׁם נְאֻם־יְהוָה וַהֲשִׁבֹתִי אֶתְכֶם אֶל־הַמָּקוֹם אֲשֶׁר־
הִגְלֵיתִי אֶתְכֶם מִשָּׁם׃

> 10 'For thus says the LORD: When seventy years are completed for Babylon, I will visit you, and I will fulfil to you my promise and bring you back to this place. [11]For I know the plans I have for you, says the LORD, plans for welfare and not for evil, to give you a future and a hope. [12]Then you will call upon me and come and pray to me, and I will hear you. [13]You will seek me and find me; when you seek me with all your heart, [14]I will be found by you, says the LORD, and I will restore your fortunes and gather you from all the nations and all the places where I have driven you, says the LORD, and I will bring you back to the place from which I sent you into exile'.

The claims for dtr. (or other) redaction in Jer. 29.10-14:

1. Driver (1906) and Streane contend that the general speech of v. 14, מכל הגוים ומכל המקומות, 'from all the nations and from all the places', does not appropriately address the particular condition of the Jehoiachin exiles abiding in Babylon. However, it is not necessary to agree with this viewpoint, for if one may assume that 'the city' mentioned in v. 7 is not the only city in which the exiles are dwelling, then the question of the exiles inhabiting many 'places' (and even residing among many 'nations') is dispensable. There is biblical testimony that the returnees under Zerubbabel emigrated from many מקומות (Ezra 1.1, בכל מלכותו 'throughout all his kingdom'; 1.4, מכל המקומות; cp. 2.59);

2. Volz eliminated vv. 10, 11, and most of v. 14 as having been produced at the end of the exilic period. From the remnant of vv. 10-14, however, it is impossible to reconstruct a prophecy of redemption (contra Volz);

3. Welch (1928:173) also erased v. 10 from the prophecy with the assertion that, 'The sentence which promised return after seventy years could only turn the men's minds away from their present tasks and opportunities . . . the well-being of Babylon became to them a thing indifferent, because transient'.

Welch accepts the words ונמצאתי לכם נאם יהוה ושבתי את שבותכם 'I will be found by you, speech of YHWH, and I will restore your fortunes' in v. 14 and excises the rest of the verse. However, he translates שבותכם as 'your fortune' (1928:174); he, too, does not envision here a prophecy promising restoration of the Jehoiachin exiles to their homeland. Welch argues that the assurance of redemption after seventy years is only insignificantly different from the views of the false prophets concerning the return to the land, and, therefore, Jeremiah could not have written it.

Welch's perception of the situation is undoubtedly incorrect, for even he

(1928:175) admits that 'the greatest issues were involved in this controversy' between the prophets. According to Welch (1928:175-77), Jeremiah opposed the false religious concept of return to the land for it would have instigated rebellion against Babylon, which in turn would have resulted in harsh treatment of the exiles. Apparently, Welch did not grasp the supreme importance of the concept of return to the land in the Bible. The promise of future restoration, even in the distant future, enables the people to continue their day-to-day life as a religio-ethnic community, and thus to pray for the welfare of their city of captivity (v. 7) instead of revolting against it. Furthermore, the exact date of return to the land is not essential, rather it is the fulfillment of the prophecy in the distant future that is important, for this will allow sufficient time for the punishment of the guilty who have not yet suffered—the people who have remained in the land with Zedekiah. Only after destruction, exile, and the raising up of a new generation, 'the generation of the desert', shall the moment come for the restoration of the people (Jer. 16.14-15 //23.7-8). This concept will be expanded upon below;

4. Hyatt (1951:86-87; 1956), as is his wont, thinks that vv. 10-14 are the product of the dtr. redactors of Jeremiah, and, thus, it is no longer possible to identify the original words of the prophet. He compares v. 13 with Deut. 4.29 and 1 Kgs 8.48 with Deut. 30.3, 5. Hyatt doubts that the promise of return after seventy years would comfort the exiles of the generation of Zedekiah. Following the Septuagint, he excises the majority of v. 14.[4] Even so, Hyatt acknowledges that one cannot completely negate any relationship between Jeremiah and the ideas expressed in these verses (especially v. 11);

5. Nicholson's views have been examined in the discussion on 24.4-7 above:

6. Weinfeld (1972:145) notes that the 'seventy years' motif is already present in the Esarhaddon inscription and that traces of Assyrian sources are well recognizable in the dtr. literature. He concludes that the 'seventy years' motif was inserted in Jeremiah by the deuteronomistic school. Yet, against Weinfield, the very fact that the 'seventy years' motif is found in Assyria in the days of Esarhaddon, approximately eighty years before the reign of Zedekiah, is proof that Jeremiah also would have been able to know it and use it;

7. Böhmer (1976:34) decrees vv. 10-14 to be inauthentic additions. He sees v. 10b as copied from Jer. 28.6b. Verse 11 compares to the dtr. passages in Jer. 18.8, 11; 26.3; and to the late exilic Isa. 55.6ff. The phrase חשב . . . מחשבות 'making . . . plans' (v. 11), Böhmer states, belongs to exilic and post-exilic texts, but he contradicts himself by admitting the exception of 2 Sam. 14.14. He concludes that vv. 10-14 are dtr.;

8. Seidl (1977:136, 139, 144) also rejects the authenticity of vv. 10-14 as in direct contradiction to vv. 3-7. However, vv. 5-7 do not indicate that the exile will be indefinite. The double use of כי in v. 10 is continuative.

In support of the Jeremianic authorship of vv. 10-14:

1. Bright (1965), who tends to follow the Septuagint in v. 14, accepts the 'seventy years' of v. 10, finding no reason to regard it as a *vaticinium ex eventu*;

2. Martens (1972:62), despite the Septuagint, sees no justification in eliding v. 14 since it is 'a recapitulation of 29.10 and so . . . an *inclusio*. This recapitulation . . . can be seen in other salvation oracles (28.4; 32.41; Ezek. 36.22)';

3. Raitt's conclusions have been presented in the discussion on 24.4-7 above.

2. *Comparison of Passages*

a. *Jer. 24.4-7 and Deut. 30.1-10*

Deut. 30.1-10

וְהָיָה כִי־יָבֹאוּ עָלֶיךָ כָּל־הַדְּבָרִים הָאֵלֶּה הַבְּרָכָה וְהַקְּלָלָה א
אֲשֶׁר נָתַתִּי לְפָנֶיךָ וַהֲשֵׁבֹתָ אֶל־לְבָבֶךָ בְּכָל־הַגּוֹיִם אֲשֶׁר
הִדִּיחֲךָ יְהוָה אֱלֹהֶיךָ שָׁמָּה׃ וְשַׁבְתָּ עַד־יְהוָה אֱלֹהֶיךָ 2
וְשָׁמַעְתָּ בְקֹלוֹ כְּכֹל אֲשֶׁר־אָנֹכִי מְצַוְּךָ הַיּוֹם אַתָּה וּבָנֶיךָ
בְּכָל־לְבָבְךָ וּבְכָל־נַפְשֶׁךָ׃ וְשָׁב יְהוָה אֱלֹהֶיךָ אֶת־שְׁבוּתְךָ 3
וְרִחֲמֶךָ וְשָׁב וְקִבֶּצְךָ מִכָּל־הָעַמִּים אֲשֶׁר הֱפִיצְךָ יְהוָה
אֱלֹהֶיךָ שָׁמָּה׃ אִם־יִהְיֶה נִדַּחֲךָ בִּקְצֵה הַשָּׁמָיִם מִשָּׁם 4
יְקַבֶּצְךָ יְהוָה אֱלֹהֶיךָ וּמִשָּׁם יִקָּחֶךָ׃ וֶהֱבִיאֲךָ יְהוָה אֱלֹהֶיךָ ה
אֶל־הָאָרֶץ אֲשֶׁר־יָרְשׁוּ אֲבֹתֶיךָ וִירִשְׁתָּהּ וְהֵיטִבְךָ וְהִרְבְּךָ
מֵאֲבֹתֶיךָ׃ וּמָל יְהוָה אֱלֹהֶיךָ אֶת־לְבָבְךָ וְאֶת־לְבַב זַרְעֶךָ 6
לְאַהֲבָה אֶת־יְהוָה אֱלֹהֶיךָ בְּכָל־לְבָבְךָ וּבְכָל־נַפְשְׁךָ לְמַעַן
חַיֶּיךָ׃ וְנָתַן יְהוָה אֱלֹהֶיךָ אֵת כָּל־הָאָלוֹת הָאֵלֶּה עַל־ 7
אֹיְבֶיךָ וְעַל־שֹׂנְאֶיךָ אֲשֶׁר רְדָפוּךָ׃ וְאַתָּה תָשׁוּב וְשָׁמַעְתָּ 8
בְּקוֹל יְהוָה וְעָשִׂיתָ אֶת־כָּל־מִצְוֹתָיו אֲשֶׁר אָנֹכִי מְצַוְּךָ
הַיּוֹם׃ וְהוֹתִירְךָ יְהוָה אֱלֹהֶיךָ בְּכֹל ׀ מַעֲשֵׂה יָדֶךָ בִּפְרִי 9
בִטְנְךָ וּבִפְרִי בְהֶמְתְּךָ וּבִפְרִי אַדְמָתְךָ לְטֹבָה כִּי ׀ יָשׁוּב
יְהוָה לָשׂוּשׂ עָלֶיךָ לְטוֹב כַּאֲשֶׁר־שָׂשׂ עַל־אֲבֹתֶיךָ׃ כִּי
תִשְׁמַע בְּקוֹל יְהוָה אֱלֹהֶיךָ לִשְׁמֹר מִצְוֹתָיו וְחֻקֹּתָיו הַכְּתוּבָה
בְּסֵפֶר הַתּוֹרָה הַזֶּה כִּי תָשׁוּב אֶל־יְהוָה אֱלֹהֶיךָ בְּכָל־
לְבָבְךָ וּבְכָל־נַפְשֶׁךָ׃

30 'And when all these things come upon you, the blessing and the curse, which I have set before you, and you call them to mind among all the nations where the LORD your God has driven you, [2]and return to the LORD your God, you and your children, and obey his voice in all that I command you this day, with all your heart and with all your soul; [3]then the LORD your God will restore your

fortunes, and have compassion upon you, and he will gather you again from all the peoples where the LORD your God has scattered you. [4]If your outcasts are in the uttermost parts of heaven, from there the LORD your God will gather you, and from there he will fetch you; [5]and the LORD your God will bring you into the land which your fathers possessed, that you may possess it; and he will make you more prosperous and numerous than your fathers. [6]And the LORD your God will circumcise your heart and the heart of your offspring, so that you will love the LORD your God with all your heart and with all your soul, that you may live.[7] And the LORD your God will put all these curses upon your foes and enemies who persecuted you.[8] And you shall again obey the voice of the LORD, and keep all his commandments which I command you this day.[9] The LORD your God will make you abundantly prosperous in all the work of your hand, in the fruit of your body, and in the fruit of your cattle, and in the fruit of your ground; for the LORD will again take delight in prospering you, as he took delight in your fathers, [10]if you obey the voice of the LORD your God, to keep his commandments and his statutes which are written in this book of the law, if you turn to the LORD your God with all your heart and with all your soul'.

Both these passages hold in common four basic concepts concerning the period of redemption:

1. YHWH will bring back the people to their land (Jer. 24.6; Deut. 30.3-5);
2. YHWH will cause the people to flourish in the land (Jer. 24.6; Deut. 30.5, 9);
3. YHWH's action upon the heart of the people will result in their knowing/loving Him (Jer. 24.7; Deut. 30.6);
4. The people will return to YHWH with all their heart (Jer. 24.7; Deut. 30.1, 2, 8, 10).

In addition to the ideological parallels, there are also linguistic similarities:

1. לטובה 'for good' (Jer.24.5, 6; Deut. 30.9; cp. v. 5);
2. שוב אל יהוה בכל לב 'return to YHWH wholeheartedly' (Jer. 24.7, כי ישבו אלי בכל לבם; Deut. 30.1, והשבת אל לבבך v. 2 ושבת עד יהוה אלהיך v. 8, ואתה תשוב; v. 10, כי תשוב אל יהוה אלהיך בכל לבבך ובכל נפשך;
3. the root נדח (Jer. 24.9[5]); Deut. 30.1, 4.

The existence of these similarities is not necessarily indicative of a direct relationship between the two passages. As has been previously noted, Raitt observed that the use of 'good' in Jeremiah is fundamentally different from that in the dtr. literature. It should be added that לטובה is not characteristic of dtr. literature since it appears only here and in Deut. 28.11. Jer. 24.6, ושמתי עיני עליהם לטובה has much more in common with Amos 9.4, ושמתי עיני עליהם לרעה ולא לטובה. לרעה ולא לטובה appears elsewhere only in Jer. 21.10; 39.16; 44.27. Similarly the root נדח in reference to exiles appears only here in Deuteronomy and dtr. historiography, while also appearing in Mic. 4.6. The closest correspondence to its use in Jer. 24.9, בכל המקומות אשר אדיחם שם, is Ezek. 4.13, בגוים אשר אדיחם שם. The root נדח, then, can hardly be termed deuteronomic phraseology.[6] Finally, בכל לב (Jer. 24.6), as opposed to בכל לבב (Deut. 30.2, 6, 10), is not characteristic of Deuteronomy and its by-products.[7]

Nonetheless, the parallel elements taken as a whole attest to a direct connection between the two passages. Yet there is a major and decisive ideological difference (cp. Raitt's remarks, above). The return to God is emphasized in Deuteronomy three times (vv. 1-2, 8, 10) from beginning to end, while in Jeremiah it appears only at the end (v. 7). The importance of this detail becomes obvious when one considers that every passage of redemption in the deuteronomic literature begins first with the element of return to God followed by YHWH's resulting mercies: Deut. 4.29-30—return, v. 31—mercy; 1 Kgs 8.33—return, v. 34—forgiveness; 1 Kgs 8.47-48—return, vv. 49-50—forgiveness and mercy. In other words, the pattern of return to YHWH followed by the ensuing mercies prove that in the deuteronomic conception redemption is conditional upon repentance, even when such repentance is assumed, not called forth, predicted,[8] not demanded ('you *shall* return'—Deut. 30.2, never '*if* you return, then . . .', or 'return!').

In Jeremiah 24, on the other hand, the element of return to YHWH does not appear at the beginning of the passage, but crops up rather unexpectedly at the end (v. 7b) after YHWH has already promised to restore the people to their land, rebuild it, and give it a heart to know him (vv. 5-7a). The postponement of the mention of return to God until the end of the passage serves witness to its secondary importance here as opposed to its place of honor in Deuteronomy 4, 30 and 1 Kings 8. While repentance and mercy are of equal weight in the deuteronomic passages, in Jeremiah 24 the primary role is played by divine mercy preceding and overshadowing the element of repentance. Indeed, repentance emerges here almost as an afterthought.

This major ideological difference clearly shows that Jeremiah 24 does not express the dtr. conception of redemption. Therefore, the assumption that Jer. 24.4-7 is the fruit of a dtr. redactor is untenable. The similarities between Jeremiah 24 and Deuteronomy 30 can only point to the conclusion that the prophet himself was familiar with Deuteronomy[9] without being subservient to its conceptions.

b. *Jer. 29.10-14 and Deut. 4.29-31*

Deut. 4.29-31

29 וּבִקַּשְׁתֶּם מִשָּׁם אֶת־יְהוָה אֱלֹהֶיךָ וּמָצָאתָ כִּי תִדְרְשֶׁנּוּ
בְּכָל־לְבָבְךָ וּבְכָל־נַפְשֶׁךָ׃ בַּצַּר לְךָ וּמְצָאוּךָ כֹּל הַדְּבָרִים ל
הָאֵלֶּה בְּאַחֲרִית הַיָּמִים וְשַׁבְתָּ עַד־יְהוָה אֱלֹהֶיךָ וְשָׁמַעְתָּ
31 בְּקֹלוֹ׃ כִּי אֵל רַחוּם יְהוָה אֱלֹהֶיךָ לֹא יַרְפְּךָ וְלֹא יַשְׁחִיתֶךָ
וְלֹא יִשְׁכַּח אֶת־בְּרִית אֲבֹתֶיךָ אֲשֶׁר נִשְׁבַּע לָהֶם׃

> [29]But from there you will seek the LORD your God; and you will find him, if you search after him with all your heart and with all your soul.[30] When you are in tribulation, and all these things come upon you in the latter days, you will return to the LORD your God and obey his voice, [31] for the LORD your God is a merciful God; he will not fail you or destroy you or forget the covenant with your fathers which he swore to them.

The striking similarity between these two passages is that of Jer. 29.13, ובקשתם אתי ומצאתם כי תדרשני בכל לבבכם , and Deut. 4.29, ובקשתם משם את יהוה אלהיך ומצאת כי תדרשנו בכל לבבך ובכל נפשך . Nonetheless, the same conceptual difference between Deuteronomy 30 and Jeremiah 24 emerges here. Unlike the passage in Deuteronomy, Jeremiah 29 precedes the mention of return to YHWH (vv. 12-13) with God's promise of restoration to the land and future security (vv. 10-11). Once again, the divergence of the Jeremiah passage from those of the deuteronomic literature is apparent. Furthermore, Deut. 4.30 speaks of obedience of God's commandments (ושמעת בקולו), an aspect absent from Jeremiah 29. Indeed, the root שוב is not even mentioned in the Jeremiah passage, and the reference seems to be more concerned with prayer (v. 12, 'you shall call me . . . and you shall pray to me') than the type of repentance expressed in Jeremiah 3. The actions of the people are minimal in comparison to those of God. As in Jeremiah 24, the conclusion must be that Jer. 29.10-14 is the product of someone who knew Deuteronomy but was not so influenced by it that he could be termed a 'deuteronomist'.

3. *Deut. 4.29-31; 30.2-20 and the Theory of the Second, Exilic Edition of the Deuteronomistic History*

The thesis of the systematic edition of Deuteronomy–2 Kings proposed by M. Noth (1981)[10] was a watershed in the study of this literature. He posited an introduction (Deut. 1–3) and a conclusion (Deut. 30–34, minus additions) attached to the core of Deuteronomy by an exilic hand (Noth believed 4.29-40 [1981:114 n. 52] and 30.1-4 [1981:17] to be later accretions). The main theme of the dtr. history was Israel's disobedience to God's laws and the resulting divine punishment.

G. von Rad (1966:205-21) accepted Noth's analysis, but proposed the contrary dtr. theme of God's eternal promise to David, which is also indicated by the last four verses of the history—the elevation of Jehoiachin (2 Kgs 25.27-30) (1966:220). Von Rad (1966:209) also lays bare the prevalent scheme of prophecy and fulfillment which he describes as 'the theological plan of the work'.

H.W. Wolff (1978:86) rejects von Rad's view by reference to the conditional aspect of the Davidic kingship in 1 Kgs 2.3-4; 9.5-7 (cp. Deut. 17.18-19; 2 Kgs 18.6; 21.8-9; 23.25); i.e. for the monarchy to survive, it must be obedient to YHWH's commandments. Wolff sees the ultimate hope of the people, according to the dtr. history, as hinging on Israel's repentance. This hope appears in three pivotal passages, assumed by Wolff (1978:92-99) to have been written after the destruction of Jerusalem—1 Kings 8; Deut. 30.1-10; 4.29-31. 1 Kings 8 refers to the destroyed sanctuary, and repentance will result only in Israel finding 'pity among the nations'. Deut. 30.1-10 presupposes the exilic portion of Deut. 28, and together these chapters have been influenced by the Jeremiah traditions. Deut. 4.29-31 is based upon Hos. 3.5; 5.15; Jer. 29.13. Wolff hypothesizes that Deut. 4.29-31; 30.1-10 are written by a second and later author of the dtr. history. He claims (1978:98-99), in some confusion, that although the return to God is *promised*, Deut. 4.29-31; 30.1-10 help compose 'an urgent invitation to a return to the God of salvation history'.

Despite the blatant promise of return to the land in Deut. 30.3-5 and 1 Kgs 8.34 (a verse ignored by Wolff), Wolff (1978:99) concludes that the dtr. historian did not combine 'his idea of return with any *specific* hope'. Wolff's final word (1978:100) is that 'the ruined temple will . . . witness for the God of Israel among the nations . . . Israel must expect, even when she turns back, to remain in affliction for "many days"... The return cannot be thought of as a ticket to restoration or betterment'. Such a summation has much more in common with anti-Jewish Christian theology than with a careful reading of the texts in question.

A milestone in this field of research was attained by F.M. Cross (1973:276-78) who found both von Rad's and Wolff's analyses deficient. The former depends too heavily on the pithy mention of Jehoiachin's rise in status as proof of the continuing messianic belief of the dtr. editor, while the latter does not take into proper consideration the attested theme of the unconditional promise to David in 2 Samuel 7; 1 Kgs 11.12, 13, 32, 34, 36; 25.4; 2 Kgs 8.19; 19.34; 20.6 (1973:281). Cross (1973:279-85), therefore, delineates two editions of the dtr. history. The first (Dtr.[1]) is Josianic and contains two major themes: Jeroboam's sin and David's faithfulness. The former stems from 'the old Deuteronomic covenant theology which regarded destruction of dynasty and people as tied necessarily to apostasy'. The latter is 'drawn from the royal ideology of Judah: the eternal promises to David... while chastisement has regularly come upon Judah in her seasons of apostasy, hope remains in the Davidic house'. Thus, the North must return to Davidic rule and to worship at the temple in Jerusalem, while the South's fate is contingent upon the nation's return to the covenant and the monarch's zeal in following in David's footsteps (1973:284).

The second edition (Dtr.[2]) is exilic (about 550 BCE) (1973:287).[12] This editor reshaped the history 'into a document relevant to exiles for whom the bright expectations of the Josianic era were hopelessly past' (1973:285). Its primary theme appears in 2 Kgs 21.2-15; Manasseh's sin resulted in the downfall of Judah (cp. 2 Kgs 22.15-20; 23.25b-27) (1973:285-286). These 'passages which appear to be addressed to exiles and to call for their repentance, or... even promise restoration of the captives to their land... are most naturally regarded as coming from the... Exilic editor'. They include Deut. 4.27-31; 30.1-10; 1 Kgs 8.46-53 (as well as Deut. 28.36-37, 63-68; 29.27; Josh. 23.11-13, 15-16; 1 Sam. 12.25; 1 Kgs 2.4; 6.11-13; 8.25b; 9.4-9; 2 Kgs 17-19; 20.17-18; 23.26–25.30) (1973:287). Cross (1973:288) finds 'remarkable' that

> there is no peroration on the fall of Jerusalem... like that upon the destruction of Samaria. The events are recorded... without theological reflection... it must be said that the Deuteronomistic historian never tires of repetition of his themes and cliches and is

> fond of bracketing events and periods with an explicit theological framework. The omission of a final, edifying discourse on the fall of chosen Zion and the Davidic crown is better explained by attributing these final terse paragraphs of the history to a less articulate Exilic editor.
>
> . . . the relatively modest extent of the Exilic editor's work and his fidelity in preserving intact the work of the Josianic Deuteronomist . . . explains the lack of a peroration on Jerusalem's fall.

This conclusion by Cross seems highly unreasonable. The hand that inserted the predictions of Jerusalem's destruction in 2 Kgs 21.10-15; 22.15-20 (not to mention 1 Kgs 9.6-9) would surely not have hesitated to report destruction in terms of the fulfillment of those predictions. Indeed, he does so in 2 Kgs 24.2-4 concerning the raids in the days of Jehoiakim! It seems much more reasonable that the editor who predicted destruction did not record that destruction. Whether he died or was deported in the exile of Jehoiachin is not known. In any case, that he wrote *prior* to the destruction of Jerusalem appears to be the logical conclusion.

Cross's students have expanded on their mentor's theories. J. Levenson's reading (1975:203-33) of Deuteronomy (and the rest of the deuteronomic history) has convinced him that the core of Deuteronomy was inserted by the exilic hand of 'Dtr.^{2}' (!) into the work of 'Dtr.^{1}' (1–3.28; 31.1-2, 3b, 7). The work of Dtr.^{2} consists of (in Deuteronomy) 3.29–4.40 (1975:204); 29.21-28; 30; 31.16-22, 24-29 and the song of Moses which he introduced (also, 29.16 and possibly 31.3a, 4-6) (1975:210, 221). Levenson (1975:208) accepts the curses of Deut. 27–28 as pre-exilic—'The mere threat and description of exile cannot be taken as a sure reflection of the events of 587. When, however, the text promises that once in exile, Israel can still return, this pressupposes an exilic audience'.

Even if this last assumption be true, given the exile of the northern tribes, why must 4.29-31 and 30.1-10 be dated post-587? Levenson attempts to prove his dating by examining the language of Dtr.^{2} Yet, he (1975:220) finds no exilic language in 4.29-31 and only והשבת אל לבבך (30.1-10) is found only in clearly exilic passages (Lam. 3.21; Isa. 44.19; 46.8). Of course, there is no reason to suppose that exilic language differed significantly from immediately pre-exilic language. Furthermore, Levenson pays no attention to the striking resemblance of Deut. 4.29-30, ובקשתם משם את יהוה אלהיך . . . בצר לך . . . ושבת עד יהוה אלהיך 'but from there you will seek YHWH your God . . . when you are in tribulation. . . you will return to YHWH your God', to Hos. 5.15–6.1, ובקשו פני בצר להם . . . ונשובה אל יהוה 'in their tribulation they will seek my face . . . let us return to YHWH'.[14] Nor does Levenson recognize the archaic usage of עד √שוב, which appears in Amos 4.6, 8, 9, 10, 11; Hos. 14.2; Isa. 9.12; 19.22. He does admit, though (1975:214), that באחרית הימים 'at the end of days' in 4.30 'well-known from prophetic literature, is otherwise unattested in Dtr'.

In later study, Levenson (1981:143-67) enlarged his research to include 1 Kings 8, and concluded that 1 Kgs 8.23-53 is also from Dtr.[2] Arguing against J. Gray's position (1970) that the exile of v. 46 refers to that of the North and that v. 48 assumes the existence of the Temple, Levenson (1981:157) opines that

> Prayers for return from exile in the Hebrew Bible almost always derive from 'the' Exile, which has left us . . . its theology in books like Lamentations, 2 Isaiah (Isaiah 40-55), and Ezekiel, all of which are marked by a fervent hope and pleas for restoration to the land. We have no counterpart to this from the earlier deportation. The burden of proof lies upon those who would identify the setting of our prayer as earlier, not upon those who see it as of the sixth century. Wellhausen . . . noted that the concern for the Temple in Jerusalem of this speech belies any Northern origin for it. Wellhausen's argument . . . would force Gray to hold that the prayer speaks of an exile other than that of its author, in other words, that a Southerner here envisions the repentance of the North, which will then reembrace the Temple in Jerusalem which it once spurned . . . the position, although logical in a way, is too forced to merit our credence. Nor does the argument that v. 48 presupposes the existence of the Temple carry weight. All that verse says is thay the exiles will pray 'turning in the direction . . . of the Temple . . . .' Nothing here implies that the temple is other than a ruin. Note that Jer. 41.5 speaks of eighty men bringing sacrifices 'to the Temple of YHWH' after its destruction. To this day, Jews speak of facing the Temple in prayer.

However, contra Levenson, as has been shown in Chapter 1, in the days of Josiah, Jeremiah prophesied the repentance of the Northern tribes who would once again worship YHWH in Jerusalem (Jer. 31.6). Indeed, Jer. 3.6-13, 19–4.2 refutes Levenson's earlier claim (above) that a text speaking of exiles repenting must assume the catastrophe of 587. The exile of the North obviated that necessity. Furthermore, Jer. 41.5 is an awkward bit of evidence to support Levenson's view of 1 Kgs 8.48, since the preceding account of the destruction of Jerusalem *does not mention* the burning of the Temple (Jer. 39.8)![15]

Indeed, 1 Kgs 8.48 does not say, as Levenson translates, 'turning in the direction . . . of the Temple', but rather, 'they shall pray to you towards their land . . . the city . . . and the house which I built to your name' (והתפללו אליך דרך ארצם . . . העיר . . . והבית אשרבנית לשמך), cp. v. 44; 1 Kgs 8.43; Ezek. 8.5; 21.2, etc. Verse 44 assumes the existence of city and Temple. Why should not v. 48? Verses 44-45 in no way presuppose the war against Babylon: v. 44 states unequivocally that *it is YHWH* who sends the people out to battle and v. 45 implies that He hears their prayers favorably. It must be concluded that Levenson has failed to prove that the verses in question are exilic. The evidence would appear to turn in the opposite direction.

R.E. Friedman (1981a:16-19; 1981b:167-92), another of Cross's students, has also assigned Deut. 4.29-31 and 30.1-10 to the exilic Dtr.^{2}, following the arguments of Levenson. Interestingly, Friedman (1981a:21) argues against Levenson that 1 Kgs 8.46-53 is pre-exilic. Friedman envisions the final notation of Dtr.^{2} to be in 2 Kgs 25.26, that the remnant of the people went to Egypt for fear of the Babylonians. This statement, he believes (1981b:189-90), is Dtr.^{2}'s way of saying that the curse of Deut. 28.68, that YHWH will cause the people to return to Egypt, is now fulfilled. 2 Kgs 25.26, then, 'accounts for the lack of a peroration on the fall of Judah which concerned Cross' (1981b:191). In conclusion, 'the Deuteronomistic history, in its final form, tells the story of Egypt . . . God abandons them to disaster because of their breaking the covenant, leaving them now back where they started, to repent and hope for restoration' (1981b:191-92).

A major problem with this ingenious solution is that 2 Kgs 25.26 depicts the people leaving *willingly* for Egypt and there is no indication that they will be slaves there, as opposed to Deut. 28.68. In fact, according to Jer. 40.7–43.7, from which 2 Kgs 25.22-26 is taken,[16] it is God's wish that the people stay in their land, and *not* leave it for Egypt (Jer. 42)! If the author of 2 Kgs 25.26 had meant for that verse to reflect Deut. 28.68, all he would have had to do would be to insert the words כדבר יהוה 'according to the word of YHWH' after the words 'and they came to Egypt' (cp. 2 Kgs 24.2). Why the ambiguity? It would appear that Deut. 28.68 has much more in common with pre-587 dispersions to Egypt, cp. Hos. 8.13; 9.5-6; 11.5, 11; 12.2; Isa. 10.24-26; 11.11. Once again, Dtr.^{2} does not record the fall of Jerusalem.

It is noteworthy that the tendency to date Deut. 4.29-30 and 30.1-10 to the exilic period has long been present in biblical scholarship;[17]

the scholars cited above are only reiterating older perspectives. The following remarks will attempt to place the dating of these passages (and 1 Kgs 8.33-53), along with the final edition(s?) of Deuteronomy and the dtr. history, in a new light:

1. Once Hilkiah gave the 'Book of the Torah' to Shaphan, the book went through *at least* three readings: one by Shaphan (2 Kgs 22.8), one by Shaphan to Josiah (v. 10) which was a complete reading (v. 13—ככל הכתוב עלינו 'according to all that is written concerning us'), one complete reading before the people (23.2—את כל דברי ספר הברית 'all the words of the book of the covenant'). Does it make sense that after the whole book had been read publicly it would have been the subject of a systematic redaction? The book was now known, remembered, referred to, and recited. To whom would any addition be acceptable?[18] It is only logical that whatever book was turned over to Shaphan was a complete work. If it was Deuteronomy, it was so in its entirety, including Deut. 4.29-31; 30.1-10.

2. The last historical event mentioned in 2 Kings is the release of Jehoiachin from prison in 561 BCE (25.27-30). As has been shown above, it is probable that these verses were not penned by a dtr. editor (in reality, the last editorial comment appears in 24.20). It may be safely assumed that, *at the least*, the dtr. redactor edited his history within approximately 25 years of the fall of Jerusalem, even though an earlier dating is opted for here (see p. 70 above).

What period is reflected in the passages on repentance and redemption in Deuteronomy 4, 30 and 1 Kings 8? All these passages emphasize repentance as a precondition for redemption from exile (though the accent on prayer in 1 Kings 8 may differentiate it from Deuteronomy 4, 30). And yet, *neither Jeremiah nor Ezekiel* (the only two prophets possibly contemporaneous with an exilic dtr. editor) *posits repentance as a precondition for national redemption for those in exile after 587*. Only Jeremiah in 24.4-7 and 29.10-14 allows for the possibility of repentance as a precondition for redemption of the exiles of 597, and he understates it while accentuating instead YHWH's mercies.

It is important to realize that the dtr. history recognizes only three vehicles of divine authority—the Torah of Moses, prophets, and rare occurrences of divine revelation (such as to Solomon). Solomon's *prayer* is only that, a prayer, not prophecy, and not a revelation. After Solomon, the word of God is found only in Torah and prophecy. As von Rad recognized, prophecy and fulfillment is the basic plan of the dtr. history (see above). Logic dictates, then, that the passages on repentance in the dtr. work also reflect prophecy. The divergence between Deuteronomy 4; 30; 1 Kings 8 and Jeremiah and Ezekiel after 597 force the conclusion that the former must reflect an earlier view of prophecy.

As has been illustrated above (Chapter 1), repentance as a precondition for the redemption of exiles *is* found in Jer. 3.6-13, 19–4.2; 31.15-22, datable to the days of Josiah (cp. also Hos. 3.5; 14.2-9).[19] But the idea of repentance preceding redemption is the common position of classical prophecy before 597, so that Deut. 4.29-31; 30.1-10; 1 Kgs 8.33-34, 44-53 reflect either eighth- or seventh-century prophecy. The relationship of Deut. 4.29-31 to Hos. 5.15–6.1 argues particularly for the influence of Hosea there. Additionally, Deut. 30.4 may be a conscious reversal of the curse of Amos 9.2 (cp. vv. 3-4):

> Deut. 30.4—אם יהיה נדחך בקצה השמים משם יקבצך ה' אלהיך ומשם יקחך '*If* your outcasts are in the uttermost parts of *heaven from there* YHWH your God will gather you and *from there* he will *take* you'; Amos 9.2—אם יחתרו בשאול משם ידי תקחם ואם יעלו השמים משם אורידם. 'If they dig into Sheol, *from* there shall my hand *take* them, *if* they climb up to *heaven*, *from there* I will bring them down.'

Thus, it may well be that Deut. 4.29-31 and 30.1-10 mirror eighth-century prophecy.

The same may be true as well of 1 Kings 8,[20] which lists several evils concerning which the people would pray and repent: war (vv. 33-34), drought (vv. 35-36), famine, pestilence (דבר), blight (שרפון), mildew (ירקון), locust (ארבה), caterpillar (all in v. 37), and war again (v. 44) and captivity (v. 46). Amos 4 has an almost identical list in nearly the same order, which like 1 Kings 8 appears in repetitive refrains, except that in Amos the complaint is that the people have not repented: famine (v. 6), drought (v. 7), blight (שרפון), mildew (ירקון), locust (גזם; all in v. 9), pestilence (דבר, v. 10), war and captivity (of horses, v. 10), earthquake (v. 11). The similarity is unique, unparalleled, and strongly signifies a direct relationship.

All of the above evidence leads to the inescapable conclusion that Deut. 4.29-31 and 30.1-10 precede Jer. 24.4-7 and 29.10-14 (as does 1 Kgs 8.33-53). Even if the author of these passages in Jeremiah was influenced by some of the idioms in the passages from Deuteronomy, there is a distinct divergence of ideology. There is no reason to suppose that the author of Jer. 24.4-7; 29.10-14 was other than the prophet Jeremiah.

B. Structure, Meaning, and Related Issues

1. *Jer. 24.4-7*

a. *Location.* Rudolph has suggested that ch. 24 was originally a continuation of 21.1-10. Accordingly, the purpose of ch. 24 is understood by him to promise the ultimate survival of the children of Israel despite the devastation which will befall Zedekiah and those remaining in Judah. Rudolph is apparently influenced by the correspondence between 21.10 and 24.2, 3, 5, 8 (the repetitive use of derivatives of the roots טוב and רעע, as well as that between 21.9 and 24.10 (the word order חרב, רעב, דבר 'sword, famine, pestilence'). Rudolph's claim may be disallowed by pointing out that 24.4-7 is in direct opposition to 24.8-10, and thus does not refer to 21.1-10. Furthermore, 21.8-9 (דרך החיים 'the way of life') introduce a hopeful tone which is completely absent in 24.8-10.

That 24.1-10 is a self-contained literary unit is unassailable. Hence, it is conceivable that it was transmitted as an independent saying of Jeremiah in isolation until it found its way to its current location. The reasons for its position between chs. 23 and 25 are most probably associative. Chapter 24, which contains a promise of divine retribution in vv. 8-10, is situated between two other units which proclaim a similar message—23.33-40 and 25.1ff. This affinity is enhanced by several linguistic parallels: 24.9, לחרפה; 23.40, חרפת 'shame'; 24.10, אשר נתתי להם ולאבותיהם 'which I gave to them and their fathers'; 23.39, אשר נתתי לכם ולאבותיכם 'which I gave to you and your fathers'; 25.5, אשר נתן יהוה לכם ולאבותיכם. Note, also, the resemblance of 24.9, ... ונתתים ... לרעה ... ולמשל לשנינה ... 'I will give them ... for evil ... a byword, a taunt', to 25.9, ושמתים לשמה ולשרקה 'I will make them a horror and a hissing'.

b. *Structure.* Chapter 24 has an obvious and cohesive structure—a vision and its attendant explanation,[21] like that of the almond sapling and bubbling pot in Jer. 1.11-12, 13-14, and those of the visions of Amos (Amos 7.1-3, 4-6, 7-9; 8.1-3; 9.1-4). The visual side appears in vv. 1-3 while the explanation is given in vv. 4-10. The 'good figs' symbolize the 'good' that YHWH will do for the Judean exiles of 597 (vv. 5-7), and the 'bad figs' represent the evil that will betide those who remained in Judah (vv. 8-10). That the structure of 24.1-10 is that of a typical prophetic vision is further testimony in favor of the authenticity of vv. 4-7.

c. *Meaning*. The language of 24.4-6 is straightforward and without difficulty. YHWH's plan for the Judean exiles of 597 is good; He will restore them to their land, and will establish them securely (with intimations of permanency) therein—'I will build them and not destroy. I will plant them and not pluck out' (v. 6). Verse 7 however, is highly problematic. What is the meaning of ונתתי להם לב לדעת אתי followed by כי אני יהוה? What is the significance of the formula והיו לי לעם ואנכי אהיה להם לאלהים 'they shall be to me a people and I shall be to them a God'? Is the subordinate, adverbial clause כי ישבו אלי בכל לבם 'because they shall return to me with all their heart' the condition for the unification of the people with God mentioned earlier in the verse, or is it the condition for the entire restoration process from v. 5 on? Answers to these questions will be sought in this section.

(1) 24.7a, ונתתי להם לב לדעת אתי כי אני יהוה. The majority of translators and scholars translate the first כי in 24.7 by the word 'that', finding support in such verses as Exod. 7.5, 17, וידעו מצרים כי אני יהוה ... בזאת תדע כי אני יהוה ... 'and Egypt shall know that I am YHWH ... by this you shall know I am YHWH' (cp. Exod. 10.2; 29.46; 31.13; Deut. 29.5). According to this interpretation, God gives his people a heart to recognize *that* He is God, and there is no other.[22] However, in all the examples cited, no object separates the verb ידע from the conjunction כי, whereas here the object אתי divides them. In order to understand the difference between לדעת אתי כי אני יהוה and לדעת כי אני יהוה, the expression דעת יהוה and its forms in the book of Jeremiah will now be surveyed:

1. 2.8, 'The priests did not say "where is YHWH?" and those who handle the Torah לא ידעוני, and the "shepherds" rebelled against me, and the prophets prophesied by Baal and followed useless things'. The words לא ידעוני are paralleled to 'did not say "where is YHWH?"' (which also appears in v. 6), 'rebelled against me' and 'prophesied by Baal and followed useless things'. 'Those who handle the Torah' are 'the priests' (or a part of them).[23] It is clear from the context that the meaning of 'they do not know me' is disobedience to YHWH's Torah which manifests itself primarily in idolatrous worship.
2. 4.22, 'For my people are foolish, אותי לא ידעו, they are stupid children without understanding. They are wise to do evil but

they do not know how to do good.' The phrase אותי לא ידעו, 'They do not know me', is collimated to 'but do not know how to do good', and see similarly Amos 5.4, 6, 14 which also compares God to the good: 'Seek me and live, seek YHWH and live, seek good and not evil that you may live'. Here אותי לא ידעו refers to immorality.

3. 9.2, '"They bent their tongue into a bow for lying and not for truth, they have become mighty in the land for they go from evil to evil ואותי לא ידעו", speech of YHWH'.
4. 9.5, '"You dwell in the midst of deceit, in deceit מאנו דעת אותי they refuse to know me" speech of YHWH'. The forms of 'knowledge of YHWH' in 9.2 and 5 are analogous to that in 4.22. The connotation of מאנו דעת אותי is comparable to those of מאנו לשוב 'they refuse to return' (5.3), 'they cling to deceit מאנו לשוב (8.5), מאנו to obey my word, and they followed other gods to serve them. The House of Israel and the House of Judah have broken my covenant...' (11.10), 'this evil people המאנים to obey my word, who walk in the stubbornness of their heart and follow other gods to serve them...' (13.10). Thus 'knowledge of God' implies worship of God, return to Him, obedience to His commandments, and fealty to His covenant.
5. 9.23, '"For in this may he who prides himself pride himself, השכל וידע אותי, that he understands and knows me, כי אני יהוה, who practices חסד משפט וצדקה, faithfulness, justice, and righteousness in the earth, for in these things I delight", speech of YHWH'. This verse appears similar to that which is written in 3.15, ורעו אתכם דעה והשכיל, 'who will shepherd you with knowledge and understanding', and 23.5, ומלך מלך והשכיל ועשה משפט וצדקה בארץ 'and shall reign as king and with understanding, and shall practice justice and righteousness in the earth'. Weinfeld (1976:41-42, n. 91) has shown that the concept of the king who behaves with knowledge and wisdom is well known in Mesopotamia. According to the dtr. literature, the leader who conducts himself with שכל is one whose wise acts are based upon observance of the Torah—'Only be very strong and courageous to keep, to do according to all the Torah which Moses my servant commanded you. Do not turn from it to the right or the left in order תשכיל, in all your doings' (Josh. 1.7); 'You shall keep the charge of YHWH your God to walk

in all His ways to keep his laws . . . as is written in the Torah of Moses in order תשכיל everything you do' (1 Kgs 2.3; cp. Deut. 29.8). On the other hand, in 9.23 השכל וידע אותי signifies righteous action which is exhibited in accordance with the mode of behavior desired by YHWH. 9.23 is thus comparable to Hos. 2.21-22 ('I shall betrothe you to me בצדק ובמשפט ובחסד and in mercy and I shall betrothe you to me in truth וידעת את יהוה'), and 6.6 ('For I desire חסד and not sacrifice, ודעת אלהים more than offerings').[24]

6. 10.25, 'Pour out your wrath upon the nations who לא ידעוך and upon the families who do not call on your name, for they have devoured Jacob . . .' 10.25, like its twin in Ps. 79.6-7, collimates לא ידעוך with 'do not call on your name'. The expression 'to call on ("in") the name of YHWH' does not appear elsewhere in Jeremiah, but its meaning can be determined by comparison with its appearances in other verses: to pray to God (1 Kgs 18.24, 'and you call in the name of your god and I will call in the name of YHWH and the God who will answer by fire is God'); to thank Him (Isa. 12.4, 'Give thanks to YHWH, call on His name, make known among the nations His deeds'; cp. the identical verses in Ps. 105.1 and 1 Chron. 16.8); to serve him (Zeph. 3.9, 'For them I shall reverse the peoples to a clear speech that all of them will call in the name of YHWH to serve Him with one shoulder'). Perhaps the meaning most suitable to the expressions 'they did not know you' and 'in your name they did not call' in 10.25 is 'they did not serve you'; the verse is a segment of a prayer and an entreaty to God that He destroy those nations which did not serve Him and 'devoured Jacob', and therefore are not worthy of His forbearance.

7. 22.15b, '". . . did not your father eat and drink and do justice and righteousness, then it was well with him. He judged the case of the poor and needy, then it was well. Is this not הדעת אתי", speech of YHWH'. The moral connotation of 'knowledge of YHWH' found in 9.23 is appropriate also for 22.15-16.

8. 31.33-34, 'For this is the covenant I shall make . . . I will put my Torah within them and write it on their heart, and I shall be their God and they shall be my people and they shall not teach one another . . . saying דעו את יהוה for כולם ידעו אותי . . . ' These verses will be discussed in depth in Chapter 3.

> Here it is sufficient to point out that all will know God after the Torah has been written on the people's heart. The appearance of the formula 'and I shall be their God and they shall be my people' bespeaks a close connection between these verses and 24.7. If so, then 'knowledge of YHWH' in 24.7 may simply refer to observance of the Torah.

The above survey may be summarized as follows:

Outside 24.7, the phrase 'knowledge of YHWH' and its variations appear nine times in the book of Jeremiah (twice in 31.34). In five of its appearances, the expression refers to moral conduct (4.22; 9.2, 5, 23; 22.16), while in the other four instances it implies service to God (2.8; 10.25; 31.34). These two meanings do not contradict each other, for the commandments of YHWH include both—morality and service together. Therefore, the preferable interpretation of 'knowledge of YHWH' would denote obedience to YHWH's words (and see the discussion on 9.5). The expression לדעת כי אני יהוה does not appear at all in Jeremiah while its most similar counterpart in the book is וידעו כי שמי יהוה (16.21).

It is abundantly clear that it is incorrect to interpret 24.16a, 'YHWH will give his people a heart to *recognize* that he is God'. Rather, 24.7a means that YHWH will give his people a heart to be obedient to him *because* He is God.[25] Thus, the expression כי אני יהוה emphasizes God's authority and Israel's subjugation to it. This interpretation also fits in 9.23, the only other place besides 24.7 where the object אתי separates the verb ידע and the conjunction כי— וידעו אתי כי אני יהוה i.e. obedience to YHWH because He is God who . . . The same definition applies in Lev. 20.8, והתקדשתם והייתם קדשים כי אני יהוה אלהיכם, 'consecrate yourselves and be holy, for I am YHWH your God', and 25.17, ויראת מאלהיך כי אני יהוה אלהיכם, 'but you shall fear your God, for I am YHWH your God'. Further support for the interpretation of לדעת אתי as obedience to God is found in a comparison of ונתתי להם לב לדעת אתי with ומל יהוה אלהיך את לבבך ואת לבב זרעך לאהבה את יהוה אלהיך, 'and YHWH your God shall circumcise your heart and the heart of your offspring so that you will love YHWH your God' in Deut. 30.6. The infinitive לאהבה has the same stress on obedience to God as does לדעת (and see the usage of the root אהב in Deut. 11.13, 22; 19.9; 30.16, 20; Josh. 22.5; 23.11).[26] In fact, both roots are used to express treaty-faithfulness in Mesopotamia.[27] The same is true of ירא,[28] and ונתתי להם לב . . . ליראה אותי appears in Jer. 32.39 along with the formula 'they shall be my people and I shall be their God' (v. 38). Similar gifts of heart in conjunction with that formula appear in Ezek. 11.19-20; 36.26, 28. The above analysis of the phrase לדעת אתי has proven beyond a doubt that it contains a dynamic meaning—'knowledge of YHWH' is not a passive recognition but, rather, a concrete activity,[29] the people's obedience to YHWH's commandments.

(2) 24.7b, והיו לי לעם ואנכי אהיה להם לאלהים. The coordinate clause 'and they shall be for me a people and I will be for them a God' has been characterized by Smend (1963) as the 'covenant formula'. Besides this verse, it appears primarily in Jeremiah (7.23; 11.4; 30.22; 31.1, 33; 32.38) and Ezekiel (11.20; 14.11; 36.28; 37.23, 27) with only slight variations. The most similar other appearances of the formula are in Lev. 26.12 and Zech. 8.8, with greater variations found in Exod. 6.7; Deut. 29.12; 2 Sam. 7.24; 1 Chron. 17.22 (cp. Exod. 19.5-6; Deut. 26.16-19; Hos. 1.9; 2.4, 25; Zech. 13.9). Smend (1963:26-27), Muffs (1965), and Weinfeld (1972:79-81) think the formula is adapted from ancient legal terminology used in marriage and adoption ceremonies (cp. 2 Sam. 7.14). Raitt (1977:194-200) holds that, rather than signifying election, in deliverance passages it stands for the *re-election* of Israel and the goal of the covenant—communion with God.

Indeed, the formula does not indicate a stage in the development of the relationship between YHWH and His people, but the ideal relationship itself. Nor is this a passive relationship; it consists of those acts which express the mutual faithfulness of God and Israel. The faithfulness of Israel to God, in the Jeremiah passages in which the covenant formula appears, is manifested by the people's obedience: 7.23, 'Obey my voice . . . (the formula) and walk in the way that I command you . . .'; 11.4, 'Obey my voice and do all that I command you . . . (the formula)'; 31.33-34, ' . . . I will put my torah within them and will write it on their hearts . . . (their formula) . . . for they shall all know me . . .'; 32.38-40, '(the formula) I will give them one heart . . . to fear me . . . and I will put my fear in their hearts that they may not turn away from me'.[30] The faithfulness of YHWH to Israel, in turn, is revealed in His actions on their behalf: 7.23, the apodosis, 'in order that it may be well with you'; 11.5, 'in order to fulfill the oath that I swore to your fathers to give them a land flowing with milk and honey'; 32.39-41, '. . . for the good of them and their children after them, I will make with them an eternal covenant, that I will not turn away from doing good to them . . . and I will rejoice over them to do good to them and I will plant them in this land in truth . . .'[31]

Thus, the formula defines the relationship between YHWH and Israel (Baltzer, 1971:102) which is established when both sides fulfill all the conditions of the covenant (see the mentions of the covenant in 11.3; 31.33; 32.40). Similarly, in 24.7 the covenant formula indicates the ideal relationship which will exist between YHWH and His people (in this case, the exiles with Jehoiachin) when the obedience of Israel (24.7a, c)[32] and YHWH's merciful acts (vv. 5-6) are manifested.

(3) 24.7c, כי ישבו אלי בכל לבם. According to the plain meaning of the text, it seems evident that כי in the last clause of 24.7 means 'because'. Thus, the subordinate clause states the condition for the ideal relationship expressed by the words immediately preceding; God and Israel will be united because the people will return to YHWH with all their heart. A question then arises: Is the people's repentance a result of God's gift of the 'heart to know me', or is it an act of the exiles' will which becomes the rationale for all the promises of restoration in vv. 6-7? The first possibility, that the giving of the heart will forcibly bring about the return of the people to YHWH, is a deterministic conception that has gained support among both exegetes and theologians.[33] Nonetheless, a comparison with the other prophecy of redemption directed towards the Jehoiachin exiles points to the legitimacy of the second possibility.

29.10-14, like 24.4-7, contains God's promise to restore the people to the land prior to any mention of repentance. 29.10, '. . . I will fulfill to you my good word to return you to this place'; 24.7, '. . . and I will return them to this land . . .' The concept of repentance appears in 29.12-13, 'You will call upon me and come and pray to me and I will hear you. You will seek me and find me because you will seek me with all your heart.' This prophecy states explicitly that the return to God will materialize while the people are still in exile, for it is only in response to this return that YHWH will restore the people to their land—14, 'and I will be found by you . . . and I will gather you from among the nations . . .' The same scheme appears in Deut. 30.1-10: vv. 1-2 speak of Israel's repentance in exile; vv. 3-5 of the restoration to the land; v. 6 of the circumcision of the heart which will cause the people to obey YHWH. Deut. 30.8-10 reemphasizes the repentance of vv. 1-2[34] which will result in a plenitude of fertility (vv. 5, 9). On the basis of these comparisons it may be concluded that in Jer. 24.4-7, also, repentance will take place in exile and will serve as the formal cause for the promise of redemption.

The foregoing analysis raises another question: If already in exile the people have returned 'with all their heart', why is it necessary for God to give them a 'heart' to be obedient to Him during the period of redemption? Two possible answers suggest themselves:

(a) It may be that the return of the people to YHWH in exile will continue only until God saves them and restores them to their land. Afterwards, the people might once again rebel against YHWH, much as the recurring pattern in Judges in which the people sin, YHWH punishes, the people call out in prayer, YHWH saves them through a judge, and, after the death of the judge, the people sin once again (e.g. Judg. 3.7-12). Therefore, God must give the people a heart to be obedient to Him in order that they should not sin again. Thereby the ideal relationship expressed by the covenant formula would be eternalized.

(b) Those who attempt to return to God are aided by God in doing so. In the words of Nahmanides,

> זהו שאמרו בא לטהר מסייעין אותו מבטיחך
> שתשוב אליו בכל לבבך והוא יעזור אותך
>
> this is what is said, 'one who comes to be purified is helped'. He promises you that you will return to Him with all your heart and He will aid you.[35]

The second answer is present in Jeremiah in 15.19, ואשיבך ואשובה, and 31.18, השיבני ואשובה. However, the first answer appears preferable, since the giving of a heart or the changing of a heart by God occurs in 31.33 and 32.39—passages in which repentance plays no part (this subject will be further investigated in Chapter 3).

d. *Authenticity (Revisited)*. It has already been established that the author of Jer. 24.4-7 could not have been a dtr. redactor. To the previous arguments are added the following:

(1) In Deuteronomy and the dtr. edition of the Former Prophets, the phrase 'to know YHWH' as denoting obedience to His words is absent. Since this term is characteristic of Jeremiah in general and plays an important role particularly in 24.7, it is clear that it is not the product of a dtr. editor.

(2) When Jeremiah addresses the conduct of the people in the time before exile, he reproaches them for their sins and frequently prophesies catastrophe if they do not return to YHWH in obedience. Nevertheless, when exile and destruction are already given realities, or when they are in the process of becoming crystallized, Jeremiah's mercies are aroused and he prophesies words of consolation and redemption to his people: compare (a) the reproof to Ephraim in 3.6-8 with the prophecy of redemption in 3.11-13, 19ff.; 31.2-9, 15-22; (b) the prophecies of reproof to Judah and Jerusalem in 4.3ff.; 5.1-6; etc. with the prophecies of redemption in 31.23-25, 38-40; (c) the prophecies of reproof to Judah and Ephraim together in 32.25-36 with the redemption prophecies in 32.36-44; (d) the prophecies of reproof of the Davidic dynasty in 17.19-27; 21.11-14; 22.1-7 with the prophecies of redemption in 23.(1-4)5-6; 33.14-26.[36]

The same pattern holds for the Jehoiachin exiles. The identical duality appears in 24.1-10. To those who have suffered exile, Jeremiah prophesies redemption (vv. 4-7). To those who have remained in the land, and have not drunk the cup of poison, Jeremiah prophesies disaster (vv. 8-10).[37] A similar relationship between exiles and those who have remained on the land is discernible in 3.11ff. There the prophet looks favorably upon the exiles of Ephraim and unfavorably upon the inhabitants of Judah.

It cannot be denied that 24.4-7 has all the signs of an authentic Jeremianic prophecy. There is no reason to reject either its authenticity or its date shortly after the Jehoiachin exile (v. 1).

2. *Jer. 29.10-14*

a. *Location*. Chapter 29 has two interests—the favorable future of the Jehoiachin exiles and the false prophets in their midst. As such, it is situated between Jeremiah's confrontation with the false prophet Hannaniah in ch. 28 and the redemption messages of the 'book of comfort' in chs. 30–31.

The fragmentary and confused character of the chapter serves notice that its components are not in their natural order. As it now stands, the chapter is structured as follows: vv. 1-3 form a biographical introduction which specifically addresses the Jehoiachin exiles; vv. 4-7 are an organic continuation and instruct the exiles as to appropriate behavior in the immediate future; vv. 8-9 are a further instruction to ignore the false prophets; vv. 10-14 speak of the redemption of the exiles in the distant future; v. 15 appears out of context and refers once again to the false prophets; vv. 16-19, although addressed to the exiles (v. 16, אתכם), are concerned with the disastrous fate of those who have remained in the land under Zedekiah, and therefore create the impression that they have no connection with the context; vv. 20-23 return once again to the problem of the false prophets, this time pertaining to specific ones—Ahab ben Kolaiah and Zedekiah ben Maaseiah; vv. 24-32 are concerned with another false prophet, Shemaiah of Nehelam, and contain both his reaction to Jeremiah's letter as well as Jeremiah's reaction to Shemaiah's words. Obviously, vv. 24-32 were written at a later date than the letter at the beginning of the chapter.

Verse 15 is most problematic since it is unconnected to either the preceding or the succeeding verses. Rudolph suggests placing vv. 8-9 after v. 15, in order to bring together all the verses dealing with false prophecy (vv. 16-20 are missing in the Septuagint). Driver and Streane put v. 15 before v. 21 (following the Lucianic recension).

Wherever v. 15 belongs, it is clear that the false prophets are those who promise the exiles: (1) a quick restoration to their land (cp. 28.3-4, 11); (2) 'the yoke of the king of Babylon' shall soon be broken (cp. 28.2, 4, 11). The transparent implication is that Judah and Jerusalem are no longer in danger (for if Judah is destroyed, the exiles would have no place to which to return). Since these proclamations contradicted all of Jeremiah's prophecies, it is reasonable that he would send a letter to the exiles accusing his opponents of false prophecy and laying out his own plan for the exiles' ultimate redemption. Thus, the letter combats the claims of the false prophets: (1) since the exiles will not enjoy a quick return to their land, they are obliged to begin building a life for themselves in exile (vv. 4-7); (2) the hegemony of Babylon will last 'seventy years' and only then will YHWH restore the exiles (vv. 10-14); (3) Judah and Jerusalem will undergo destruction and their inhabitants will be exiled (vv. 16-19);[38] (4) sensibly, the letter also contains words condemning the false prophets (vv. 8-9, 20-23). With the exception of the statements concerning the false prophets, the chapter parallels ch. 24 and even assumes it—both chapters prophesy good tidings to the Jehoiachin exiles and evil ones to those who were not exiled in 597 (29.18 has a chiastic relationship to 24.9-10; the phrase כתאנים השערים אשר לא תאכלנה מרע, 'like vile figs which are so bad they cannot be eaten', reflects the nearly identical one in 24.2, 8).

b. *The Shorter Version in the Septuagint*. Verses 10-13 are nearly identical in both the Hebrew and the Greek. The largest difference in these appears in v. 11 where the Septuagint is missing אנכי ידעתי את המחשבות אשר 'I know the plans which'. The absence of these five words is most probably due to a homoioteleuton—the double appearance of the word אנכי in the masoretic text. On the other hand, v. 14, except for the first two words in Hebrew, is missing entirely from the Greek. Nevertheless, this loss does not detract from the meaning of the passage since only the *repetition* of God's promise to restore the people to their land (v. 10) is missing in the Septuagint. The Greek still contains the key elements of the promise of restoration and the people's repentance.

As mentioned above, an argument for the retention of v. 14 has been advanced by Martens (1972:62), who notes that v. 14 is 'a recapitulation of 29.10 and so . . . an *inclusio*'. Martens finds other examples of this phenomenon in 28.2, 4; 32.37, 41; Ezek. 36.22, 32.

c. *Structure and Meaning*. In common with 24.4-7, 29.10-14 opens with YHWH's unconditional promise to restore the exiles to their land (v. 10). It is conceivable that the phrase דברי הטוב 'my good word' looks back to the prophecy of 24.4-7.[39] 'My word', in the sense of the word of YHWH which has already been spoken, appears in Jer. 1.12; Num. 11.23 (cp. Jer. 33.14; Josh. 21.45; 23.15; 1 Kgs 6.12; 8.56). Verse 11 expresses God's good intentions to the exiles in similar fashion to 24.5-6. Verses 12-13 speaks of the repentance of the people in exile which serves as the formal reason for their return to the land (v. 14).

It is noteworthy that the root שוב does not appear in this passage. This raises the question of the significance of the terms וקראתם אתי 'you shall *call* me',. . . והתפללתם אלי, 'you shall *pray* to me'. . ., ובקשתם אתי, 'you shall *seek* me' . . ., כי תדרשני בכל לבבכם, 'when you *seek* me with all your heart' in vv. 12-13;

1. וקראתם אתי—'Calling to God' signifies fealty in 3.4, 19; in the latter verse it implies repentance, כי תקראי לי ומאחרי לא תשובו. The most instructive parallel may be found in Isa. 55.6-8, דרשו יהוה בהמצאו, 'seek YHWH while He may be found' . . . , קראהו בהיותו קרוב, 'call upon Him while He is near' . . . , וישב אל יהוה וירחמהו, 'let him return to YHWH and He will

have mercy upon him'.... The similar usage of terms in chiastic order may indicate a line of influence from Jeremiah to II Isaiah. In any case, קרא is here associated with repentance.

2. והתפללתם אלי—the classical term for prayer, it also appears in v. 7.
3. ובקשתם אתי—the root בקש appears elsewhere in connection with repentance in Deut. 4.29-31; Hos. 3.5; 5.15–6.1; 7.10; Isa. 65.1; Zeph. 1.6; 2 Chron. 7.14; 15.4. However, Wagner cautions that several of these occurrences, as well as that in Jer. 50.4-5 (הלך ובכה ילכו ואת יהוה אלהיהם יבקשו ציון ישאלו, 'weeping as they walk and they shall seek YHWH their God, they shall ask for Zion'),[40] may reflect a cultic rite (Wagner, 1977:237-39).
4. כי תדרשני בכל לבבכם—the root דרש, which, like בקש, means 'seek', is used theologically to express 'a loyal, positive, devoted commitment to Yahweh' (Wagner 1978:300). It appears in the context of repentance in Deut. 4.29-30; Hos. 10.12; Amos 5.4, 6; Isa. 9.12; 31.1; 55.6; Pss. 14.1-3; 53.2-4; 78.34.[41] Similarly, it appears elsewhere in Jeremiah in 10.21.

The above survey indicates that, despite the absence of the root שוב, 29.12-13 are concerned with acts of repentance. Nonetheless, there may be some small psychological significance to the absence of שוב here, for it will never be used again by Jeremiah to refer to repentance in a prophecy of redemption. It may also be of some importance that there is no *direct* mention of obedience to YHWH. Indeed, perhaps, the reference to prayer and 'calling' may place the emphasis on the contrition aspect of repentance (as does 1 Kgs 8.47-50).

C. **Jer. 24.4-7; 29.10-14: Summary and Conclusions**

The second stage in the development of Jeremiah's thought concerning repentance and redemption is represented by the prophecies in Jer. 24.4-7 and 29.10-14. Both are addressed to the Jehoiachin exiles and both (24.4-7 first) originate in the days between the exiles of 597 and 587. In both cases the repentance of Israel is the formal rationale for God's restoration of the exiles to their land. However, whereas in Jeremiah's early prophecies to Ephraim (see

Chapter 1) Israel's repentance and YHWH's mercies are both of primary importance, in these prophecies repentance takes a secondary position and God's promise of redemption takes center-stage.

The appearance of the theme of repentance at the end of 24.4-7 and at the middle of 29.10-14 repudiates the popular theory of the dtr. edition of those prophecies and throws into question the entire theory of an exilic dtr. redactor of Deuteronomy and the Former Prophets (as well as Jeremiah).

The preponderant stress placed upon YHWH's merciful acts in the prophecies of redemption to the Jehoiachin exiles and the diminished prominence attached to repentance symbolize the dawn of Jeremiah's despair of the people's ability to return of its own free will to its God. And yet, despite the continuous disdain of his people for his words (cp. 25.3, 5, 7), at this stage Jeremiah is still unable to give up all hope for repentance.

Chapter 3

PROPHECIES OF REDEMPTION TO JUDAH AND EPHRAIM ON THE NIGHT[1] OF DESTRUCTION

A. Jer. 31.27-37

26 הִנֵּה יָמִים בָּאִים נְאֻם־יְהוָה
וְזָרַעְתִּי אֶת־בֵּית יִשְׂרָאֵל וְאֶת־בֵּית יְהוּדָה זֶרַע אָדָם וְזֶרַע
27 בְּהֵמָה׃ וְהָיָה כַּאֲשֶׁר שָׁקַדְתִּי עֲלֵיהֶם לִנְתוֹשׁ וְלִנְתוֹץ
וְלַהֲרֹס וּלְהַאֲבִיד וּלְהָרֵעַ כֵּן אֶשְׁקֹד עֲלֵיהֶם לִבְנוֹת וְלִנְטוֹעַ
28 נְאֻם־יְהוָה׃ בַּיָּמִים הָהֵם לֹא־יֹאמְרוּ עוֹד אָבוֹת אָכְלוּ
29 בֹסֶר וְשִׁנֵּי בָנִים תִּקְהֶינָה׃ כִּי אִם־אִישׁ בַּעֲוֺנוֹ יָמוּת כָּל־
הָאָדָם הָאֹכֵל הַבֹּסֶר תִּקְהֶינָה שִׁנָּיו׃ הִנֵּה יָמִים בָּאִים ל
נְאֻם־יְהוָה וְכָרַתִּי אֶת־בֵּית יִשְׂרָאֵל וְאֶת־בֵּית יְהוּדָה בְּרִית
31 חֲדָשָׁה׃ לֹא כַבְּרִית אֲשֶׁר כָּרַתִּי אֶת־אֲבוֹתָם בְּיוֹם
הֶחֱזִיקִי בְיָדָם לְהוֹצִיאָם מֵאֶרֶץ מִצְרָיִם אֲשֶׁר־הֵמָּה הֵפֵרוּ
32 אֶת־בְּרִיתִי וְאָנֹכִי בָּעַלְתִּי בָם נְאֻם־יְהוָה׃ כִּי זֹאת הַבְּרִית
אֲשֶׁר אֶכְרֹת אֶת־בֵּית יִשְׂרָאֵל אַחֲרֵי הַיָּמִים הָהֵם נְאֻם־
יְהוָה נָתַתִּי אֶת־תּוֹרָתִי בְּקִרְבָּם וְעַל־לִבָּם אֶכְתֲּבֶנָּה וְהָיִיתִי
33 לָהֶם לֵאלֹהִים וְהֵמָּה יִהְיוּ־לִי לְעָם׃ וְלֹא יְלַמְּדוּ עוֹד אִישׁ
אֶת־רֵעֵהוּ וְאִישׁ אֶת־אָחִיו לֵאמֹר דְּעוּ אֶת־יְהוָה כִּי כוּלָּם
יֵדְעוּ אוֹתִי לְמִקְטַנָּם וְעַד־גְּדוֹלָם נְאֻם־יְהוָה כִּי אֶסְלַח
34 לַעֲוֺנָם וּלְחַטָּאתָם לֹא אֶזְכָּר־עוֹד׃ כֹּה ׀ אָמַר יְהוָה
נֹתֵן שֶׁמֶשׁ לְאוֹר יוֹמָם חֻקֹּת יָרֵחַ וְכוֹכָבִים לְאוֹר לָיְלָה
רֹגַע הַיָּם וַיֶּהֱמוּ גַלָּיו יְהוָה צְבָאוֹת שְׁמוֹ׃ אִם־יָמֻשׁוּ לה
הַחֻקִּים הָאֵלֶּה מִלְּפָנַי נְאֻם־יְהוָה גַּם זֶרַע יִשְׂרָאֵל יִשְׁבְּתוּ
36 מִהְיוֹת גּוֹי לְפָנַי כָּל־הַיָּמִים׃ כֹּה ׀ אָמַר יְהוָה אִם־
יִמַּדּוּ שָׁמַיִם מִלְמַעְלָה וְיֵחָקְרוּ מוֹסְדֵי־אֶרֶץ לְמָטָּה גַּם־
אֲנִי אֶמְאַס בְּכָל־זֶרַע יִשְׂרָאֵל עַל־כָּל־אֲשֶׁר עָשׂוּ נְאֻם־
יְהוָה׃

27 'Behold, the days are coming, says the LORD, when I will sow the house of Israel and the house of Judah with the seed of man and

the seed of beast.[28] And it shall come to pass that as I have watched over them to pluck up and break down, to overthrow, destroy, and bring evil, so I will watch over them to build and to plant, says the LORD. [29]In those days, they shall no longer say:

> The fathers have eaten sour grapes,
> and the children's teeth are set on edge.

[30]But every one shall die for his own sin; each man who eats sour grapes, his teeth shall be set on edge.

31 'Behold, the days are coming, says the LORD, when I will make a new covenant with the house of Israel and the house of Judah, [32]not like the covenant which I made with their fathers when I took them by the hand to bring them out of the land of Egypt, my covenant which they broke, though I was their husband, says the LORD. [33]But this is the covenant which I will make with the house of Israel after those days, says the LORD: I will put my law within them, and I will write it upon their hearts; and I will be their God, and they shall be my people. [34]And no longer shall each man teach his neighbor and each his brother, saying, "Know the LORD", for they shall all know me, from the least of them to the greatest, says the LORD; for I will forgive their iniquity, and I will remember their sin no more.'

> [35]Thus says the LORD,
> who gives the sun for light by day
> and the fixed order of the moon and the stars for light by night,
> who stirs up the sea so that its waves roar—
> the Lord of hosts is his name:
> [36]'If this fixed order departs
> from before me, says the LORD,
> then shall the descendants of Israel cease
> from being a nation before me for ever'.

> [37]Thus says the LORD:
> 'If the heavens above can be measured,
> and the foundations of the earth below can be explored,
> then I will cast off all the descendants of Israel
> for all that they have done, says the LORD'.

It will be the thesis of this section that Jer. 31.27-37 is an organic unity authentic to the prophet. It will be demonstrated that the meaning of its three segments—vv. 27-30, 31-34, 35-37—can only be fleshed out when understood as part of an interlocking whole. This radical claim runs contrary to the unanimity of established scholarship. Since the focal point of the unit is the 'New Covenant' prophecy in vv. 31-34, the review of scholarship will start there.

1. *Review of Scholarship*

a. *31.31-34.* Jer. 31.31-34 has been a popular subject for research due to its phrase 'New Covenant', which has been applied as the appellation for the most important Christian holy works (the Latin *testamentum* is translated both by 'covenant' and 'testament'). The phrase is also referred to often in those works (Mt. 26.28; Mk 14.24; Lk. 22.20; 1 Cor. 11.25; the cup of wine=the blood of Jesus=the new covenant. See also Jn 13.34-35; 2 Cor. 3.1-18; Heb. 8.6-13; 9.15; 12.24; 1 Jn 2.8-11). It is therefore not surprising, although regrettable, that too often Christian scholars have perceived this prophecy in Jeremiah in a distorted fashion,[2] hampering an objective understanding of the text (see below on תורתי).

Additionally, scholarship is confused on the issues of authenticity, meaning, and dating the text. Some typical examples follow:

(1) Welch (1928:229-30), following Skinner, accepts both the authenticity of the prophecy and its relatedness to the entire people. Since the new covenant forgives the breaking of the old one, he claims that the new one is richer in content than the old:

> It had all the content of forgiveness . . . it could unfold its meaning to men who understood their need for forgiveness . . . it was new to men . . . who recognized that the past relationship had been destroyed by their own act and needed to be renewed in spite of it. The new relation unfolded its meaning to their new experience. Because it involved this experience, it was inward and it was incommunicable. Men could now learn the terms of a law which God ordered and man obeyed. There was something there which involved a personal experience of sin and grace.

(2) Rudolph contends that vv. 31-34 continue from vv. 18-22, and thus are the authentic words of the prophet which address only Ephraim (following Volz). He dates the prophecy to the days of Josiah, and, more precisely, to Josiah's attempt to conquer Samaria.[3] There is nothing new in the content of the covenant, and the only reason for the use of the term 'new' is because of this covenant's eternality. God's forgiveness (v. 34) is His response to Ephraim's plea 'turn me back and I shall return' (v. 18). The mention of Judah in v. 31 is a later gloss, based on its absence in v. 33.

(3) Hyatt (1956), admits the possibility that the idea of the new covenant is Jeremiah's. Nonetheless, the prophecy in its current formulation was reworked after the book had received a dtr. redaction (following Mowinckel). The prophecy relates to both Ephraim and Judah, but contains nothing new.

(4) Nicholson (1970:82-84, 138), following Hermann, considers the reference to a covenant ceremony at a crucial time, as well as the similarity

to Deut. 30:6, to be decisive in determining that 31.31-34 is, in its origin, a dtr. invention.

Carroll (1981:217), in Nicholson's footsteps, asserts that 'For Jeremiah, the only grounds for national deliverance is the return of the people of Yahweh' and since that element is lacking in 31.31-34 it must have originated with the deuteronomists. The deuteronomists are merely substituting a new covenant with 'A few alterations and modifications' for the old one 'which was a complete failure from the beginning'. This substitution is 'perhaps . . . more folly than despair' (1981:219) and negates the 'moral force' of prophecy which seeks 'to persuade the people to turn . . . from present policies' (1981:220):

> to encounter a passage in a prophetic book which promises a golden future and a new covenant without repentance, and which envisages a period when there will be no need for such moral change *by* the people because Yahweh will change them automatically, is to enter a world where the prophets have conceded defeat and have withdrawn from the moral struggle . . . If people will not change, then to hope for God to change them is to move from the moral sphere to piety and transcendentalism. It is in this sense that the motif of the new covenant is a counsel of despair *if* it is to be attributed to Jeremiah (contrast the role of repentance in restoration in Jer. 31.18-20). This . . . [is] one very good argument for not attributing the new covenant passage to Jeremiah.[4]

Carroll's limited view of morality is problematic. Is it not moral to hope that the tragedy of the catastrophe of 587 will never be repeated?[5] Would it not be moral of the prophet to be true to the lessons of his own experience? Is not the promise of righteous behavior a moral dream? Is the pouring forth of divine mercy an immoral hope? The investigation below will nullify Carroll's gratuitous comments.

b. *The Authenticity of 31.27-30*. The authenticity of 31.27-30 has been questioned by many. Duhm and Rudolph doubt vv. 27-28; according to Rudolph they are a prose summary of 31.2-26. However, v. 27 matches Hos. 2.25 in both language and contents: v. 27, וזרעתי את בית ישראל ואת בית יהודה; Hos. 2.25, וזרעתיה לי בארץ, 'I will sow her for myself in the land'.

Nicholson (1970:85), following Hermann, claims that v. 28 is a reworking of the conditional dtr. promise of salvation found in 18.7-10 and points to the similar terminology (the use of the roots בנה, נטע, רעע, אבד, נתץ, נתש). Nicholson ignores Bach (1961:23) who notes that it is Jeremiah who links together the four roots נטע, בנה, נתץ, נתש.[6] It should be noted that v. 28 is apparently a conscious conflation of Jeremiah's call and inaugural visions:

> v. 28, כאשר שקדתי עליהם לנתוש ולנתוץ ולהרס
> ולהאביד ולהרע כן אשקד עליהם לבנות ולנטוע;
> 1.10, 12, 14, ראה הפקדתיך היום... לנתוש ולנתוץ ולהאביד
> ולהרס לבנות ולנטוע... כי שקד אני על דברי

> See I have set you this day . . . to pluck up and to break down, to destroy and to overthrow, to build and to plant . . . for I am watching over my word to perform it . . . the evil.

The prophesied destruction has already materialized. It is time for the prophecies of restoration to come to the fore.

c. *The Authenticity of 31.35-37*. Doubts have also been raised concerning the authenticity of vv. 35-37. Duhm, Welch (1928:226), Hyatt (1956), Raitt (1977:251 n. 6), and Böhmer (1976:79) assert that these verses are influenced by II Isaiah and were inserted here by the editor of chs. 30–31. The words of II Isaiah are recognizable in v. 35, רגע הים והמו גליו יהוה צבאות שמו, which is identical to Isa. 51.15, Raitt comments that vv. 35-37 'employs an argument from nature to history utterly unlike and contradictory to Jeremiah elsewhere'. Carroll (1981:214), in his inimitable manner, states of this promise of the eternality of the relationship of YHWH to His people,

> In many ways this very strong nationalistic conviction is precisely the kind of belief opposed by the early oracles of Jeremiah . . . The irony of the developed tradition carrying views so antagonistic to his spirit should not be overlooked by the modern analyst of the book of Jeremiah.

Carroll has failed to take into consideration that vv. 35-37 speak to a different historical reality than do Jeremiah's earlier prophecies. All Carroll proves is that vv. 35-37 do not belong to the prophet's early prophecies, not that Jeremiah did not author these verses later. Carroll appears incapable of conceiving of the possibility that the prophet can be affected by changing historical realities and his own personal experience.

The following points are brought in refutation of the claim that vv. 35-37 were influenced by II Isaiah: (1) the phrase יהוה צבאות recurs more often in Jeremiah than in any other biblical book—57 times as opposed to 8 times in II Isaiah, and the expression יהוה צבאות שמו is found 8 times in Jeremiah and only 4 times in II Isaiah.[7] (2) the root המה appears 9 times in Jeremiah (see especially 5.22; 6.23// 50.42; 51.55) and twice in II Isaiah (the other occurrence is 59.11).[8] (3) the words ישבתו, מהיות, כל הימים (v. 36) do not appear in II Isaiah. The root שבת appears 6 times in Jeremiah, the word מהיות 3 times, and the phrase כל הימים 4 times. (4) גם אני אמאס בכל זרע ישראל in v. 37 appears to be at the basis of Isa. 41.8-9 (cp. Jer. 33.24-26). The root מאס appears 11 times in Jeremiah and only twice in II Isaiah (41.9; 54.6). (5) the poetic-rhetorical style of 31.36-37 (and 33.20-21, 25-26), אם . . . גם . . ., as well as their content is borrowed from Gen. 13.16 (cp. Rashi on both texts). Furthermore, Jeremiah's affection for rhetorical style is well attested (Held, 1969:76; Brueggemann, 1973:358-74).

All of the above evidence points to the conclusion that II Isaiah was influenced by Jeremiah, and not the reverse (see below).

2. *The Interconnection of 31.27-30, 31-34, 35-37*

It is the considered opinion of scholarship (e.g. Duhm; Lofthouse, 1925:89-90; Blank, 1961:210) that vv. 31-34 form an independent unit or have been separated from their natural context. However, an investigation of their immediate context will reveal that vv. 27-37 form a single literary unit.

In Chapter 1 it was determined that 31.22 ends a literary unit concerned with Ephraim, while vv. 23-26, like vv. 10-14, have Judah as their subject. Of the remaining verses, 27-40, vv. 38-40 are stylistically different from their predecessors. In vv. 27-37, YHWH always appears in the first person (with the exception of the stereotypical Jeremianic, and non-dtr. phrase, נאם יהוה), and the verbs are in active speech. In vv. 38-40, though, YHWH appears in indirect object (vv. 38, 40) and the verbs נתש, הרם, בנה are passive. It is doubtful, then, that vv. 38-40 are directly related to the preceding ones. It seems much more probable that vv. 38-40 were placed after vv. 27-37 due to associative-linguistic connections: (1) הנה ימים באים נאם יהוה in vv. 27, 31, 38 (this expression also appears in the context of prophecies of redemption in 23.5; 33.14 as here without the transition word לכן, 'therefore'; (2) the root בנה appears in vv. 28, 38 and the roots נתש, הרם are mentioned in vv. 28, 40 (these roots also appear together in 1.10; 24.6; 42.10; 45.4).

a. *31.27-30, 31-34*. An extraordinary resemblance exists between vv. 27-30, 31-34:

(1) Verses 27 and 31 refer to both Israel and Judah, but in reality the affinity is much deeper:

> הנה ימים באים נאם ה׳ וזרעתי את בית ישראל ואת בית יהודה זרע אדם וזרע בהמה (v. 27)
>
> הנה ימים באים נאם ה׳ וכרתי את בית ישראל ואת בית יהודה ברית חדשה (v. 31)

The two verses, except for the verb and the direct object, are identical. There is no other verse in the Bible which is as similar to these two verses as they are to each other.[9]

(2) A strong resemblance also characterizes vv. 29-30, 34:

> לא יאמרו עוד... כי... איש... כל האדם (vv. 29-30)
>
> ולא יאמרו עוד... כי כולם... למקטנם ועד גרולם. (v. 34)

The components of the correspondence are: (a) the formula A לא

B כי ... עוד;[10] (b) the people shall no longer say in the future what they say in the present (אבות אכלו בסר, דעו את יהוה); (c) there will be a transformation in individual responsibility towards sin.

(3) Verses 28 and 32-33 portray a change between the results of YHWH's actions in the past and those of the future:

> (v. 28) 'as I have watched over them to ... pluck out and to destroy ... so I will watch over them to build and to plant',
> (vv. 32-33) 'not according to the covenant which I made with their fathers ... but this is the covenant I shall make with the house of Israel'.

(4) In vv. 29 and 32 the sins of the fathers are mentioned—v. 29, אבות אכלו בסר, v. 32, אבותם ... אשר המה הפרו את בריתי.

The above lines of relationship testify to an organic connection between vv. 27-30 and 31-34.

b. *31.31-34, 35-37*. The endings of vv. 34 and 37 are similar in their mention of God's good intentions towards His people despite their past sinful behavior:

> (v. 34) 'For I shall forgive *their iniquities* and *their sins* I shall no longer remember.'
> (v. 37) 'If the heavens above can be measured ... then I will also reject all the seed of Israel for *all they have done*.'

This resemblance is itensified in the Septuagint, where v. 37 precedes vv. 35-36. Thereby, the references to the people's sins are placed next to one another.

Another link between vv. 31-34 and 35-37 is the statements concerning the giving of laws by YHWH (v. 33) נתתי את תורתי, (v. 35) ... נתן ... חקת ... (cp. v. 36, החקים האלה).

c. *Summary*. A chain of linguistic, stylistic, and ideological similarities links together 31.27-30, 31-34, 35-37. The logical conclusion is that these three segments form a single literary unit. Further evidence for this unity is adduced from the fact that the unit ends in the manner that it begins. Verse 27 speaks of the 'seeding' of Israel and Judah זרע אדם וזרע בהמה. Similarly, in v. 37 YHWH gives his oath never to reject all זרע ישראל.[11] Thus, by use of the root זרע an *inclusion* is created at the extremities of the prophecy.

3. *Structure and Meaning*

a. *31.27-34*

In vv. 27-28, YHWH promises material abundance to the exiles of Ephraim and Judah. At the time of redemption, 'they shall no longer say, "The fathers have eaten sour grapes and the children's teeth are set on edge", rather, "Each one shall die for his own sin; every man who eats sour grapes, his teeth shall be set on edge"' (vv. 29-30). The meaning of these words has been the subject of much scholarly controversy (e.g. Driver, 1906; Binns, 1919; Tur-Sinai, 1954:458-71; Weiss, 1962:255-56). The vast majority of exegetes have discovered here a great innovation in the doctrine of retribution in the book of Jeremiah and the Bible in general (e.g. Buber, 1960:185; Greenberg, 1960:22, 25; 1970:xxviii).[12]

The prophet announces that at the time of redemption the people will no longer claim that their generation has been punished for the sins of their forbears. Rather, the people will come to the recognition that it is the sinner who will die for his sin. This prophecy implies that during the days of Jeremiah the people believe that their own suffering is derived from the sins of previous generations, punishment for crimes which they themselves did not commit. In the future, says the prophet, the people will understand that individual retribution is the rule, and not the vertical retribution which places upon the shoulders of the children the burden of their parents' sins.

If this explanation is correct, though, a contradiction, or at least tension, is established between vv. 29-30 and the words of God at the end of v. 34, 'for I shall forgive their sins and will no longer remember their iniquities': If sins are forgiven, then how shall a person die for his sin?[13]

A second contradiction arises between vv. 29-30 and vv. 33-34, 'I shall put my torah within them . . . all shall know me'. How can it be possible for a person to sin when God puts His torah into the hearts of His people so that they shall not be able to sin any more, but rather be obedient (ידעו) to Him?[14]

The solution to these two problems is dependent upon the meaning of the unique expression in v. 33, 'after (אחרי) those days'. Which days? If the new covenant shall be given 'after those days', then the words 'those days' refer to a period of time before the giving of the new covenant—a period of time mentioned previously by the prophet.[15] Since the 'days' which 'are coming' in v. 31 are the days of the new covenant, it is obvious that they are not the referent of the words 'those days' in v. 33. In order to find the 'days' mentioned in v. 33, one is forced to go back to the 'days' predicted in v. 27—the days of redemption depicted in vv. 27-30. Thus, the expression 'after those days' relates to a time after the redemption mentioned in vv. 27-30. In other words, between the period of restoration to the land and the time of the establishment of the new covenant, an indeterminate amount of time shall pass.[16] Only afterwards will the new covenant be given.

By this understanding of 'after those days', the door is open for the dismissal of the contradictions presented above. It is entirely conceivable that even in the days of restoration the people will continue to sin. However, 'after those days', i.e. from the hour of the establishment of the new covenant, the people will cease to sin, 'they shall all know me'. Thus the second contradiction is eliminated.

The first contradiction is disposed of when one realizes that the subordinate clause 'for I shall forgive their sins and no longer remember their iniquities' is concerned with the forgiveness which will precede the giving of the new covenant. The location of this subordinate clause in the segment of vv. 31-34 is identical to the one at the end of 24.4-7, 'for they shall return to me with all their heart' (see Chapter 2). Both clauses make the crystallization of God's mercies conditional on a preceding action.[17] Verses 27-34 should therefore be understood as positing the following chronological order: at the time of restoration to the land the people shall say,[18] 'Each one shall die for his own sin (etc.)'. *Afterwards* YHWH will forgive the sins of the people and after the forgiveness He will give them the new covenant.

Jeremiah and his people are not occupied here with a theoretical theological-philosophical problem. The people's complaint that 'the fathers have eaten sour grapes and the children's teeth are set on edge' is based on the reality within which it lives. The people's protest reflects the spiritual despair of a nation which has felt the lash of punishment on its own flesh. Their grievance states that generations of ancestors were guilty of manifold transgressions, and yet did not die by pestilence, famine, the sword of the Chaldeans, or in exile, whereas they themselves have been made to suffer and to pay back with their lives the debt of their ancestors. To this bitter remonstration of the people, Jeremiah responds with a prophecy of redemption: those who will experience restoration will understand that those who suffered in the destruction and exile were sinful and evil, and deserved the tribulations that befell them. There will thus be agreement with the concept expressed by Jeremiah in most of his prophecies, that the generation of the destruction is one rebellious against God, deserving of punishment. Therefore, those who will be restored will abandon the proverb of their fathers and will say, instead, 'Each one will die for his own sin . . .' Just as the complaint, 'the fathers have eaten sour grapes . . .' is based upon human experience, so, too, the saying 'Each one shall die for his own sin' will find support in the coming reality.[19] 'In those days', in the days of redemption, Israel shall affirm 'Each one shall die for his own sin' and then God, who has begun to reveal His mercies during the period of exile, will forgive the sins of those who are restored[20] in order to purify their hearts[21] and to prepare them to receive the new covenant.

b. *The New Covenant*

According to v. 32, the new covenant will not be 'like the covenant, which I made with their fathers on the day that I held them by the hand to bring them out of the land of Egypt, my covenant which they broke even though I had been their husband'. This verse implies that the Israelites will not break the new covenant as they broke the Sinaitic one. What is the basis for this assurance? An examination of vv. 33-34 will provide the answer.

1. 31.33, נתתי את תורתי בקרבם ועל לבם אכתבנה. The words 'I will put my torah within them and will write it on their hearts' depict the method by which the torah will be transmitted from God to Israel. This will be accomplished without any intermediary—a direct transmission without the use of an agent, neither human (a prophet or a priestly instructor) nor material (tablets or book). Furthermore, the re-giving of the torah will not be accompanied by a revelation which affects the senses of sight and hearing.

The giving of the new covenant may be described, perhaps, as an internal act which takes place within the recipient and transforms the torah into an organic part of the individual. Thus, at the time of the giving of the new covenant, the transmission of the torah as well as its acceptance will entail an entirely different experience than that of the covenant at Sinai.

2. 31.33, תורתי. For many Christian scholars, the main stumbling block on the path to understanding the new covenant has been the meaning of the term 'my torah'. These scholars, who seem to be

influenced by their own religious theology, have been hard put to accept the legal context of 'torah'. For example:

(1) Streane contends that the placement of the torah in the heart abrogates any need for a 'complex system of ordinances. The inner life, emotional and intellectual alike, will be in full harmony with Jehovah's will'.

(2) According to Skinner (1922:332), 'The true Tora of Yahwe is the revelation of the essential ethical will of God . . . the Tora of Yahwe is the living principle of religion which is ever new, which exists perfectly in the mind of God'.

(3) Hyatt (1941:394-96) remarks that 'the concept of Torah was not a very important one in Jeremiah's thinking', and that Jeremiah 'denied that true Torah was contained in some written book, probably including Deuteronomy'. Hyatt identifies the 'true Torah' with the ethical will of God and with the commandment, given to Israel in the desert, to worship God alone. In his opinion, it is possible that Jeremiah thought that the essence of the torah was contained in the 'ethical decalogue'.

(4) Ostborn (1945:155) and Davies (1952:26-28) do not identify the torah of the Sinaitic covenant with that of the new covenant, and both talk of an obvious tension that exists between the first and the second. They claim that a contradiction exists between the law of God and His will. Even though Ostborn (1945:169-71) recognizes that the term 'torah' can denote 'guidance', 'instruction', and 'law', he does not consider the possibility that 'torah' can be interpreted as 'legal instruction'.

(5) In contradistinction to the viewpoints presented above, Duhm accepts the interpretation of 'torah' as first and foremost law. He therefore rejects these verses as Jeremianic, since they express the narrow perspective of a late editor who wishes to bind Judaism with the bonds of formalistic legalities. According to Duhm this is a step backwards in the evolution of the religion. Duhm's words are echoed, apparently unconsciously, by Carroll (1981:222),[22] who seems to consider that 'torah' in v. 33 is 'confined to ritual practices' and that the new covenant is 'a variation on the standard presentation of life in the community' limited by 'communal observances'.

It should be remembered that the definition of 'torah' as 'law' does not reflect the original meaning of the word, which is 'instruction' or 'teaching':

(Prov. 6.20-21) 'Keep, my son, the commandment of your father,

> and do not forsake the *torah* of your mother, bind them on your heart always, tie them upon your neck';
> (7.1-3) 'My son, observe my sayings and store up my commandments with you. Observe my commandments and live, and my *torah* as the apple of your eye. Bind them on your fingers, write them of the tablet of your heart.'[23]

Nonetheless, the numerous occurrences of 'torah' in the Bible, particularly in a legal context and in relationship to the statutes given by YHWH, point to the necessity of understanding 'torah' as 'divine legal instructions'. The meaning of 'the torah of YHWH' is thus similar to that of 'the commandment of YHWH'[24] (see e.g. Exod. 16.28, 'How long will you refuse to observe my commandments and my *torot*'; similarly, cp. Exod. 24.12; Josh. 22.5). The conscious usage of the term 'torah' as 'divine legal instruction' appears often in the Bible. Verses in which the noun 'torah' occurs next to the verb ירה 'instruct', 'teach'—are Exod. 24.12; Lev. 14.54-57; Deut. 17.8-11; 33.10; Isa. 2.3//Mic. 4.6; Ezek. 44.23-24; Ps. 119.33-34; 2 Chron. 15.3. In other verses the verb למד, the synonym of ירה, appears with 'torah': Deut. 31.12-13; 17.18-19; Isa. 8.16; Pss. 94.12; 119.71-73; Ezra 7.10; 2 Chron. 17.9; Jer. 9.12-13.

The meaning of 'torah' as 'divine legal instruction' fits the context under discussion perfectly, as clarified by the continuation in v. 34, 'and no longer shall each man teach ילמדו his neighbor and each man his brother, saying, "Know YHWH", for they shall all know me'. In light of the fact that the only result of the placement of the Torah in the heart is 'they shall all know me', it may be assumed that a close connection exists between teaching the law of YHWH and learning the knowledge of YHWH. This assumption is supported by Jer. 2.8, 'the priests did not say "where is YHWH" and the handlers of the Torah did not know me'. Despite the reference in v. 34 to the anonymous members of the people ('each man his neighbor and each man his brother'), the responsibility for dissemination of the torah in Israel is borne primarily by the priests and Levites:[25]

(1) the verb ירה signifies the actions of these two groups in Lev. 10.11; 14.57; Deut. 17.8-11; 24.8; 33.8-10; 2 Kgs 12.3; 17.27-28; Ezek. 44.23; 2 Chron. 15.3. See also the critique of the priests in Isa. 9.14 and Mic. 3.11.

(2) Similarly, the verb למד in 1 Chron. 25.8; 2 Chron. 17.9. See also Deut. 4.1, 5, 14 concerning Moses and Ezra 7.10 concerning Ezra.

(3) Similarly, also, the verb בין in the late texts of Neh. 8.3-9; 1 Chron. 25.8; 2 Chron. 35.3.

(4) It appears that Jeremiah and his listeners knew a priestly formula used for the instruction of the torah of YHWH. This conclusion arises from a comparison of Jer. 3.1 with Hag. 2.11-13:[26]

Hag. 2.11-13	*Jer. 3.1*
כה אמר ה' צבאות שאל נא הכהנים תורה	
לאמר	לאמר
הן ישא איש בשר קדש בכנף בגדו	הן ישלח איש את אשתו והלכה מאתו
ונגע בכנפו אל הלחם ואל הנזיד ואל	והיתה לאיש אחר
היין ואל השמן ואל כל מאכל	
היקדש ויענו הכהנים	הישוב אליה עוד
ויאמרו לא ויאמר חגי אם יגע	
טמא נפש בכל אלה היטמא ויאמרו יטמא	
[11]Thus says the LORD of hosts: 'Ask the priests to decide this question, [12]"If one carries holy flesh in the skirt of his garment, and touches with his skirt bread, or pottage, or wine, or oil, or any kind of food, does it become holy?"' The priests answered, 'No'. [13]Then said Haggai, 'If one who is unclean by contact with a dead body touches any of these, does it become unclean?' The priests answered, 'It does become unclean'.	If a man divorces his wife and she goes from him and becomes another man's wife, will he return to her?'

The formula הן . . . ו . . . ה appears only in these two passages in the Bible.[27]

In view of the above discussion, it may be concluded that the image of the priest who teaches the torah was one of the central factors lying at the basis of the words 'each man shall not teach his neighbor' etc.

However, the priests (2.8; 5.31; 6.13; 8.8-10; 18.18; and cp. Ezek. 7.26; Mal. 2.1-9) and the prophets (2.8; 5.31; 6.13; 8.10; 14.14; 18.18; 23.11, 13-17, 21, 25-32; 27.9-10, 16; 29.8-9), the parents (7.18, 31; 9.11-13; 11.7-10; 14.20; 16.11, 19; 23.27; 34.14; and cp. Deut. 6.7; 11.13, 16, 18-19) and the children (5.7; 7.18, 26; 16.12), the 'shepherds' (2.8; 10.21; 23.1-2; 50.6) and the entire people (2.7, 11, 13, 19-27; 3.1-3; 5.1-9, 20-29; 6.13; 7.16-18; 8.7; 9.1-8, 12-13, etc.) refused again and again to fulfill the commandment of God and His torah, and did not accept the yoke of responsibility to teach one another the torah. It is not surprising, then, that in this prophecy of redemption it is God Himself who transforms the heart of the people so that they shall know Him.

In reality, the promise that YHWH will teach His torah to Israel without the benefit of an intermediary is only the reflection of a common biblical image. This idea is expressed in the following verses through use of the verb ירה: Isa. 2.4// Mic. 4.2; 1 Kgs 8.36//2 Chron. 6.27; Pss. 25.8, 12; 27.11; 86.11; 119.33, 102 (cp. Judg. 13.8; Isa. 28.26; Job 34.32).[28] Elsewhere this concept appears in connection with the verb למד: Isa. 48.17; 50.4; 54.13; Pss. 25.4, 5, 9; 71.17; 94.10, 12; 119.12, 26, 54, 66, 68, 71, 73, 108, 124, 135, 171; 132.12; 143.10 (and compare 114.1 with Judg. 3.2). Jer. 31.33-34, like the above-cited verses which express the same aspiration, was cast in the mold inspired by the central event of the giving of the torah on Sinai, as described in Exod. 24.12, 'and I will *give you* the stone tablets and the *torah* and the commandment which I have written *to instruct them*'. In other words, the torah of the new covenant is none other than the same torah upon which was established the covenant at Sinai.

3. *The Knowledge of YHWH and the Covenant Formula*. The conclusions of the discussion concerning the knowledge of YHWH in Chapter 2 apply also to the understanding of the terms דעו את יהוה and ידעו אותי in v. 34. These expressions indicate the people's fealty to God which is realized in complete obedience to His torah.

The direct transmission of the commandments from God to the hearts of the people will result, then, in absolute obedience which will close out any possibility of sin, 'for they shall all know me from the least of them to the greatest' (v. 34). Thereby, the necessity of one person teaching another to know YHWH will become superfluous (v. 34). In this manner the new covenant will result in the creation of the ideal positive relationship between YHWH and His people, 'I will be their God, and they shall be my people' (v. 33, and see the discussion in Chapter 2).

It is noteworthy that the new covenant passage contains no mention of any initiative by the people to return to their God.

Further conclusions concerning vv. 31-34 will be presented below.

c. *31.35-37*

As indicated earlier, the majority of scholars do not credit vv. 35-37 with Jeremianic authorship. However, a comparison with other passages in Scripture will testify to the exact opposite. These passages, all of which may be described as the positive promises of YHWH, serve witness to the literary development of an ideological motif—the eternal existence of the people of Israel which is comparable to the existence of natural phenomena. The following remarks refer to the tables on pp. 104f.

(1) Gen. 13.16 is the source which lies at the basis of the literary development presented here, as its short and prosaic formulation evinces. Note the pattern ... גם ... אם and the use of the noun זרע.

(2) Jer. 31.35-37 demonstrates a longer, more balanced, and more poetic form. Several affinities with Gen. 13.16 can be pointed out: (a) the use of the noun זרע in reference to the entire people; (b) the pattern ... גם ... אם; (c) the existence of Israel is compared to the existence of natural phenomena.

(3) Jer. 33.20-22, 25-26 are considered by most scholars to be a late textual addition (they will be discussed more fully in Chapter 4). Unlike the previous passages, the main subjects are a specific part of the people—the descendants of David, the priests and the Levites. Nonetheless, the similarities with Gen. 13.16 are readily recognizable: (a) the use of the noun זרע, and even זרע אברהם (v. 26); (b) the pattern ... גם ... אם; (c) the motif of numerical infinity; (d) the comparison between the existence of Israel and that of nature. It is significant to note that only in Gen. 13.16; Jer. 31.36-37; 33.20-21, 25-26 does the ... גם ... אם pattern appear.

(4) An essential difference divides Isa. 54.10 from the other verses cited here: the mountains and hills are not eternal. Thus, the relationship between Israel and God is *more* stable than the existence of nature. Only in this verse in the series is there a comparison between unequals (similarly, cp. Isa. 49.15, 25; 51.6, 8).[29]

(5) Isa. 54.10 paves the way for 66.22: existing nature has disappeared and has been replaced by the creation of a new nature. Unlike the old, this new nature is eternal and is therefore comparable to the never-ending existence of Israel.

The evolution of the motif in II Isaiah to a degree not attained in the prophecies of Jeremiah is critical for an understanding of the historical development of this type of comparison. The passages in Jeremiah represent an earlier stage than do those in II Isaiah in the literary development of the motif which compares the existence of Israel to that of natural phenomena. Thus, the argument that Jer. 31.35-37 was influenced by II Isaiah is invalidated, and the doubts

Gen. 13.16

(16) ושמתי
זרעך כעפר
הארץ
אם יוכל
איש למנות
את עפר הארץ
גם זרעך
ימנה

[16]I will make your descendants as the dust of the earth; so that if one can count the dust of the earth, your descendants also can be counted.

Jer. 31.35-37

(35) כה אמר ה׳ נתן שמש
לאור יומם חקת ירח וכוכבים
לאור לילה רגע הים ויהמו
גליו ה׳ צבאות שמו
(36) אם ימשו החקים האלה
מלפני נאם ה׳
גם זרע ישראל ישבתו מהיות
גוי לפני כל הימים
(37) כה אמר ה׳
אם ימדו שמים למעלה ויחקרו
מוסדי ארץ למטה
גם אני אמאס בכל זרע ישראל
על כל אשר עשו נאם ה׳

[35]Thus says the LORD,
who gives the sun for light by day
and the fixed order of the moon
and the stars for light by night,
who stirs up the sea so that its waves
roar—
the LORD of hosts is his name:
[36]'If this fixed order departs
from before me, says the LORD,
then shall the descendants of Israel
cease
from being a nation before me for
ever.'
[37]Thus says the LORD:
'If the heavens above can be
measured,
and the foundations of the earth
below can be explored,
then I will cast off all the
descendants of Israel
for all that they have done,
says the LORD.'

Jer. 33.20-22, 25-26

(20) כה אמר ה׳ אם תפרו את
בריתי היום ואת בריתי הלילה
ולבלתי היות יום ולילה בעתם
(21) גם בריתי תופר את דוד עבדי
מהיות לו בן מלך על כסאו ואת
הלוים הכהנים משרתי (22) אשר
לא יספר צבא השמים ולא ימד חול
הים כן ארבה את זרע דוד עבדי ואת
הלוים משרתי (25) כה אמר ה׳
אם לא בריתי יומם ולילה חקות
שמים וארץ לא שמתי
(26) גם זרע יעקוב ודוד עבדי
אמאס מקחת מזרעו משלים אל זרע
אברהם ישחק ויעקב כי
אשיב את שבותם ורחמתים

[20]'Thus says the LORD: If you can
break my covenant with the day and
my covenant with the night, so that
day and night will not come at their
appointed time, [21]then also my covenant
with David my servant may be broken,
so that he shall not have a son to reign
on his throne, and my covenant with
the Levitical priests my ministers.
[22]As the host of heaven cannot be
numbered and the sands of the sea
cannot be measured, so I will multiply
the descendants of David my servant,
and the Levitical priests who minister
to me.'
[25]'Thus says the LORD: If I have not
established my covenant with day and
night and the ordinances of heaven
and earth, [26]then I will reject the
descendants of Jacob and David my
servant and will not choose one of his
descendants to rule over the seed of
Abraham, Isaac, and Jacob. For I will
restore their fortunes, and will have
mercy upon them.'

Isa. 54.9-10

(9) כימי נח
זאת לי אשר
נשבעתי מעבר
מי נוח עוד
על הארץ כן
נשבעתי מקצף
עליך ומגער בך
(10) כי ההרים
ימושו והגבעות
תמוטנה וחסדי
מאתך לא ימוש
וברית שלומי
לא תמוט
אמר מרחמך ה׳

[9]'For this is like the days of Noah
to me:
as I swore that the waters of
Noah
should no more go over the earth,
so I have sworn that I will not be
angry with you
and will not rebuke you.
[10]For the mountains may depart
and the hills be removed,
but my steadfast love shall not
depart from you,
and my covenant of peace shall
not be removed,
says the LORD, who has
compassion on you.

Isa. 66.22

(22) כי כאשר
השמים החדשים
והארץ החדשה
אשר אני עשה
עמדים לפני
נאם ה׳
כן יעמד
זרעכם ושמכם

[22]'For as the new heavens and the new
earth
which I will make
shall remain before me, says the
LORD;
so shall your descendants and
your name remain.

	a comparison between	*in terms of*	*result*	*pattern*
Gen. 13.16	the seed of Abraham *and* the dust of the earth	numerical infinity[30]	equal	אם . . . גם . . .
Jer. 31.35-37	the relationship of the seed of Israel to God (twice) *and* the divine order of day and night, the sea and its waves; the height of the heavens and the depth of the earth	eternality	equal	אם . . . גם . . .
Jer. 33.20-22, 25-26	the relationship of the seed of David (twice), the priests, and the Levites (also, Jacob's seed) to God *and* (1) the covenant between God and day and night (twice); (2) the host of the heavens and the sand of the sea; (3) the laws of the heavens and the earth.	eternality (twice); numerical infinity	equal	אם . . . גם . . . אשר . . . כן . . .
Isa. 54.9-10	(1) the end of God's anger and punishment on the earth *and* the end of God's anger and punishment on Israel (symbolized by the unique, single occasion of the flood);	(1) eternality	(1) equal	אשר . . . כן . . .
	(2) the impermanence of the hills and mountains *and* God's faithfulness and covenant of peace with Israel.	(2) eternality	(2) unequal! In contrast to the hills, Israel is permanent.	כי . . . ו . . . לא
Isa. 66.22	the seed and name of Israel *and* the new heavens and the new earth.	eternality	equal	כי . . . כאשר . . . כן

concerning the authenticity of the passage are eliminated.

Verses 35-37 play a substantial role in the prophecy of the new covenant, without which that prophecy could not be fully comprehended. The purpose of these verses is to assure the people of the eternality of the ideal relationship which will be established by the new covenant and to reinforce the statement concerning the forgiveness of sins in v. 34—Israel's past behavior will not be a barrier to its security (v. 37).

4. *Date*

No precise date is mentioned in 31.27-37. Nevertheless, the references to 'the house of Israel and the house of Judah' in vv. 27, 31 attest to a date after the Jehoiachin exile. Furthermore, vv. 27-30 assume that the threat of destruction has fully materialized. There is no real reason to block the acceptance of the date recounted in 32.1-2 as the date, more or less, of 31.27-37: 'The word that came to Jeremiah from YHWH in the tenth year of Zedekiah king of Judah, which was the eighteenth year of Nebuchadrezzar. Then the army of the king of Babylon was besieging Jerusalem, and Jeremiah the prophet was imprisoned in the court of the guard which was in the palace of the king of Judah' (see also 33.1, 'The word of YHWH came to Jeremiah a second time, and he was still shut up in the court of the guard'). In those days, on the verge of the fall of Jerusalem, the land had already been devastated and a considerable portion of the populace had already been carried off into exile. One did not have to be a prophet in order to realize that the kingdom of Judah was finished. The hour of rapidly approaching darkness would have been highly suitable for the hopeful expressions of prophecies of redemption.

Indeed, chs. 32–33, to which this date is applied, teem with prophecies of redemption. Special attention will be paid below to the prophecy in 32.36-44—a prophecy which resembles a short version of that of the new covenant. That 33.8, 'I will purify them from all the transgression that they have sinned against me and I will forgive all their transgressions which they sinned against me and which they rebelled against me', which is similar to 31.34, 'for I will forgive their transgression and will no longer remember their sin', is related to this date further strengthens the claim that 31.27-37 originates at the time of the destruction of Jerusalem and the exile of Zedekiah.

5. *Summary and Conclusions*

The investigation that has been presented above led to the conclusion that Jer. 31.27-37 comprises a single literary unit spoken by Jeremiah at the time of the destruction of Jerusalem and the exile of Zedekiah. In this prophecy, YHWH's mercies are the only condition for the restoration of the people to its land and the creation of the ideal relationship between Him and His people. The condition of repentance, which was present at previous times, has now disappeared completely.

(a) The prophecy opens in vv. 27-30 with two promises which are combined, in reality, into one—(1) YHWH will restore both halves of the people to their land, in which they will be rebuilt (vv. 27-28); (2) Their implantation in the land will bring about the people's acknowledgment of YHWH's righteousness and justice (vv. 29-30). If during the time of destruction and exile (v. 28a) the children of Israel complained that 'the fathers have eaten sour grapes and the children's teeth have been set on edge' (v. 29), at the time of rebuilding and replanting (v. 28b) their eyes will be opened to the recognition that 'each man dies for his own transgression' (v. 30). This last saying reflects the perspective which will be adopted by the restored people in the future. Due to the new reality of redemption, the nation will declare that individual retribution does exist, thereby justifying God's actions.

(b) Jeremiah, however, does not deem this recognition to be sufficient. After years of fighting losing battles to turn his people from their obdurate ways, he knows that 'the heart is deceitful above all things and incurable' (17.9). To his calls to return to YHWH, the people have answered, 'there is no hope, we will follow our own plans, and will act each of us according to the wicked stubbornness of his own heart' (18.12). The people fulfilled their rebellious promise and all revolted against God (5.1-6).[31] Jeremiah was well aware that, left to their own devices, there was no surety that those who would experience redemption would not eventually repeat the crimes of their ancestors. The prophet was fearful that the restored people, like their forefathers, would be unable to behave properly and return to YHWH: 'Can the Ethiopian change his skin or the leopard its spots? So you, who are trained to do evil, could do good' (13.23); 'the sin of Judah is inscribed with an iron pen, engraved with a point of adamant on the tablet of their heart, and the horns of your altars' (17.1). Indeed, if there is no security, and rebelliousness has become second nature to Israel, then it is palpably predictable that even those who will be redeemed will sin.

The restored people, though, will have an advantage over their ancestors. The generation which followed the iniquities of its predecessors was destroyed. According to Jeremiah, the destruction and exile slammed the door on an era in the history of the relationship between YHWH and His people, an epoch which would not bear repetition—the traumatic tragedy had proven too overwhelming. The ensuing redemption opens a new age in which the relationship of YHWH to His people takes on a fundamentally different character. A new generation has arisen in Israel, a generation, though, whose faults are the faults of all people in that they are human. At this point, the novel transformation takes place—the people are going out in a new exodus from exile to freedom in the land of Israel ('Therefore, behold, the days are coming, says YHWH, when it shall no longer be said, "As YHWH lives who brought up the children of Israel from the land of Egypt", but, "As YHWH lives who brought up the children of Israel from the land of the North and from all the lands which He had driven them there", and I will return them to their land which I gave to their forefathers'—16.14-15//23.7-8). This exodus is precipitated by the death of a new 'generation of the desert', as indicated by 25.12, 'Then, after seventy years are fulfilled, I will punish the king of Babylon . . . for their transgression'; 27.7, 'All the nations shall serve him and his son and his son's son until the time comes for his land'; 29.6, 10, 'Take wives and bear sons and daughters, and take wives for your sons and give your daughters to husbands that they may bear sons and daughters . . . for thus says YHWH, when seventy years are fulfilled for Babylon I will visit you . . . to bring you back to this place'. These verses signify the lifespan to which a human can aspire, 'the days of our years are seventy years' (Ps. 90.10).

Just as there will be a new exodus, so, too, there will be established a new covenant (31.31-34). Just as the old covenant was preceded by the purification of the people (Exod. 19.10-11), so, too, purification will precede the new one, only on this occasion the people do not purify themselves, but rather YHWH purifies them, 'for I shall forgive their transgression and will no longer remember their sin' (v. 34). With these words, Jeremiah, in opposition to his previous prophecies, totally reverses himself. While in his message of redemption to the Jehoiachin exiles he still adheres to the possibility of repentance, here he completely abandons the idea, as illustrated by the following:

24.6-7	*31.28, 33-34*
ושמתי עיני עליהם לטובה והשבתים אל	והיה כאשר שקרתי עליהם לנתוש ולנתוץ
הארץ הזאת ובניתים ולא אהרס	ולהרס ולהאביד ולהרע כן אשקד עליהם
ונטעתים ולא אתוש	לבנות ולנטוע...
ונתתי להם לב לדעת אתי כי אני ה׳	נתתי תורתי בקרבם ועל לבם אכתבנה
והיו לי לעם ואנכי אהיה להם לאלהים	והייתי להם לאלהים והמה יהיו לי לעם
כי ישבו אלי בכל לבם	...כי כולם ידעו אותי...
	כי אסלח לעונם ולחטאתם לא אזכר עוד

The above comparison vividly displays the strong resemblance between 31.28, 33-34 and 24.6-7. Nonetheless, an essential divergence must be singled out: in the very place in v. 34 where one would expect to find an expression of the return of the people to God in congruence with 24.7, there appears instead YHWH's promise to wipe out the people's sin. To put it differently, while the aim of repentance, where it is mentioned, is to motivate divine forgiveness (cp. Jer. 4.1, 4; 7.3-7; 15.19; 18.7-8, 11; 26.3, 13), here complete forgiveness is given without the necessity of the people initiating any action at all.[32]

Although it is not clearly stated here, God's forgiveness of sins may be based in part on His mercies which were stirred up the severity of the destruction. Compare

> 30.12-18, 'your injury is incurable, your wound is grievous . . . there is no healing for you . . . I have struck you the blow of an enemy, cruel chastisement . . . therefore, all who devour you shall be devoured . . . for I will bring you a cure, I will heal your wounds . . . I will turn the fortunes of the tents of Jacob and have mercy on his dwellings';
>
> 33.6-11, 'I will bring her a cure and a healing, I will heal them and will reveal to them a wealth of peace and stability . . . I will forgive all their sins . . . once again will be heard in this place, which you say "it is a waste . . .", the voice of joy and the voice of happiness . . . for His faithfulness is forever . . .';
>
> 33.26, '. . . for I will turn their fortunes and have mercy upon them' (see also 50.17-20).

The nature of the new covenant also emphasizes God's activity and the nation's passivity. God takes upon Himself the raising up of His relationship to the Israelites to an ideal height in that He Himself, without any intermediary, places His legal instructions within the heart of His people. This 'heart surgery'[33] was necessary because of the inability or refusal of the people to do it for themselves—compare 4.4, 'Circumcise yourselves to YHWH and remove the foreskins of your heart', with 17.1 cited above.[34] God's act upon the heart abrogates all need, and even all possibility, of 'each man shall teach his neighbor and each man his brother saying, "Know YHWH"'. The saying of the people, 'Know YHWH', was mere lip service, and it is possible that Jeremiah was influenced here by the false words of repentance mentioned by Hosea: 'Let us know, let us pursue the knowledge of YHWH' (Hos. 6.3) (Unterman 1982:545). Note also Jer. 5.2, 'and if they say, "As YHWH lives", they are swearing falsely'. These delusory words stand in direct opposition to the people's obedience to the commandments of God in the future—'for they shall all know me'. The new covenant effectively nullifies human freedom of choice to act in accordance with God's will or not.[35]

(c) Finally, Jeremiah, who no longer entertains the possibility of a turn for the worse in the relationship between YHWH and His people, presents God's assurance of the inviolability and eternality of that relationship, despite the people's past transgressions. This promise is reminiscent of the promise to Abraham (Gen. 13.16), but, in this longer form, this prophecy emphasizes the everlasting nature of the new covenant.

B. Jer. 32.36-44

וְעַתָּה לָכֵן כֹּה־אָמַר יְהוָה אֱלֹהֵי
יִשְׂרָאֵל אֶל־הָעִיר הַזֹּאת אֲשֶׁר ׀ אַתֶּם אֹמְרִים נִתְּנָה בְּיַד
37 מֶלֶךְ־בָּבֶל בַּחֶרֶב וּבָרָעָב וּבַדָּבֶר׃ הִנְנִי מְקַבְּצָם מִכָּל־
הָאֲרָצוֹת אֲשֶׁר הִדַּחְתִּים שָׁם בְּאַפִּי וּבַחֲמָתִי וּבְקֶצֶף גָּדוֹל
38 וַהֲשִׁבֹתִים אֶל־הַמָּקוֹם הַזֶּה וְהֹשַׁבְתִּים לָבֶטַח׃ וְהָיוּ לִי
39 לְעָם וַאֲנִי אֶהְיֶה לָהֶם לֵאלֹהִים׃ וְנָתַתִּי לָהֶם לֵב אֶחָד
וְדֶרֶךְ אֶחָד לְיִרְאָה אוֹתִי כָּל־הַיָּמִים לְטוֹב לָהֶם וְלִבְנֵיהֶם
מ אַחֲרֵיהֶם׃ וְכָרַתִּי לָהֶם בְּרִית עוֹלָם אֲשֶׁר לֹא־אָשׁוּב
מֵאַחֲרֵיהֶם לְהֵיטִיבִי אוֹתָם וְאֶת־יִרְאָתִי אֶתֵּן בִּלְבָבָם
41 לְבִלְתִּי סוּר מֵעָלָי׃ וְשַׂשְׂתִּי עֲלֵיהֶם לְהֵטִיב אוֹתָם וּנְטַעְתִּים
42 בָּאָרֶץ הַזֹּאת בֶּאֱמֶת בְּכָל־לִבִּי וּבְכָל־נַפְשִׁי׃ כִּי־
כֹה אָמַר יְהוָה כַּאֲשֶׁר הֵבֵאתִי אֶל־הָעָם הַזֶּה אֵת כָּל־
הָרָעָה הַגְּדוֹלָה הַזֹּאת כֵּן אָנֹכִי מֵבִיא עֲלֵיהֶם אֶת־כָּל־
43 הַטּוֹבָה אֲשֶׁר אָנֹכִי דֹּבֵר עֲלֵיהֶם׃ וְנִקְנָה הַשָּׂדֶה בָּאָרֶץ
הַזֹּאת אֲשֶׁר ׀ אַתֶּם אֹמְרִים שְׁמָמָה הִיא מֵאֵין אָדָם וּבְהֵמָה
44 נִתְּנָה בְּיַד הַכַּשְׂדִּים׃ שָׂדוֹת בַּכֶּסֶף יִקְנוּ וְכָתוֹב בַּסֵּפֶר ׀

וְחָתוֹם וְהָעֵד עֵדִים בְּאֶרֶץ בִּנְיָמִן וּבִסְבִיבֵי יְרוּשָׁלַםִ וּבְעָרֵי
יְהוּדָה וּבְעָרֵי הָהָר וּבְעָרֵי הַשְּׁפֵלָה וּבְעָרֵי הַנֶּגֶב כִּי־אָשִׁיב
אֶת־שְׁבוּתָם נְאֻם־יְהוָה׃

36 'Now therefore thus says the LORD, the God of Israel,
concerning this city of which you say, "It is given into the hand of
the king of Babylon by sword, by famine, and by pestilence":
37Behold, I will gather them from all the countries to which I drove
them in my anger and my wrath and in great indignation; I will
bring them back to this place, and I will make them dwell in safety.
38And they shall be my people, and I will be their God. 39I will give
them one heart and one way, that they may fear me for ever, for
their own good and the good of their children after them. 40I will
make with them an everlasting covenant, that I will not turn away
from doing good to them; and I will put the fear of me in their
hearts, that they may not turn from me. 41I will rejoice in doing
them good, and I will plant them in this land in faithfulness, with
all my heart and all my soul.

42 'For thus says the LORD: Just as I have brought all this great
evil upon this people, so I will bring upon them all the good that I
promise them. 43Fields shall be bought in this land of which you
are saying, It is a desolation, without man or beast; it is given into
the hands of the Chaldeans. 44Fields shall be bought for money,
and deeds shall be signed and sealed and witnessed, in the land of
Benjamin, in the places about Jerusalem, and in the cities of Judah,
in the cities of the hill country, in the cities of the Shephelah, and
in the cities of the Negeb; for I will restore their fortunes, says the
LORD.'

1. *Review of Scholarship*

Jer. 32.36-44 is viewed by many scholars as a late addition, in part or in toto, to the book. Some representative perspectives will be presented here:

(1) Hyatt (1951:87) states that 32.17-44 'are an excellent summary of D's theology of history including his interpretation of the Babylonian exile and his hope for the future', although he does acknowledge that the redactor repeats 'some of the genuine material in vv. 43-44'.[36] Böhmer (1976:43-44), following Hermann (1965:187) and Nicholson (1970:84) is more explicit. He argues that the formulas used in these verses are more predominantly found in Deuteronomy and dtr. literature: v. 37. ובחמתי ובקצף גדול באפי, and Deut. 29.27; v. 39, ליראה אותי, and Deut. 6.24; 8.6; 10.12, 20; 13.5; 14.23 (but also Jer. 5.22, 24); v. 40, להיטיבי אותם, and Josh. 24.20; 4.41, וששתי עליהם להיטיב אותם, and Deut. 28.63; v. 41, בכל לבי ובכל נפשי, and cp. Deut. 4.29; 6.5; 10.12; 26.16; 30.2, 6, 10; 1 Kgs 2.4; 8.48; 2 Kgs 23.25. The

rest of Böhmer's comparative 'evidence' is based upon other texts in Jeremiah, such as 24.7; 29.14; 31.33, which he claims are dtr. and upon the affinity of v. 40, וכרתי להם ברית עולם, with Isa. 55.3; 61.8.[37] Like Hyatt, he recognizes vv. 42-44 as an authentic prophetic word which has been broadened and reinterpreted.

As has been shown previously, the methodology employed by Böhmer is flawed—if text A and text B contain similar terminology, it does not necessarily mean (so Hyatt, Nicholson, Böhmer, Carroll, etc.) that the two texts are the product of the same hand or school.[38] The key question, which is ignored by these researchers, is whether or not the ideological content is the same in both texts.

(2) Martens (1972:84-85) finds other grounds for rejecting vv. 37-41, 'The structure of the salvation statement . . . is . . . problematic because . . . it is quite jumbled in form'. Following Volz and Rudolph, he (1972:85-86) posits vv. 42-44 to be authentic, but also accepts v. 36 as Jeremianic since it is the logical predecessor of v. 42.

The other viewpoint, that vv. 36-44 are wholly authentic, is asserted by a minority of recent scholars. These are best represented by Raitt (1977:180-81, 202-204) and, before him, von Rad (1965:214-15). Raitt notes (1977:115-19) that 32.36-41 and 32.6-15, 42-44 (Raitt treats these as two separate deliverance messages) contain most of the same components that appear in 24.4-7; 29.4-7, 10-14; 31.31-34; 33.6-9. He (1977:120) remarks on the lack of '*any* reference to repentance as a precondition for God's gracious act' which differentiates these passages from the dtr. redemption promises. Raitt (1977:119) concludes that these Jeremianic passages 'were addressed to the same audience, belong in their first formulation ιo within less than a decade of one another, and speak to the same constellation of concerns from the same basic theological perspective'. The affinities among them 'are too strong to permit serious doubt that they are all from the same source'.[39]

2. *Structure and Meaning*

Jer. 32.36-44 is best understood as YHWH's response to Jeremiah's cry of astonishment in vv. 23-25:

Jer. 32.23-25	*vv. 36, 42-44*
(23)... ותקרא אותם את כל הרעה	(36)... כה אמר ה'... אל העיר הזאת אשר
הזאת (24)... והעיר נתנה ביד הכשדים	אתם אמרים נתנה ביד מלך בבל בחרב
הנלחמים עליה מפני החרב והרעב	וברעב ובדבר... (42) כי כה אמר ה' כאשר
והדבר ואשר דברת היה והנך ראה	הבאתי... את כל הרעה הגדולה הזאת כן
(25) ואתה אמרת אלי אדני ה' קנה לך	אנכי מביא עליהם את כל הטובה... (43)
השדה בכסף והעד עדים והעיר נתנה	ונקנה השדה בארץ הזאת אשר אתם אמרים
ביד הכשדים	... נתנה ביד הכשדים (44) שדות בכסף
	יקנו וכתוב בספר וחתום והעד עדים...
(cp. vv. 6-15)	כי אשיב את שבותם

That YHWH, in the midst of the calamitous Babylonian siege of Jerusalem, should order Jeremiah to buy a field in Anatoth creates a paradox that requires explanation. That explanation is found in vv. 36-44.

Verse 36 is an opening statement which refers back to the prophet's words cited above. It provides an introduction and sets the stage for the following prophecy of redemption.

Verses 37-44 are divided into two segments: 37-41 and 42-44. In the first part, God promises (1) to return Israel and Judah (cp. vv. 30, 32) to the land and cause them to dwell in security (v. 37), and (2) to make them an eternal covenant (v. 40, ברית עולם) which will result in the people's permanent obedience and YHWH's everlasting favors (vv. 39-41), and thus the establishment of an ideal relationship based upon mutual faithfulness (vv. 38, 40). The segment closes with a reiteration of v. 37b, an assurance of YHWH's positive intentions to reconstitute the people in its land (v. 41). The second part, which is concerned with the kingdom of Judah (as attested by the geographical list in v. 44, paralleled by 17.26; 33.13), reaffirms God's intentions (v. 42) to restore the fortunes of the people on its land (v. 44, paralleled by 33.11-12).

a. *Verse 39*, ונתתי להם לב אחד ודרך אחד ליראה אותי

The nouns לב and דרך are not synonymous here, but complementary. לב most commonly refers to the mind and will of the individual (Jer. 3.15, 17; 5.21; 7.24; 12.3, 11; 17.1, 10; 24.7; 31.33, etc.). דרך, on the other hand, often denotes behavior (2.23, 33; 3.21; 6.27; 7.3, 5; 16.17; 17.10; 18.11, 15; 26.13; 32.19, etc.). The will and ensuing behavior of humans are subject to God's scrutiny and judgment—'I YHWH search the heart and investigate the livers to give to each man according to his way, according to the fruit of his doings' (17.10). Israel's דרך has been contrary to YHWH's will (3.21; 7.3, 5; 10.2; 23.22; 25.5; 26.3; 35.15; 36.3, 7, etc.). Jeremiah's concept of the proper דרך of action appears to be influenced by Deuteronomy (Deut. 11.22, 28; 19.9; 26.17; 28.9; 30.16, etc.). More to the point, Deut. 8.6, like v. 39, combines √דרך and (אתו) ליראה; Deut. 10.12-13, like v. 39, combines √דרך, (את יהוה) ליראה, and (לך) לטוב (also cp. בכל לבבך ובכל נפשך with v. 41). The greatest terminological resemblance to Jer. 32.39-40, though, is Deut. 5.26, 29, 30:

מי יתן והיה לבבם זה ליראה אתי... כל הימים
למען ייטב להם ולבניהם לעלם... לא תסרו ימין
ושמאל בכל הדרך אשר צוה ה׳ ... וטוב לכם

'who would give that this their heart would fear me . . . all the days in order that it would be well with them and their children forever . . . you shall not turn aside to the right or to the left in all the way which YHWH has commanded . . . that it may go well with you'.

The verb ירא in vv. 39 and 40 (as mentioned in Chapter 2) has the same meaning as the verbs אהב and ידע in the sense of obedience to YHWH. This is its sense also in Jer. 5.22-24 (and cp. Deut. 4.10; 5.26; 6.24; 8.6; 10.12; 14.23; 17.19; 28.50; 31.12-13; Isa. 11.2-3; 29.13; Hos. 10.3; Ps. 86.11).[40]

In sum, the phrase לב אחד ודרך אחד ליראה אותי refers to the unification of will and action in obedience to YHWH,[41] which has, in the past, been so lacking in Israel.

b. *The relationship of 32.36-44 to 31.27-37*

Despite the linguistic similarities to Deuteronomy, mentioned above, the prophecy of 32.35-44 is best understood in comparison to that of 31.27-37. The lines of affinity are:

(1) YHWH has punished his people and now will cause them to dwell securely in their land—31.27; 32.37. In particular, compare 31.28, כאשר שקדתי עליהם לנתוש... ולהרע כן אשקד עליהם לבנות ולנטוע, and 32.42, כאשר הבאתי אל העם הזה את כל הרעה הגדולה הזאת כן אנכי מביא עליהם את כל הטובה.

(2) the covenant formula in 31.33 and 32.38.

(3) YHWH's gift associated with the heart: 31.33, 'I will put my torah within them and I will write it on their heart'; 32.39, 40, 'I will give them one heart . . . and I will put my fear in their heart'.

(4) וכרתי ברית—31.31; 32.40.

(5) the people will be obedient to YHWH and will not sin again—31.34, 'For they shall all know me'; 32.39, 40, 'to fear me all the days . . . so not to turn away from me'.

(6) YHWH will not abandon his people—31.36-37; 32.40, 'that I will not turn away from doing good to them'.

(7) the motif of eternality—31.36-37; 32.40, 'an eternal covenant'.

(8) the root נטע—31.28; 32.41.

(9) האדם and בהמה—31.27; 32.43.

The many connections between 32.36-44 and 31.27-37 are strong testimony to their direct relationship. This testimony is enhanced upon notice that the linguistic similarities of 32.36-44 are in chiastic relationship to 31.27-37; 32.38-40 parallels 31.31-37, while 32.41-43 complements 31.27-28. Perhaps this is the reason why the covenant formula appears before the 'gift' in 32.39, but after it in 31.33. Perhaps, too, this is why the two clauses of the formula in 32.38 are reversed from that of 31.33, and why the mention of the covenant succeeds that of the heart in 32.39-40, but precedes it in 31.33. Whatever the case may be, one would certainly be inclined to agree with von Rad's remark (1965:215) on the two passages, 'The best explanation is . . . that Jeremiah spoke of the new covenant on two different occasions, both times in a different way . . .'[42] It should be noted, also, that 32.36-44 is a shorter, less complete prophecy than 31.27-37.

3. *Date*

There is no reason to doubt the date (and the setting) of 32.1-3, particularly, since this prophecy is organically related to the events described in 32.6-15. Nor is there reason to deny the possibility that a prophecy of redemption could be pronounced while Jerusalem was being destroyed (see above, concerning the date of 31.27-37). In the hour of crisis an individual will respond with despair or with hope. Jeremiah, who believed in redemption and the eternal relationship between God and Israel, hoped.

4. *Summary and Conclusions*

Jer. 32.36-44 is an authentic prophecy of redemption originating during the period of the destruction of Jerusalem. In this prophecy, as in its larger cousin, 31.27-37, God's mercies, expressed by His commitment to His relationship with His people, are the only cause and condition for redemption. Repentance is not a factor. Thus, the prophecy could not be a product of a dtr. redactor.[43] The passage focuses on two aspects: the return of the people to its land where it will dwell in security (vv. 37, 41-44); the establishment of an eternal covenant which will result in the ideal, faithful relationship between YHWH and Israel—the transformation of the people's will and attendant behavior will ensure their fealty (vv. 38-40).

C. Jer. 31.27-37 and 32.36-44: Conclusions

The final stage in Jeremiah's prophecies of redemption reflects his response to the trauma of 587 and the experiences of a lifetime. For forty years and more he has pleaded, threatened, cajoled, and warned his people to return to their God, and his words have been as unheeded as a voice crying in the wilderness. His prophecies failed to arouse the people to return to YHWH of their own free will. Finally, Jeremiah became convinced that Israel was not capable of repentance. Thus was completed the transfer of emphasis from the primary role of repentance in the early prophecies to Ephraim, to its secondary position in the redemption message to the Jehoiachin exiles, to its disappearance[44] in his prophecies of restoration on the night of the destruction of Jerusalem.

Nonetheless, Jeremiah's belief in the eternality of YHWH's commitment to His relationship with Israel was never shaken. YHWH would always be the God of Israel, despite the absence of repentance. Thus, in the darkest hour of Israelite history, the prophet was able to depict a new reality, a new relationship based upon a mutual and eternal faithfulness between YHWH and His people. The necessity of the eternal existence of this relationship obligated the abandonment of the principle of free choice between the good (obedience to YHWH) or the evil (disobedience). At the end of days, there would reign complete harmony between the will of YHWH and the behavior of Israel.

Chapter 4

MISCELLANEOUS PROPHECIES OF REDEMPTION

A. **Introduction**

The analysis of the six prophecies presented in the three previous chapters has revealed an historical development in Jeremiah's thought in terms of repentance and redemption. These prophecies were all good subjects for analysis since they were rather complete and coherent portrayals of the prophet's contemplation of the topic at hand. Often the text conveniently provided a date which was of assistance in their interpretation. These six, however, by no means exhaust the prophecies of redemption in the book. Of the remaining ones, though, many have no direct relationship to the topic and, thus, are beyond the purview of this study. These include:[1]

1. Prophecies which imply redemption or the continued existence of the people without explanation: 1.10 ('to build and to plant'); 4.27; 5.10, 18; 29.32 ('and he shall not see the good I am doing for my people', cp. 29.10-14 in Chapter 2.B, above); 51.45.
2. Prophecies which refer only to the physical benefits of redemption: 30.18-22 (23-24?); 31.10-14, 23-26 (to Judah, see Chapter 1.B, above), 38-40 (the rebuilding of Jerusalem); 49.2 (cp. Obad. 17).
3. The redemption of the temple sancta: 27.21-22.
4. The redemption of individuals: 32.5 (Zedekiah? cp. 27.22); 39.15-18 (Ebed-melech the Cushite); 45.1-5 (Baruch ben Neriah).
5. Unexplained redemption to the nations: 1.10; 12.14-17; 46.26 (Egypt); 48.47 (Moab); 49.6 (Ammon), 11 (Edom?), 39 (Elam).

Nevertheless, there are several other prophecies which relate, if only tangentially, to the theme of this study. These passages will be surveyed here in the order in which they appear in the text. The extent of the investigation of these passages will be determined by the degree of their relevant elements.

B. 3.14-18

שׁוּבוּ בָנִים שׁוֹבָבִים נְאֻם־יְהוָה כִּי אָנֹכִי בָּעַלְתִּי בָכֶם 14
וְלָקַחְתִּי אֶתְכֶם אֶחָד מֵעִיר וּשְׁנַיִם מִמִּשְׁפָּחָה וְהֵבֵאתִי
אֶתְכֶם צִיּוֹן׃ וְנָתַתִּי לָכֶם רֹעִים כְּלִבִּי וְרָעוּ אֶתְכֶם דֵּעָה טו
וְהַשְׂכֵּיל׃ וְהָיָה כִּי תִרְבּוּ וּפְרִיתֶם בָּאָרֶץ בַּיָּמִים הָהֵמָּה 16
נְאֻם־יְהוָה לֹא־יֹאמְרוּ עוֹד אֲרוֹן בְּרִית יְהוָה וְלֹא יַעֲלֶה עַל־
לֵב וְלֹא יִזְכְּרוּ בוֹ וְלֹא יִפְקֹדוּ וְלֹא יֵעָשֶׂה עוֹד׃ בָּעֵת הַהִיא 17
יִקְרְאוּ לִירוּשָׁלִַם כִּסֵּא יְהוָה וְנִקְווּ אֵלֶיהָ כָל־הַגּוֹיִם לְשֵׁם
יְהוָה לִירוּשָׁלִָם וְלֹא־יֵלְכוּ עוֹד אַחֲרֵי שְׁרִרוּת לִבָּם הָרָע׃
בַּיָּמִים הָהֵמָּה יֵלְכוּ בֵית־יְהוּדָה עַל־בֵּית יִשְׂרָאֵל וְיָבֹאוּ 18
יַחְדָּו מֵאֶרֶץ צָפוֹן עַל־הָאָרֶץ אֲשֶׁר הִנְחַלְתִּי אֶת־
וְאָנֹכִי אָמַרְתִּי אֵיךְ אֲשִׁיתֵךְ בַּבָּנִים וְאֶתֶּן־לָךְ

14Return, O faithless children, says the LORD;
for I am your master; I will take you, one from a city and two
from a family,
and I will bring you to Zion.

15'And I will give you shepherds after my own heart, who will feed you with knowledge and understanding. 16And when you have multiplied and increased in the land, in those days says the LORD they shall no more say "The ark of the covenant of the LORD". It shall not come to mind, or be remembered, or missed; it shall not be made again. 17At that time Jerusalem shall be called the throne of the LORD, and all nations shall gather to it, to the presence of the LORD in Jerusalem, and they shall no more stubbornly follow their own evil heart. 18 In those days the house of Judah shall join the house of Israel, and together they shall come from the land of the north to the land that I gave your fathers for a heritage.

The importance of 3.14-18 in this study is apparent in the opening words of v. 14, שובו בנים שובבים. Does שובו demand a spiritual return to God or a physical return to the land? The answer will depend upon the immediate context, but does that context include all of vv. 14-18 or are vv. 14-18 made up of two or more separate literary units brought together by a compiler? Furthermore, is this complex datable? It has already been shown (in Chapter 1.A) that vv. 14-18 are an insertion.

1. *Review of scholarship on authenticity and date*

Scholarship on the authenticity and date of 3.14-18 falls into three major positions: (a) 3.14-18 is inauthentic and, therefore, late; (b) the passage contains both Jeremianic and non-Jeremianic elements; (c) all the verses are from the prophet.

(a) *3.14-18 is inauthentic and late.*
Those who view 3.14-18 as inauthentic may further be subdivided into two categories: (1) those who hold that 3.14-18 is dtr. and (2) those who see these verses as dtr. and, even, post-exilic.

(1) *3.14-18 is dtr.* Hyatt (1942:170) notes the similarities between 3.17, 'and they shall no longer walk after the stubbornness of their heart', and Deut. 29.18, 'but I shall walk in the stubbornness of my heart', although he states (1956) that '"stubbornly follow their own evil heart" is a favorite expression of Jeremiah, but he applies it to Israel rather than the foreign nations'.[2] Hyatt (1942:170) also remarks on the resemblance between 3.18 (the use of the hiphil of נחל) and Deut. 1.38; 3.28; 12.10; 19.3; 31.7. However, it should be noted that in Jeremiah, as in the core of Deuteronomy (12.10; 19.3) נחל in the hiphil conjunction with the land of Israel is in reference to God. In the framework of Deuteronomy (1.38; 3.28; 31.7), it is used in reference to Joshua. The same use of נחל as in Jeremiah appears in the old Song of Moses (Deut. 32.8-9). Thus, even according to those who would claim a late edition of Deuteronomy, there is no evidence here for a dtr. editor of Jeremiah.

Hyatt (1956) concludes that 'These verses are editorial, expressing ideas foreign to Jeremiah but are frequently found in exilic and post-exilic apocalyptic passages' (Ezek. 37.16-28; Isa. 12–14), although he admits the possibility that 3.16 could be from Jeremiah.

Nicholson (1970:88) ties in 3.15, an 'isolated saying', with 23.1-4 as both products of the dtr. prose tradition which emphasizes 'the solemn obligations and responsiblities of the monarchy in the life of Israel'. Why Jeremiah could not have held such a view is beyond reason (cp. 21.12; 22.13-19). Furthermore, Coppens (1966:48) sees no grounds for denying Jeremianic authorship of 3.15 and 23.1-4 since the term רועה 'shepherd' for king is used elsewhere in unquestioned Jeremiah poetry in 2.8; 22.22; 25.34-36. Holladay (1966:420-24) has shown conclusively and in detail that 23.1-4 is indeed poetry, and thus authentic. His study was ignored by Nicholson (1973) who concludes that 3.14-18 is a dtr. elaboration on 3.12-13.

(2) *3.14-18 is dtr. and post-exilic.* According to Mowinckel (1914:43), 3.14-18 is post-exilic and refers to the circumstances of the second temple. It is a quasi-parallel to 3.19ff. and an insertion (1914:48).

Skinner (1922:80) views 3.14-18 as 'a series of detached oracles loosely strung together' which expresses a post-exilic perspective.

Welch (1928:83) also sees this passage as derived from the returning exiles, for Jeremiah insisted that the South was worse than the North and 'It is especially incredible that Jeremiah could have believed . . . that a return to Zion should . . . be a blessed thing for Israel' (Welch also rejects 31.6 as post-exilic, which, as has been shown in Chapter 1.B above, is untenable).

Thiel (1973:91-93), followed by Böhmer (1976:37-38), conceives of 3.14-18 as post-dtr. and post-exilic, with v. 18 later than vv. 14-17 because the former refers to the united people in opposition to v. 14b. In his mind, the small numbers of returnees of v. 14b and the pilgrimage to Zion in v. 17 reflect the experiences and disappointments of the early post-exile. The phrase לשם יהוה in v. 17 belongs to post-exilic texts such as Isa. 60.9 and 18.7, although Thiel allows for the possibility that this phrase is a gloss (לשם יהוה לירושלים is absent in the Septuagint). עלה√ על לב where the subject is human also appears in the late texts of Isa. 65.17 and Jer. 51.50. Against these arguments, it should be noted that Ezek. 38.10 uses יעלו דברים על לבבך in reference to humans (cp. Ezek. 14.3), and there is no reason to assume that he was the first to do so. Further, לשם יהוה already appears in Ps. 122.4 and is used by the pre-exilic dtr. editor of Joshua (9.9) and Kings (1 Kgs 3.2; 5.17, 19; 8.17, 20; 10.1), so Jeremiah certainly could have known it.

(b) *3.14-18 contains both Jeremianic and non-Jeremianic elements.* Giesebrecht divides the passage in two: 3.14-16 is authentic, vv. 17-18 are late. Verses 14-15 were either originally addressed to Judah alone or Israel and Judah together. If the latter, they suitably follow 31.28. Verse 16 may be from Jeremiah, but, if so, was written in the period of exile immediately after destruction, similarly to Jeremiah 32.

Streane sees much in 3.14-18 as a later insertion. The limited number of captives returning in v. 14 is contradicted by 31.7ff. Verse 17 is an addition since 'we have no warrant for thinking that Jeremiah . . . expected all nations to gather at Jerusalem to worship'. The mention of the ark in 3.16, however,

> is probably a genuine fragment . . . for the prophet's attitude towards the Ark, as symbolical of the old Covenant which was destined to yield to the new one for which he looked . . . is paralleled by his view as to the Temple (vii 4).

Volz holds that vv. 14-15 were originally followed by the last phrase of v. 18, 'on the land that I gave your fathers for a possession'. These words are an authentic prophecy to Ephraim (627-625 BCE) which was later redacted with the non-Jeremianic words of 3.16-18 (excluding the last phrase of v. 18 just mentioned) and 'I will bring you to Zion' (v. 14).

Rudolph posits vv. 14-17 as possibly Jeremianic. Verse 16 assumes that the ark is no longer existent, thus, if from Jeremiah then from his final words. From ונקוו in v. 17 through the end of the verse is an addition and does not reflect Jeremiah's ideology. Verse 18 is the work of an editor who combined vv. 6-13 and 14-17, and presents a summary of those verses. Leslie (1954:40, 323) takes a similar position, but states that v. 18 is dtr.

According to Bright (1965), vv. 14-15 form a prose parallel to vv. 12b-13 and may continue them, but vv. 16-18 'are probably of anonymous origin, although the ideas expressed are in no way inconsistent with Jeremiah's thought' after 587.

Raitt's position (1974:179-80) is unique. In comparison to the six authentic redemption passages of Jeremiah on the one hand (24.4-7; 29.4-7, 10-14; 31.31-34; 32.6-16, 42-44; 32.36-39; 33.6-9) and the three deuteronomic promises of hope on the other (Deut. 4.26-31; 30.1-10; 1 Kgs 8.46-53), Raitt makes the following observations on twelve 'prose oracles' which he considers un-Jeremianic: 3.15-18 (he sees [1974: 178] 3.12-13, 14, 22; 4.1-2 as calls to repentance); 16.14-15; 23.3-4, 5-6; 30.2-3, 8-9; 31.38-40; 33.14-16, 17-18, 19-22, 23-26; 50.18-20.

> 1. There is a more relaxed tone than in the earlier authentic six. The problem here is not the people's sin, . . . nor in what has happened to the personal relationship between God and Judah . . . The problem is presented as being simply the fact of the exile. These oracles seem to have been spoken at a time when the Exile as God's justified punishment was forgotten, or so thoroughly accepted as to no longer be an issue. 2. Given this perception of what the people need deliverance from, the solution is not regeneration of their humanity, cleansing, or reinitiating the relationship. The distress is resolved simply with the promised return of the people from exile to Judea and the reestablishment there of the visible signs of the theo-political state (faithful rulers patterned after David; Levitical priests; restoration of Jerusalem; repossession of the land as the people's promised inheritance). 3. It is difficult to see how these oracles could escape the charge of being false prophecy unless they had been delivered well after the fall of Jerusalem was an accomplished fact.* Had they been delivered before 587 they would be promising a continuation of all the reassuring tokens of God's favor as manifest in the visible signs of the theo-political state without any regard to the people's sin and without realism concerning the impending invasion by Nebuchad-nezzar (interpreted as God's judgment). 4. These twelve prose oracles find their closest correlation with two promises added to

> the end of Amos, probably after the fall of Samaria . . . (9.11-12 and 9.13-15) and with Jer. 30.18-22, 31.2-6 . . . perhaps those are oracles of salvation for the Northern State Israel written by disciples of Amos, Hosea, Isaiah, and Micah and added editorially to Jer. . . Jer. 30.18-22; 31.2-6, would have all the shallow optimism of false prophecy if those words were spoken to Judah before 587 and meant to have their application then. The only realistic position . . . is to affirm that the two Amos passages, the two Jeremianic poetic oracles, and the twelve prose promises . . . of Jer. . . were addressed to an audience not in peril of imminent historical cataclysm, but were spoken well after such a judgment had taken place. 5. Because of the dissimilarity between these twelve (late) prose promises in Jer, and the undoubtedly d'istic promises considered above, I think . . . that the d'istic editors of Deut—2Kgs were of a different generation or circle than the authors of the (late) prose promises in Jer. . . the prose material [was] seemingly added after the death of Jeremiah and his first circle of disciples . . . 6. Compared with the twelve (late) prose promises in Jer., the six (earlier-authentic) Jeremianic oracles promise deliverance in awareness of the exile *as God's judgment*, and with a conviction that the people of deliverance must be transformed from the condition of the people who went into judgment. In these six the relationship between God and Judah is . . . negotiable. But, there is no sense that restoration will mean a return to the status quo before the judgment.
>
> *The problem with the oracles of weal of the false prophets was that they 'whitewashed' (overlooked) the sin of the people . . . and failed to read accurately the connection between the people's guilt and the forthcoming doom as God's conscious, just punishment. In the determination of the false prophetic promise from the true one it is crucial . . . to know when it was spoken, when it was to take effect, and to whom the promise was directed.

Against Raitt, point by point, the following arguments may be brought to bear:

1. To assume that Jeremiah could only prophesy redemption in connection with transformation of character (a) allows for no human diversity, no capability to emphasize certain aspects of redemption without mentioning others, (b) ignores the possibility that Jeremiah might be announcing these promises against the backdrop of previous prophecies which speak of the transformation of character, (c) does not consider that Jeremiah may be following earlier prophetic patterns (see Raitt's fourth point, as well as, for example, Hos. 11.8-11;[3] Isa. 11.11-16), (d) fails to appreciate the

effect that the trauma of the actual destruction might have had on the prophet, impelling him to burst out with prophecies of comfort. Furthermore, Raitt contradicts the text itself—for example, 3.15 resolves the issue of sinful rulers who led the people astray, and 3.17 speaks of the future obedience of all mankind.

2. Again the text contradicts Raitt: 'cleansing' is mentioned in 50.20, 30.9 speaks of 'reinitiating the relationship', and the 'visible sign' of the ark will be replaced with the holiness of Jerusalem (3.16-17; 31.40. Of course, Raitt could counter that since the ark was not viewed by the public, it was not 'visible', but that would be specious). Since 'repossession of the land as the people's promised inheritance' is the focus of 32.6-16, 42-44 (cp. 24.6; 29.10, 14; 32.37; 33.7, all recognized as authentic by Raitt), there is no difficulty in accepting that concept in these other restoration prophecies.
3. The difference between the false prophets and Jeremiah was not just that one spoke 'weal' and one 'woe', but rather that when Jeremiah spoke of 'weal' he referred to the somewhat distant, and not immediate future (contrast 29.10-14 with 28.1-17). Thus, Jeremiah never negated or down-played the harshness of destruction and exile. Nothing in the passages under discussion implies otherwise. They could easily have been delivered by Jeremiah on the night of destruction.
4. The comments in 1. and 3. above are applicable here. There is no reason to assume that these passages (including Amos 9.11-15) 'were spoken well after . . . a judgment had taken place'.
5. That these passages differ from the deuteronomic ones is agreed. Again, though, there is no sufficient reason to assume that they were 'added after the death of Jeremiah and his first circle of disciples'. Such a circle is, in any case, conjecture.
6. 'Exile as God's judgment' is apparent in 16.15; 23.3-8; 30.8; 31.40; 33.16, 24. Raitt's excision of 23.1-2 and 3.14 from their succeeding verses naturally helps his case, but is methodologically indefensible (on 3.14, see below). That 'restoration will mean a return to the status quo before judgment' is found in 32.15, 43-44; 33.7—passages authenticated by Raitt. On the other hand, the existence of God-fearing rulers (3.15; 23.4-6; 32.15-16), Jerusalem as YHWH's throne to which all nations will flow, Israel's obedient service to God, and the absence of sins due to forgiveness (50.20) are all hardly representative of 'the status quo before judgment'. Raitt's criteria are not supported by the text.

(c) *All of 3.14-18 should be attributed to Jeremiah.*

Kaufmann (1967: III, 466) divides 3.14-18 in two: vv. 14-15 continue v. 12 and parallel v. 22, while vv. 16-18 are a later prophecy of Jeremiah's similar in style to 23.1-4. Indeed, in his opinion, vv. 16-18 would be a fine continuation to 23.4, although Kaufmann (1967: III, 470) also relates vv. 16-18 ideologically to the new covenant passage.

Driver (1967:251) sees 3.6-18 as a unit from the early days of Josiah:

> only when the ideal Zion of the future has been established by the restoration of *Israel*, so that even heathen nations flock towards it (v. 15-17), will *Judah* abandon its sin and return from banishment (which the prophet here presupposes) to dwell with Israel upon its own land, v. 18.

Weiser holds a similar view and contends that the statement on the ark in v. 16 refers to a debate among the priests of Josiah's time concerning its importance.[4] Weiser is followed by Martens (1972:38), who defends v. 18 as a 'statement . . . not so far-fetched even in the days of Josiah, for a future removal from the Land is conceivable from Jeremiah's early vision' of 1.15-16. Martens (1972:39-41) also repeats the arguments of Cazelles (1968:149-58) that vv. 14-16 should be taken as a recital of past events (!) which serve as a motivational statement for the people's repentance. This repentance will be manifested in Ephraim's recognition of Jerusalem as the throne of God. Repentance would then be rewarded with restoration (v. 18) (Martens, 1972:40-41). Generally, Martens holds that 3.11-20 is one unit.

The most detailed analysis of vv. 16-17, until now, has been attempted by Weinfeld (1976:19-26). He (1976:17) notes that four passages in Jeremiah which 'relate to values and principles' are 'set in the form of thesis and antithesis' (3.16-17; 16.14-15 // 23.7-8; 31.29, 30, 31-34). Furthermore, these passages follow set formulas (1976:18), which, in 3.16-17 take the form of בימים ההם . . . לא יאמרו עוד . . . בעת ההיא יקראו (√אמר and √קרא are interchanged also in 7.32//19.6) (1976:20). Thus, 3.16-17 are definitely united (1976:19). When once only the ark and cherubim were acknowledged as the footstool and throne of God, now all Jerusalem will be recognized as such (1976:20). Furthermore, 'even as the concept of the throne is enlarged and extended, so too does the circle of those who adore Him become wider, and accordingly not only the children of Israel but all the nations go up to Jerusalem' (1976:24). The idea that the ark has no future significance and is spiritually replaceable is paralleled and supported by the new covenant passage which predicts no future role for the externally written covenant (1976:26). Weinfeld (1976:28) tends to include the new covenant passage with Jeremiah's early prophecies to Ephraim, although he admits that 'this cannot be substantiated'.

Weinfeld (1976:21-23) argues that 3.6-17 are a unity and are addressed to Ephraim. The mention of Zion in v. 16 is no problem since it appears in 31.6, 11 in relation to Ephraim (1976:21). The concept of the nations flowing to Jerusalem in v. 17 is well known from Isa. 2.2-3; 18.7; 25.6; Mic. 4.1-4 and occurs in Jer. 16.19 as well as Pss. 68.30ff. and 72.8-11 (1976:21-22).

Weinfeld (1976:22) points out that Jer. 3.17 is similar to Isa. 2.2-4 in spiritual significance, whereas Isa. 60.9 (a late text) is concerned with the material needs of the temple, reflecting the prevailing circumstances of that later time (cp. Hag. 2.3, 9). Verse 18 may be a later, but Jeremianic, addition uttered during or after the destruction of the temple (1976:23).

Finally, Thompson refers 3.12-15 to Jeremiah's prophecies to the North, although 'they could easily have been taken up again later and set in a wider context'. Verses 16-18 are from a later period, but may well be from the prophet. As Thompson cogently remarks, 'we are hardly in a position to assert what Jeremiah might or might not have thought about a whole range of topics'.

2. *Authenticity, Date, and Unity*

The above discussion has shown that there are no convincing reasons for denying the authenticity of 3.14-18 (cp. Weinfeld's comments particularly). What about its date and unity? There are no clear indications concerning the date. As mentioned above, the statement on the ark proves nothing. On the other hand, v. 18, at least, with its reference to the Judean exiles, would seem to presuppose the events of 587. But is v. 18 organically related to vv. 14-17?

a. *Survey of similarities*

It appears that the only method available for determining the date of these verses is the comparative one. To which passages are vv. 14-18 most similar in terms of philology and ideology? An investigation of the passage reveals the following:

3.14a, שובו בנים שובבים, is identical to the opening words of 3.22, an early passage (from Josiah's time), but 3.14b, כי אנכי בעלתי בכם, most resembles 31.32, ואנכי בעלתי בם, from the end of the Judean state. There is a slight similarity between 3.14cd, ולקחתי אתכם. . . ממשפחה, והבאתי אתכם ציון and 25.9 ולקחתי את כל משפחות צפון. . . והבאתים על הארץ הזאת 'I will take all of the families of the North . . . and I will bring them upon this land', dated to the fourth year of Jehoiakim (25.1; 605 BCE). בוא in the hiph'il in reference to the restoration of Israel to its land also appears in 23.8 and 31.8 (an early verse). The return to 'Zion' appears in 30.17-18 (implied? questionable date), 31.6 (Josianic), and 50.5 (date?). The idea of a restored remnant is contained in 23.3; 31.7 (but 31.8 depicts a large return); 50.20 (date?).

3.15, ונתתי לכם רעים כלבי ורעו אתכם דעה והשכיל, is most closely reminiscent of 23.4, 5, והקמתי עליהם רעים ורעום... ומלך מלך והשכיל (cp. 10.21 in a negative context).

3.16, כי תרבו ופריתם (a P term!), has its only parallel in the book in 23.3, ופרו ורבו. As noted above, Weinfeld observed the affinity of 3.16-17, בימים ההמה נאם יהוה לא יאמרו עוד... כי אם, and 31.29-30, בימים ההם לא יאמרו עוד ... כי אם (cp. 31.31-34). The most similar usage of the phrase √עלה על לב (cp. 7.31; 19.15; 32.35—idolatry) with the verb זכר (cp. 44.21) appears in 51.50 (date?). √זכר and √פקד appear together in 15.15 (cp. 14.10). For √זכר alone see 23.36 and 11.19. The reference in 3.16 may be to a cultic sense, as in Hos. 2.19; Amos 6.10; Pss. 20.8; 45.18, which supports Streane, for example, in his contention that 3.16 is reminiscent of Jeremiah's attitude towards the temple in 7.4 (datable, from the parallel passage in 26.1-6, to the beginning of the reign of Jehoiakim, 609/608 BCE).[5] ולא in a series of three or more appears also in Jer. 5.22; 13.14; 14.14; 16.6; 21.7; 23.4; 25.33; 35.7; 42.14; 44.10. ולא יִפָּקֵדוּ has the same consonants as ולא יִפָּקֵדוּ in 23.4, if not the same meaning.

In 3.17, the calling of Jerusalem in the future 'the throne of YHWH' is reminiscent of 33.16 in which Jerusalem will be called 'YHWH is our righteousness'. 23.6, the parallel to 33.16, refers the latter name to the messianic king. The change in reference to the throne of YHWH appears to be conceived of later than the references to the more limited throne in 14.21 and 17.12. שרירות לב occurs elsewhere in Jer. 7.24; 9.13; 11.8; 13.10; 16.12; 18.12; 23.17. As Weinfeld has mentioned, 16.19 also speaks of the nations coming to God.

Other verses which, like 3.18, predict the restoration of Judah and Israel, explicitly, to their land are 30.3 and 50.4. 'Israel' as the collective name in the context of return to the land of the fathers given by God appears in 16.15//23.8 and 30.3. אשר הנחלתי also appears in 12.14. מארץ צפון in restoration contexts occurs in 16.15 // 23.8; 31.8. It should be noted that the Septuagint adds to 3.18 καὶ ἀπὸ πασῶν τῶν χωρῶν, ומכל הארצות, which strengthens its relationship to the Hebrew of 16.15 and 23.8.

b. *23.1-8*

הוֹי רֹעִים מְאַבְּדִים וּמְפִצִים אֶת־צֹאן מַרְעִיתִי נְאֻם־יְהוָה׃ 1
לָכֵן כֹּה־אָמַר יְהוָה אֱלֹהֵי יִשְׂרָאֵל עַל־הָרֹעִים הָרֹעִים 2
אֶת־עַמִּי אַתֶּם הֲפִצֹתֶם אֶת־צֹאנִי וַתַּדִּחוּם וְלֹא פְקַדְתֶּם
אֹתָם הִנְנִי פֹקֵד עֲלֵיכֶם אֶת־רֹעַ מַעַלְלֵיכֶם נְאֻם־יְהוָה׃
וַאֲנִי אֲקַבֵּץ אֶת־שְׁאֵרִית צֹאנִי מִכֹּל הָאֲרָצוֹת אֲשֶׁר־הִדַּחְתִּי 3

אֹתָם שָׁם וַהֲשִׁבֹתִי אֶתְהֶן עַל־נְוֵהֶן וּפָרוּ וְרָבוּ׃ וַהֲקִמֹתִי 4
עֲלֵיהֶם רֹעִים וְרָעוּם וְלֹא־יִירְאוּ עוֹד וְלֹא־יֵחַתּוּ וְלֹא יִפָּקֵדוּ
נְאֻם־יְהוָה׃ הִנֵּה יָמִים בָּאִים נְאֻם־יְהוָה וַהֲקִמֹתִי 5
לְדָוִד צֶמַח צַדִּיק וּמָלַךְ מֶלֶךְ וְהִשְׂכִּיל וְעָשָׂה מִשְׁפָּט
וּצְדָקָה בָּאָרֶץ׃ בְּיָמָיו תִּוָּשַׁע יְהוּדָה וְיִשְׂרָאֵל יִשְׁכֹּן לָבֶטַח 6
וְזֶה־שְּׁמוֹ אֲשֶׁר־יִקְרְאוֹ יְהוָה ׀ צִדְקֵנוּ׃ לָכֵן הִנֵּה־יָמִים 7
בָּאִים נְאֻם־יְהוָה וְלֹא־יֹאמְרוּ עוֹד חַי־יְהוָה אֲשֶׁר הֶעֱלָה
אֶת־בְּנֵי יִשְׂרָאֵל מֵאֶרֶץ מִצְרָיִם׃ כִּי אִם־חַי־יְהוָה אֲשֶׁר 8
הֶעֱלָה וַאֲשֶׁר הֵבִיא אֶת־זֶרַע בֵּית יִשְׂרָאֵל מֵאֶרֶץ צָפוֹנָה
וּמִכֹּל הָאֲרָצוֹת אֲשֶׁר הִדַּחְתִּים שָׁם וְיָשְׁבוּ עַל־אַדְמָתָם׃

23 'Woe to the shepherds who destroy and scatter the sheep of my pasture!' says the LORD. [2]Therefore thus says the LORD, the God of Israel, concerning the shepherds who care for my people: 'You have scattered my flock, and have driven them away, and you have not attended to them. Behold, I will attend to you for your evil doings, says the LORD. [3]Then I will gather the remnant of my flock out of all the countries where I have driven them, and I will bring them back to their fold, and they shall be fruitful and multiply. [4]I will set shepherds over them who will care for them, and they shall fear no more, nor be dismayed, neither shall any be missing, says the LORD.

5 'Behold, the days are coming, says the LORD, when I will raise up for David a righteous Branch, and he shall reign as king and deal wisely, and shall execute justice and righteousness in the land. [6]In his days Judah will be saved, and Israel will dwell securely. And this is the name by which he will be called: "The LORD is our righteousness".

7 'Therefore, behold, the days are coming, says the LORD, when men shall no longer say, "As the LORD lives who brought up the people of Israel out of the land of Egypt," [8]but "As the LORD lives who brought up and led the descendants of the house of Israel out of the north country and out of all the countries where he had driven them". Then they shall dwell in their own land'.

A perusal of the above paragraphs leads inexorably to the conclusion that by far the most similar passage to 3.14-18 from the perspective of both phraseology and content is 23.1-8. These two passages are also ordered similarly: a promise to ingather the remnant back to their land—3.14; 23.3; the people will then be ruled by divinely ordained rulers—3.15; 23.4; the new spiritual situation will be indicated by a new name given to a focal point of the people's life—3.17 (Jerusalem); 23.6 (David's descendant); the reiteration of the promise of return from the land of the North to the homeland—3.18; 23.8. Another point of contact is that the events associated with the exodus will be superseded by the new reality—3.16-17 (the ark will be forgotten); 23.7-8 (the exodus will be forgotten); cp. 31.31-34. It appears likely that 3.14-18 and 23.1-8 are complementary units from the hand of one author.

Nonetheless, like 3.14-18, scholars are divided on the questions of the dating, the authenticity, and the unity of 23.1-8. Volz, for example, divides 23.1-8 into three sections: 1-4, 5-6, 7-8. The first he considers authentic from the last days of Zedekiah, but the last two, to him, are later and later additions. Rudolph holds a similar position, with minor variations (he denies 23.3 but accepts 23.5-6). Hyatt accepts 23.1-2, 5-6 (Zedekianic), but rejects 23.3-4, 7-8 (presuppose exile, like 3.14-18). Streane and Weiser accept these verses as authentic, Bright (1965) accepts 23.1-6 as Zedekianic, but views vv. 7-8 as presupposing the exile. Holladay (1966:420-24) investigated 23.1-4 and found it to be primarily poetry. Coppens (1966:48-54) accepts 23.1-4 and argued extensively for the authenticity of vv. 5-6. Both these last two studies were ignored by Nicholson (1970:88-91), who rejects all of 23.1-8 as dtr. or later. Martens (1972:48) sees 23.1-8 as a 'text unit, for Jer. 22.30 concludes the words about Coniah, and Jer. 23.9 takes up a new subject, the prophets'. Noting the possible wordplay on Zedekiah's name (23.5-6, also noted by Bright and many others), as well as the fact that since this prophecy comes in an ordered survey of recent kings of Judah, Zedekiah logically follows Jehoiachin (22.24-30), Martens (1972:50) concludes that these verses belong to the last monarch's time. Böhmer (1976:34-37), following Nicholson and Thiel (1973:246-48), views 23.1-4 as dtr., vv. 7-8 as exilic, but raises the possibility that vv. 5-6 may be an authentic Jeremianic insertion. As stated above, Raitt rejects the authenticity of 23.3-8. Carroll (1981:147-48) views 23.3-4 as exilic and belonging to the same redaction as 3.15-18. He also rejects vv. 7-8 as exilic, but admits the possibility that 23.5-6 may be from the time of Zedekiah (like Böhmer). In a footnote, Carroll (1981:317 n. 23) makes a rather revealing statement of his bias:

> On messianism in the Hebrew Bible I take the view that it only developed in the Roman period as an apocalyptic-political movement, so only metaphors and images within such a movement are derived from biblical traditions. J.L. McKenzie . . . sensibly states the issue thus: '. . . messianism is a Christian interest and a Christian theme; . . . it is a Christian response to the Old Testament and should be treated as such; . . . in a theology of the Old Testament . . . messianism would appear neither in the chapter headings nor in the index. It is not only not a dominant theme, but in the proper sense of the word it is doubtfully a theme of the Old Testament at all. This theme is imposed upon the theologian by theological

> factors foreign to his area of study'. To this statement I would add it is also very much a *Jewish* interest and theme, though one belonging to the post-biblical period and utilizing motifs from biblical traditions.

One hardly knows how to react to such a confession. A simple statement will have to suffice: Carroll's perception of messianism (or the lack of it) in the Hebrew Bible is not surprising when one considers that he conceives of most of the book of Jeremiah as a spiritually inferior forgery.

Kaufmann's association of 3.16-18 with 23.1-4 has already been mentioned. It is interesting that Kaufmann (1967: III, 466-67) attributes 3.14-15; 23.5-6, 7-8 all to the days of Josiah. Weinfeld (1976:41-42) following Kaufmann, notes the similar mentions of divinely appointed shepherds who would lead Israel with understanding, of the terms 'multiply and increase', and the 'spiritual change of values'. However, he (1976:43) concludes that 23.1-8 alludes to Zedekiah (like Martens), while in 3.14-17 the ideal king is Josiah.

Given the diversity of scholarly opinions, is it possible to arrive at a conclusion concerning the unity and authenticity of 23.1-8? Building upon the pioneering work of Miller (1955:106), Weinfeld (1976:45-46) observes that

> Ezekiel devotes a lengthy chapter to the shepherds of Israel (ch. 34), and like Jeremiah he too commences the prophecy with 'Woe'. All the motifs that occur in the brief prophecy in Jer. 23.1-8 were taken up, developed, and enlarged upon by Ezekiel. The lost, driven away, and scattered sheep, alluded to by Jeremiah (23.1-2), are allegorically embodied in Ezekiel (v. 4, 12, 16, 21). The other expressions in Jer. 23.1-6 also occur there; . . . 'the sheep of my pasture' (v. 31), the restoration of the sheep to their fold (. . . v. 14, and cf. Jer. 23.3), the setting up of a shepherd (v. 23), the dwelling safely (. . . v. 25, 27, 28).

Additionally, Miller (1955:106) noted that Jer. 23.1-2 was reflected in Ezek. 34.1-16, as well as the similarity between Jer. 23.5, והקמתי לדוד, and Ezek. 34.23, והקמתי . . . את עבדי דוד. To these remarks the following may be added: the substance of Jer. 23.8 is enlarged upon in Ezek. 34.8, 12-13, 25, 27—cp. the former, חי יהוה אשר . . . הביא את זרע בית ישראל . . . וישבו על אדמתם, with חי אני נאם אדני יהוה (Ezek. 34.8), והביאותים אל אדמתם (34.13), וישבו (34.25), והיו על אדמתם (34.27). Further, the implicit reference to freedom from bondage, which the exodus motif in Jer. 23.7-8 assumes, appears in Ezek. וידעו כי אני יהוה בשברי את מטות עלם והצלתים מיד העבדים בהם (34.27), which in phraseology is drawn from Lev. 26.13, אני יהוה אלהיכם אשר הוצאתי אתכם

מארץ מצרים מהית להם עבדים ואשבר מטות עלכם (Weinfeld, 1976:47).[6] It is undeniable, then, that the author of Ezek. 34 was influenced by Jer. 23.1-8 as it now stands, and that he considered those verses to be a genuine prophecy of Jeremiah. It may further be concluded that Jer. 23.1-8 was written no later than the early exile for, as Greenberg (1978:1090-91) has determined,

> Information supplied by contemporary records suffices to test the claim of the book that its contents fall between July 593 and April 571 BCE . . .
> [conclusion:] In sum: no post-571 anachronism has left its mark in the book to necessitate the assumption of another hand than Ezekiel's.

It is time to resolve the status of Jer. 23.1-8. The prophecy is a literary unit, authentic to Jeremiah, written, at the very earliest, after the 597 exile. This last conclusion may be inferred from vv. 1-3, which assume that Judean kings have contributed to the exile of the people. The name of v. 6 does *not* refer to Zedekiah as the hoped-for Davidide (as Weinfeld and others suppose). If Jeremiah had wished to imply that Zedekiah was the awaited 'branch', he would have given the precise name צדקיהו just as Haggai (2.23) and Zechariah (3.1-6; 4.1-14; 6.9-15) did when they indicated messianic figures. Instead, the name given by Jeremiah is an *inversion* of Zedekiah and a change of meaning from '*my* righteousness (or salvation) is YHWH' to 'YHWH is *our* righteousness (or salvation)'. The implication is that Zedekiah is a perversion of what a Davidide should be and that God will not bring salvation to him but to the people through a true 'righteous branch'. Thus Jer. 23.5-6 expresses the prophet's disappointment with Zedekiah. This negative evaluation matches those concerning Jehoiakim and Jehoiachin in Jeremiah 22 and serves as an inclusion, along with the negative prophecy to Zedekiah in the beginning of Jeremiah 21, to this complex of prophecies on the kings of Judah. Therefore, it is most probable that 23.1-8 emanates from some time during the reign of Zedekiah.

That this prophecy is spoken on the night of destruction may be inferred from v. 8. The depiction of a new exodus fits in well with the idea of the new covenant, which originated at the time of the destruction of Jerusalem. The fact that 23.7-8 is written in a similar form to 31.31-34 appears only to strengthen this conclusion. However, Jeremiah may have used the same form and similar ideas over a longer period than just that of the actual destruction, and v. 8 may have the 597 exile in mind.

c. *The Date of 3.14-18*

The remnant that will be increased resembles not only 23.3 but also 31.27-28 and 32.43-44. The ark, the ancient vessel which houses the written covenant, is extraneous when the new covenant is to be written on the heart. The concept that the nations will no longer tread the evil path laid out by the stubbornness of their hearts is reminiscent of the assurance of 31.34 that the people will be obedient to YHWH. The promise of future kings who will rule according to God's wishes echoes 23.4. In sum, 3.14-18 was written some time in the reign of Zedekiah—in the midst of the maelstrom that enveloped Jerusalem between 597 and 587.

3. *The Meaning of* שובו בנים שובבים

What then is the correct interpretation of the words שובו בנים שובבים in 3.14? Scholars are divided on this question, as indicated earlier. Most, such as Bright (1965), Nicholson (1973), Martens (1972:40-41) and Raitt (1974:178), simply apply the meaning of repentance in the similar language of v. 12 and the identical words of v. 22. Others hold that 'return' here refers to the physical restoration of the exiles: Rudolph sees v. 14 in the light of 33.8—God has forgiven the people's sins and, therefore, the return is physical; Hyatt (1956) states, on these words, that they are

> genuine, though the editor... has misunderstood the meaning of *Return*. Jeremiah meant it as a plea to all the Hebrews to return to God in true confession of sin and repentance; the editor understood it as a summons to the Northern Kingdom to return from exile (vs. 14b).

Böhmer (1976:37) and Thompson also understand the return as restoration.

Although the word שובבים is normally translated 'backsliding', which might suggest that שובו means 'repent', this is not necessarily the case. On the basis of Semitic parallels, Avishur (1970:76) translates שובב (and משבה) from the root שבב as meaning 'wounded' or 'destroyed'. This accords somewhat with the position of Morag (1975:70-71) who, although defining שובב as one who has been turned aside or removed from the straight path and משבה as 'a sharp deviation from the straight path', sees this as 'a type of sickness—its correction is done by healing'.

Indeed, since Ammon was never under obligation to follow God's commandments, it is difficult to understand הבת השובבה in Jer. 49.4 as meaning 'backsliding'. A word like 'wounded' would be much more suited to the context. Furthermore, the imperative of √שוב is not always used in Jeremiah to mean 'return to YHWH' but can be used, as in 31.21, to mean 'return to the land', שובי בתולת ישראל שובי אל עריך אלה. Thus, there is no cause for denying the possibility that the first words of 3.14 call for the people to return to the land. It is conceivable that the prophet has reapplied an earlier phrase (v. 22) to a later condition; the older phrase may have received a new meaning in a different context. Nonetheless, one must be cautious—there is no certainty that שובו here does not mean 'return to YHWH'.

4. *Conclusions*

The fact is that either interpretation of שובו is difficult in the context of the last days of Judah, as the above analysis has supposed. If שובו means 'repent!', then it flies in the face of the more developed prophecies from this period which eliminate the theme of repentance. On the other hand, if it means 'return to the land!', then the attendant immediacy of the imperative is confusing when one recalls that Jeremiah predicted a redemption that would be fulfilled only in seventy years. If one then posits that v. 14a organically follows v. 13, there is no reason for the insertion to begin with v. 14b.

Perhaps, it is most sensible to date 3.14-18 fairly early in the reign of Zedekiah, placing it near the time of 24.1-10. If 3.14-18 was originally directed to the exiles of Jehoiachin, then the meaning of שובו as 'repent' would complement the use of ישבו in 24.7. 3.14-18 would then belong to the middle stage of Jeremiah's thought on the relationship of repentance to redemption. It would resemble the deuteronomic promise of redemption in that it begins with the call to repentance, but its concentration and emphasis on redemption is another indication of Jeremianic authorship. Thus, 3.14-18 would present a stage in Jeremiah's thought leading up to the new covenant prophecy. This appears to be the most plausible of solutions. Jeremiah would then indeed have reused an old phrase in a new context, but with its meaning retained.

C. **Jer. 30.1-17**

הַדָּבָר אֲשֶׁר־הָיָה אֶל־יִרְמְיָהוּ מֵאֵת יְהוָה לֵאמֹר׃ כֹּה־
אָמַר יְהוָה אֱלֹהֵי יִשְׂרָאֵל לֵאמֹר כְּתָב־לְךָ אֵת כָּל־הַדְּבָרִים

אֲשֶׁר־דִּבַּרְתִּי אֵלֶיךָ אֶל־סֵפֶר׃ כִּי הִנֵּה יָמִים בָּאִים נְאֻם־ 3
יְהוָה וְשַׁבְתִּי אֶת־שְׁבוּת עַמִּי יִשְׂרָאֵל וִיהוּדָה אָמַר יְהוָה
וַהֲשִׁבֹתִים אֶל־הָאָרֶץ אֲשֶׁר־נָתַתִּי לַאֲבוֹתָם וִירֵשׁוּהָ׃
וְאֵלֶּה הַדְּבָרִים אֲשֶׁר דִּבֶּר יְהוָה אֶל־יִשְׂרָאֵל וְאֶל־יְהוּדָה׃ 4
כִּי־כֹה אָמַר יְהוָה קוֹל חֲרָדָה שָׁמָעְנוּ פַּחַד וְאֵין שָׁלוֹם׃ ה
שַׁאֲלוּ־נָא וּרְאוּ אִם־יֹלֵד זָכָר מַדּוּעַ רָאִיתִי כָל־גֶּבֶר יָדָיו 6
עַל־חֲלָצָיו כַּיּוֹלֵדָה וְנֶהֶפְכוּ כָל־פָּנִים לְיֵרָקוֹן׃ הוֹי כִּי 7
גָדוֹל הַיּוֹם הַהוּא מֵאַיִן כָּמֹהוּ וְעֵת־צָרָה הִיא לְיַעֲקֹב וּמִמֶּנָּה
יִוָּשֵׁעַ׃ וְהָיָה בַיּוֹם הַהוּא נְאֻם ׀ יְהוָה צְבָאוֹת אֶשְׁבֹּר 8
עֻלּוֹ מֵעַל צַוָּארֶךָ וּמוֹסְרוֹתֶיךָ אֲנַתֵּק וְלֹא־יַעַבְדוּ־בוֹ עוֹד
זָרִים׃ וְעָבְדוּ אֵת יְהוָה אֱלֹהֵיהֶם וְאֵת דָּוִד מַלְכָּם אֲשֶׁר 9
אָקִים לָהֶם׃ וְאַתָּה אַל־תִּירָא עַבְדִּי יַעֲקֹב נְאֻם־יְהוָה י
וְאַל־תֵּחַת יִשְׂרָאֵל כִּי הִנְנִי מוֹשִׁיעֲךָ מֵרָחוֹק וְאֶת־זַרְעֲךָ
מֵאֶרֶץ שִׁבְיָם וְשָׁב יַעֲקֹב וְשָׁקַט וְשַׁאֲנַן וְאֵין מַחֲרִיד׃
כִּי־אִתְּךָ אֲנִי נְאֻם־יְהוָה לְהוֹשִׁיעֶךָ כִּי אֶעֱשֶׂה כָלָה בְּכָל־ 11
הַגּוֹיִם ׀ אֲשֶׁר הֲפִצוֹתִיךָ שָּׁם אַךְ אֹתְךָ לֹא־אֶעֱשֶׂה כָלָה
וְיִסַּרְתִּיךָ לַמִּשְׁפָּט וְנַקֵּה לֹא אֲנַקֶּךָּ׃ כִּי כֹה אָמַר 12
יְהוָה אָנוּשׁ לְשִׁבְרֵךְ נַחְלָה מַכָּתֵךְ׃ אֵין־דָּן דִּינֵךְ לְמָזוֹר 13
רְפֻאוֹת תְּעָלָה אֵין לָךְ׃ כָּל־מְאַהֲבַיִךְ שְׁכֵחוּךְ אוֹתָךְ לֹא 14
יִדְרֹשׁוּ כִּי מַכַּת אוֹיֵב הִכִּיתִיךְ מוּסַר אַכְזָרִי עַל רֹב עֲוֺנֵךְ
עָצְמוּ חַטֹּאתָיִךְ׃ מַה־תִּזְעַק עַל־שִׁבְרֵךְ אָנוּשׁ מַכְאֹבֵךְ טו
עַל ׀ רֹב עֲוֺנֵךְ עָצְמוּ חַטֹּאתַיִךְ עָשִׂיתִי אֵלֶּה לָךְ׃ לָכֵן 16
כָּל־אֹכְלַיִךְ יֵאָכֵלוּ וְכָל־צָרַיִךְ כֻּלָּם בַּשְּׁבִי יֵלֵכוּ וְהָיוּ שֹׁאסַיִךְ
לִמְשִׁסָּה וְכָל־בֹּזְזַיִךְ אֶתֵּן לָבַז׃ כִּי אַעֲלֶה אֲרֻכָה לָךְ 17
וּמִמַּכּוֹתַיִךְ אֶרְפָּאֵךְ נְאֻם־יְהוָה כִּי נִדָּחָה קָרְאוּ לָךְ צִיּוֹן
הִיא דֹּרֵשׁ אֵין לָהּ׃

The word that came to Jeremiah from the LORD: [2]'Thus says the LORD, the God of Israel: Write in a book all the words that I have spoken to you. [3]For behold, days are coming, says the LORD, when I will restore the fortunes of my people, Israel and Judah, says the LORD, and I will bring them back to the land which I gave to their fathers, and they shall take possession of it'.

4 These are the words which the LORD spoke concerning Israel and Judah:

[5]'Thus says the LORD:
We have heard a cry of panic,
of terror, and no peace.
[6]Ask now, and see,
can a man bear a child?
Why them do I see every man

with his hands in his loins like a woman in labor?
Why has every face turned pale?
7 Alas! that day is so great
there is none like it;
it is a time of distress for Jacob;
yet he shall be saved out of it.

8 'And it shall come to pass in that day, says the LORD of hosts, that
I will break the yoke from off their neck, and I will burst their
bonds, and strangers shall no more make servants of them. 9 But
they shall serve the LORD their God and David their king, whom I
will raise up for them.

10 'Then fear not, O Jacob my servant, says the LORD,
nor be dismayed, O Israel;
for lo, I will save you from afar,
and your offspring from the land of their captivity.
Jacob shall return and have quiet and ease,
and none shall make him afraid.
11 For I am with you to save you, says the LORD;

I will make a full end of all the nations
among whom I scattered you,
but of you I will not make a full end.
I will chasten you in just measure,
and I will by no means leave you unpunished.

12 'For thus says the LORD:
Your hurt is incurable,
and your wound is grievous.

13 There is none to uphold your cause,
no medicine for your wound,
no healing for you.

14 All your lovers have forgotten you;
they care nothing for you;
for I have dealt you the blow of an enemy,
the punishment of a merciless foe,
because your guilt is great,
because your sins are flagrant.

15 Why do you cry out over your hurt?
Your pain is incurable.
Because your guilt is great,
because your sins are flagrant,
I have done these things to you.

16 Therefore all who devour you shall be devoured,

and all your foes, every one of them, shall go into captivity;
those who despoil you shall become a spoil,
and all who prey on you I will make a prey.
17For I will restore health to you,
and your wounds I will heal, says the LORD,
because they have called you an outcast:
'It is Zion, for whom no one cares!'

Jer. 30.1–31.1 comprises the first half of the 'Book of Comfort'. As the introduction (30.1-4) indicates, it is a series of sayings concerning the theme of restoration. Since neither repentance nor forgiveness of sins is mentioned in this section, it is not necessary to analyze its contents in depth. For the purpose of this study, a survey will suffice.

1. *30.5-7*

After the introduction of 30.1-4, vv. 5-7 depict fear, wailing (v. 5), men suffering like women in childbirth (v. 6), a time of trouble for 'Jacob', and yet an assurance that Israel shall be saved (v. 7). According to Duhm, this is a poem based upon Joel 2 and Isaiah 13 with ideas similar to Isa. 26.20–27.1, 12, 13 and which derives from the second or third century BCE. However, the authenticity of these verses has not recently been doubted, the main issue of contention being, rather, that of the date. Rudolph and Hertzberg (1952:92) see it as Josianic, while Hyatt places it late in Jeremiah's career. The meaning of וממנה יושע has been particularly questioned by Holladay (1962:53-54). Pointing to the unusual word order, he translates 'and from such as *this*, he shall be "*saved*"?!', thus interpreting the passage as a prophecy of judgment and an ironic 'mockery of the people's hope for rescue'. However, the compiler of Jeremiah 30 understood these words in a positive sense (and see below on vv. 10-11), else he would not have included them here.

2. *30.8-9*

Verses 8-9 may be an insertion since '*his* yoke' of the MT is unidentified (the Septuagint reads simply 'yoke', but this may be a correction), which may indicate that vv. 8-9 are a fragment belonging to another unit. Nonetheless, there is no need to see here the hand of a redactor (as do Volz, Rudolph, Hyatt [1956], Nicholson [1973], *et al.*, although Hertzberg [1952:92], Weiser [1960], and Thompson defend it as early Jeremiah). Verse 8, which depicts the 'breaking' of the 'yoke' and 'bonds' of foreign servitude, echoes unquestioned Jeremianic passages: 2.20 and 5.5 (cp. chs. 27, 28 and Nah. 1.13). זרים in reference to foreigners is known from Hos. 7.9 (cp. Prov. 5.10); 8.7; Isa. 1.7: Ps. 54.5, and so should not be considered an exilic term (against Böhmer, 1976:60). Verse 9 appears to be influenced by Hos. 3.5[7] (the penchant of Jeremiah for Hoseanic passages is acknowledged by all). Verses 8-9 were apparently placed after vv. 5-7 because of the similar images of the man bent under the yoke (v. 8) and the man with his hands on his loins (v. 6; cp. Abarbanel).

3. *30.10-11*

Verses 10-11 are parallel to 46.27-28 but are generally considered original here. The Septuagint 'omits them here, as it frequently does on the second occurrence of a doublet (which this is in the LXX order)' (Bright 1965).

The inauthenticity of these verses is maintained, for example, by Hyatt (1956) who mentions the resemblance of v. 10 to Isa. 41.8-10, 13-14; 43.1, 5; 44.1-2, and therefore posits the influence of II Isaiah (similarly, Nicholson). Böhmer (1976:62) dates it early in the second half of the exilic period. Both Hyatt and Böhmer acknowledge the affinities of v. 11 to other passages in Jer.: 1.8, 19; 4.27; 5.10, 18; 10.24; 15.20; 25.29; 49.12. Carroll (1981:206) deems vv. 10-11 a priestly oracle which echoes II Isaiah. That these verses are genuine is asserted by Rudolph, who sees them as the continuation of vv. 5-7. This view is challenged by Bright, 'It is probable that a Jeremianic nucleus (vv. 5-7) . . . has by means of a conventional priestly oracle (vv. 10f.) been made to apply to the situation of the exiles'. Berridge (1970:187), however, defends Rudolph's position, dating vv. 5-7, 10-11 just prior to 587. He (1970:194) relates v. 11 specifically to 10.24 and claims that Jeremiah feared that God would let 'His anger . . . override His justice' (1970:196). Martens (1972:72) views vv. 10-11 as an earlier Jeremiah prophecy to the Northern exiles, prior to 597.

It should be noted that v. 10 can just as easily be cited as evidence for Jeremiah's influence upon II Isaiah (Cassuto, 1973:149-52). Further, 1.8, 17; 10.2; 17.18; 23.4 all have affinities to 30.10a. The root זרע followed by מארץ in the context of restoration appears in 23.8. The idea of 'saving from afar' reappears in 31.3, 7-9. The mention of 'Jacob' and the root ישע are indications of the organic attachment of vv. 10-11 to vv. 5-7. Indeed, vv. 10-11 pick up where vv. 5-7 left off. 'Jacob' is now assured that, despite the apparently hopeless conditions, YHWH will bring about the restoration of the people and the elimination of fear (cp. v. 6). Verse 11 is YHWH's promise that Israel's punishment will be justly carried out, but this does not entail ultimate destruction. Rudolph understands v. 11 as emphasizing that Israel's punishment is in fair measure for her sins, and that God's love is the motivating factor for redemption.

4. 30.12-17

Duhm, Volz, Hyatt (1956), Böhmer (1976:63), and Carroll (1981:207) all divide 30.12-17 in two: vv. 12-15 as Jeremianic, vv. 16-17 as a later (exilic) edition. The major reason for this division is the abrupt change from a discussion of the people's deserved destroyed condition (vv. 12-15) to a promise of the punishment of Israel's enemies (v. 16) accompanied by God's alleviation of the people's suffering (v. 17). Welch (1928:226) rejects the entire passage:

> it is entirely destitute of any demand for repentance, and it is not easy to believe that Jeremiah could have uttered anything which even appeared to suggest that Yahweh would take back the people on any but his own terms. Yet here He is made to appear promising to bring relief... merely because it has been called 'the rejected', Zion for whose state no man cares.

The opposite perspective is taken by Rudolph, who accepts vv. 12-17 as authentic and addressed to the Northern tribes. The nations will now see the manifestation of the true God and will suffer because of their cruelty against Israel. 'Zion' in v. 17 is a scribal error, and one should read צידנו, 'our quarry', with the Septuagint. To soften the transition, Rudolph deletes the first two letters of v. 16 as a dittography of the last two of v. 15. He then turns the third letter from a 'כ' into a 'ו', thus starting v. 16 with the word וכל. Bright (1956) argues that the transition from v. 15 to v. 16 'may not... be as sharp as it seems. Moreover, vv. 16-17... are fully in keeping with Jeremiah's style... It is quite possible... that the entire piece was composed by the prophet... just after Jerusalem fell' (similarly, Nicholson). Martens (1972:148-49) suggests replacing ציון with צאן on the basis that the Septuagint is also in error and that 'נדחה and דרש are easily used of sheep' (Ezek. 34.4, 6, 8, 11, 16; cp. Jer. 23.2-3).

Whether or not 'Zion' replaces another word, examples of Zion being termed a negative which arouses God's positive action occur in 32.43 and 33.10. Further, it is not necessary to rewrite the first word of v. 16. As March (1974:284) has concluded,

> the primary function of *laken* is seen in those numerous contexts in which *laken* serves as 'conversation director'. That is, *laken* reminds the hearer that a discussion, a dialogue, is in process. The

> preceding words make what follows necessary or understandable. With an emphatic term which signals,... the speaker acknowledges what has gone before and makes ready to reveal his next move, his response. *Laken* in such instances functions to heighten expectancy, to move the hearer to the edge of his seat.

Elsewhere, March (1974:260) states that לכן 'forbids that hearer or reader to stop prematurely or fail to recognize the proper context crucial for understanding... *laken* lends emphasis by directing attention to what will follow'.

Ideologically, vv. 16-17 repeat the thoughts of vv. 10-11. The language of vv. 16-17 appears in other Jeremiah verses: 2.3; 3.22; 8.22; 10.25; 15.18; 33.6. לבז and אתן appear next to each other in the Bible only here and Jer. 2.14; 15.13; 17.3 (cp. Ezek. 23.46). Literarily, v. 17 seems purposely to recall vv. 12-14 (cp. the use of the roots נכה, רפא, דרש). The evidence defends the authenticity of vv. 12-17 as a Jeremiah prophecy describing the coming divine healing of the people's cruel suffering (as well as the destruction of Israel's enemies).

5. *Significance*

30.1-17 appear to comprise a series of Jeremianic prophecies or prophetic fragments of undecided date. Their significance for the purpose of this study lies in the theme which unites these verses: the cruel suffering of punishment will be replaced by God's merciful acts of redemption. Two complementary conclusions emerge: (1) punishment for sin obviates the necessity for repentance as a precondition for redemption; (2) the punishment results in Israel's great suffering which, in turn, arouses God's merciful response to end the suffering and restore the people.

Conclusion (1) would seem to imply that 30.5-17 were all written after Jeremiah's messages to the Jehoiachin exiles in chs. 24 and 29, for how could the prophet maintain both that punishment excludes the need for repentance and that repentance is necessary for redemption? Nonetheless, to date all of 30.5-17 about the time of the fall of Judah is not a necessary logical deduction, despite the seeming paradoxical alternative. It is quite possible that, at one time in his life, Jeremiah, like his predecessor Hosea (see Excursus I), had two views concerning redemption. On the one hand, strict justice demanded that the people should repent before they could enjoy restoration. On the other, the suffering of the punishment would evoke the prophetic mercy. The prophet would then have vacillated between justice and mercy, on occasion demanding repentance as a precondition for redemption, at other times believing that the suffering of the punished was sufficient cause for mercy. Thus, some of the verses in 30.5-17 may have been originally directed to the northern tribes during the time of Judah. If so, it would have been probable that in the course of time, as Jeremiah became disillusioned with the people's ability to repent and as the tragedy of 597 materialized, the prophet turned away from the hope for repentance and grew more and more dependent upon the divine mercy to effect redemption. This greater emphasis upon YHWH's mercy as a reponse to Israel's suffering is reflected in 30.5-17 and elsewhere (see below).

D. **33.1-26**

א וַיְהִי דְבַר־יְהוָה אֶל־יִרְמְיָהוּ שֵׁנִית וְהוּא עוֹדֶנּוּ עָצוּר
2 בַּחֲצַר הַמַּטָּרָה לֵאמֹר׃ כֹּה־אָמַר יְהוָה עֹשָׂהּ יְהוָה יוֹצֵר
3 אוֹתָהּ לַהֲכִינָהּ יְהוָה ׀ שְׁמוֹ׃ קְרָא אֵלַי וְאֶעֱנֶךָּ וְאַגִּידָה
4 לְּךָ גְּדֹלוֹת וּבְצֻרוֹת לֹא יְדַעְתָּם׃ כִּי כֹה אָמַר יְהוָה
אֱלֹהֵי יִשְׂרָאֵל עַל־בָּתֵּי הָעִיר הַזֹּאת וְעַל־בָּתֵּי מַלְכֵי יְהוּדָה
ה הַנְּתֻצִים אֶל־הַסֹּלְלוֹת וְאֶל־הֶחָרֶב׃ בָּאִים לְהִלָּחֵם אֶת־
הַכַּשְׂדִּים וּלְמַלְאָם אֶת־פִּגְרֵי הָאָדָם אֲשֶׁר הִכֵּיתִי בְאַפִּי
וּבַחֲמָתִי וַאֲשֶׁר הִסְתַּרְתִּי פָנַי מֵהָעִיר הַזֹּאת עַל כָּל־
6 רָעָתָם׃ הִנְנִי מַעֲלֶה־לָּהּ אֲרֻכָה וּמַרְפֵּא וּרְפָאתִים וְגִלֵּיתִי
7 לָהֶם עֲתֶרֶת שָׁלוֹם וֶאֱמֶת׃ וַהֲשִׁבֹתִי אֶת־שְׁבוּת יְהוּדָה
8 וְאֵת שְׁבוּת יִשְׂרָאֵל וּבְנִתִים כְּבָרִאשֹׁנָה׃ וְטִהַרְתִּים מִכָּל־
עֲוֺנָם אֲשֶׁר חָטְאוּ־לִי וְסָלַחְתִּי לְכוֹל־עֲוֺנוֹתֵיהֶם אֲשֶׁר
9 חָטְאוּ־לִי וַאֲשֶׁר פָּשְׁעוּ בִי׃ וְהָיְתָה לִּי לְשֵׁם שָׂשׂוֹן לִתְהִלָּה
וּלְתִפְאֶרֶת לְכֹל גּוֹיֵי הָאָרֶץ אֲשֶׁר יִשְׁמְעוּ אֶת־כָּל־הַטּוֹבָה
אֲשֶׁר אָנֹכִי עֹשֶׂה אוֹתָם וּפָחֲדוּ וְרָגְזוּ עַל כָּל־הַטּוֹבָה וְעַל
י כָּל־הַשָּׁלוֹם אֲשֶׁר אָנֹכִי עֹשֶׂה לָּהּ׃ כֹּה ׀ אָמַר
יְהוָה עוֹד יִשָּׁמַע בַּמָּקוֹם־הַזֶּה אֲשֶׁר אַתֶּם אֹמְרִים חָרֵב
הוּא מֵאֵין אָדָם וּמֵאֵין בְּהֵמָה בְּעָרֵי יְהוּדָה וּבְחֻצוֹת
יְרוּשָׁלִַם הַנְשַׁמּוֹת מֵאֵין אָדָם וּמֵאֵין יוֹשֵׁב וּמֵאֵין בְּהֵמָה׃
11 קוֹל שָׂשׂוֹן וְקוֹל שִׂמְחָה קוֹל חָתָן וְקוֹל כַּלָּה קוֹל אֹמְרִים
הוֹדוּ אֶת־יְהוָה צְבָאוֹת כִּי־טוֹב יְהוָה כִּי־לְעוֹלָם חַסְדּוֹ
מְבִאִים תּוֹדָה בֵּית יְהוָה כִּי־אָשִׁיב אֶת־שְׁבוּת־הָאָרֶץ

12 כבראשנה אמר יהוה׃ כה אמר יהוה צבאות
עוד יהיה ׀ במקום הזה החרב מאין־אדם ועד־בהמה
13 ובכל־עריו נוה רעים מרבצים צאן׃ בערי ההר בערי
השפלה ובערי הנגב ובארץ בנימן ובסביבי ירושלם
ובערי יהודה עד תעברנה הצאן על־ידי מונה אמר
14 יהוה׃ הנה ימים באים נאם־יהוה והקמתי את־
הדבר הטוב אשר דברתי אל־בית ישראל ועל־בית
טו יהודה׃ בימים ההם ובעת ההיא אצמיח לדוד צמח
16 צדקה ועשה משפט וצדקה בארץ׃ בימים ההם תושע
יהודה וירושלם תשכון לבטח וזה אשר־יקרא־לה
17 יהוה ׀ צדקנו׃ כי־כה אמר יהוה לא־יכרת לדוד
18 איש ישב על־כסא בית־ישראל׃ ולכהנים הלוים לא־
יכרת איש מלפני מעלה עולה ומקטיר מנחה ועשה
19 זבח כל־הימים׃ ויהי דבר־יהוה אל־ירמיהו לאמור׃
כ כה אמר יהוה אם־תפרו את־בריתי היום ואת־בריתי
21 הלילה ולבלתי היות יומם־ולילה בעתם׃ גם־בריתי
תפר את־דוד עבדי מהיות־לו בן מלך על־כסאו ואת־
22 הלוים הכהנים משרתי׃ אשר לא־יספר צבא השמים
ולא ימד חול הים כן ארבה את־זרע דוד עבדי ואת־
23 הלוים משרתי אתי׃ ויהי דבר־יהוה אל־ירמיהו
24 לאמר׃ הלוא ראית מה־העם הזה דברו לאמר שתי
המשפחות אשר בחר יהוה בהם וימאסם ואת־עמי
כה ינאצון מהיות עוד גוי לפניהם׃ כה אמר יהוה
אם־לא בריתי יומם ולילה חקות שמים וארץ לא־
26 שמתי׃ גם־זרע יעקוב ודוד עבדי אמאס מקחת מזרעו
משלים אל־זרע אברהם ישחק ויעקב כי־אשוב את־
שבותם ורחמתים׃

33 The word of the LORD came to Jeremiah a second time, while he was still shut up in the court of the guard: 2"Thus says the LORD who made the earth, the LORD who formed it to establish it—the LORD is his name: 3Call to me and I will answer you, and will tell you great and hidden things which you have not known. 4For thus says the LORD, the God of Israel, concerning the houses of this city and the houses of the kings of Judah which were torn down to make a defense against the siege mounds and before the sword: 5The Chaldeans are coming in to fight and to fill them with the dead bodies of men whom I shall smite in my anger and my wrath, for I have hidden my face from this city because of all their wickedness. 6Behold, I will bring to it health and healing, and I will

heal them and reveal to them abundance of prosperity and security. [7]I will restore the fortunes of Judah and the fortunes of Israel, and rebuild them as they were at first. [8]I will cleanse them from all the guilt of their sin against me, and I will forgive all the guilt of their sin and rebellion against me. [9]And this city shall be to me a name of joy, a praise and a glory before all the nations of the earth who shall hear of all the good that I do for them; they shall fear and tremble because of all the good and all the prosperity I provide for it.

10 'Thus says the LORD: In this place of which you say, "It is a waste without man or beast", in the cities of Judah and the streets of Jerusalem that are desolate, without man of or inhabitant or beast, there shall be heard again [11]the voice of mirth and the voice of gladness, the voice of the bride, the voices of those who sing, as they bring thank offerings to the house of the LORD:

'Give thanks to the LORD of hosts,
  for the LORD is good,
  for his steadfast love endures for ever!'

For I will restore the fortunes of the land as at first, says the LORD.

12 'Thus says the LORD of hosts: In this place which is waste, without man or beast, and in all of its cities, there shall again be habitations of shepherds resting their flocks. [13]In the cities of the Shephelah, and in the cities of the Negeb, in the land of Benjamin, the places about Jerusalem, and in the the cities of Judah, flocks shall again pass under the hands of the one who counts them, says the LORD.

14 'Behold, the days are coming, says the LORD, when I will fulfil the promise I made to the house of Israel and the house of Judah. [15]In those days and at that time I will cause a righteous Branch to spring forth for David; and he shall execute justice and righteousness in the land. [16]In those days Judah will be saved and Jerusalem will dwell securely. And this is the name by which it will be called: "The LORD is our righteousness".

17 'For thus says the LORD: David shall never lack a man to sit on the throne of the house of Israel, [18]and the Levitical priests shall never lack a man in my presence to offer burnt offerings, to burn cereal offerings, and to make sacrifices for ever.'

19 The word of the LORD came to Jeremiah: [20]'Thus says the LORD: If you can break my covenant with the day and my covenant with the night so that day and night will not come at their appointed time, [21]then also my covenant with David my servant may be broken, so that he shall not have a son to reign on his throne, and my covenant with the Levitical priests my ministers.

[22]As the host of heaven cannot be numbered and the sands of the sea cannot be measured, so I will multiply the descendants of David my servant, and the Levitical priests who minister to me.'

23 The word of the LORD came to Jeremiah: [24]'Have you not observed what these people are saying, "The LORD has rejected the two families which he chose"? Thus they have despised my people so that they are no longer a nation in their sight. [25]Thus says the LORD: If I have not established my covenant with day and night and the ordinances of heaven and earth, [26]then I will reject the descendants of Jacob and David my servant and will not choose one of his descendants to rule over the seed of Abraham, Isaac, and Jacob. For I will restore their fortunes, and will have mercy upon them.'

Chapter 33, which is almost wholly devoted to the promise of restoration, is divided by most scholars into two parts—vv. 1-13, 14-26. This division is predicated primarily on the absence of vv. 14-26 in the Septuagint, a void that many critics accept as supporting their contention that these verses are not Jeremianic (so Volz, Rudolph, Hyatt [1956], Bright [1965], and Nicholson [1973], to name a few). However, to assume that a text is secondary just because it did not exist in the *Vorlage* of the LXX is a faulty presupposition. Who is to say that already in the exilic period there were not several different recensions of Jeremiah in circulation, and that the *Vorlage* of the LXX was only one of these?[8] One can logically deduce from the septuagintal version no more than that a shorter recension of Jeremiah than the MT existed at the time of the Greek translation One cannot conclude anything either about the existence of other recensions at that time, or about the inauthenticity of passages such as 33.14-26.[9]

The other major obstacle to critical acceptance of vv. 14-26 as Jeremianic is the prediction of an eternal priesthood (vv. 18-22). In the words of Welch (1928:231),

> I find it impossible to believe that a prophet who had declared that the sacrificial system formed no integral part of its religion could have stultified himself by erecting this and the restored Davidic line into the leading factors of the community's restored life.

Similarly, Leslie writes (1954:330),

> this author adds the expectation of a permanent line of legitimate priests who are charted with responsibility for supervision of the sacrifices in the temple, a thought quite foreign to Jeremiah's

> conception of religion, but perfectly at home in late post-exilic Judaism.

Welch's belief that Jeremiah held 'that the sacrificial system formed no integral part of its religion' is apparently based upn 7.22, 'for I did not speak to your fathers or command them in the day that I brought them out of the land of Egypt concerning עולה וזבח'. Weinfeld (1976:52-54) has pointed out that the style of thesis and antithesis which appears in 7.21-23 is Jeremianic and concludes that Jeremiah was referring to the deuteronomic position that the covenant at Sinai contained no injunction of sacrifice, but that sacrifice was only enjoined in the covenant in the plains of Moab (Weinfeld [1976:55] dismisses 33.14-26 from consideration for the solitary reason that 'The passage . . . does not occur in the LXX').

Weinfeld's statement on Jeremiah's view of sacrifice has been attacked by Milgrom. Milgrom (1977:273) notes that 'Jeremiah's rebuke specifies only two sacrifices, the *'ola* and *zaebaḥ*' which, as evidenced by many biblical texts, appear in combination 'only in the context of individual voluntary sacrifices . . . and never . . . the required staple of the cult'.

> Furthermore, the fact that Jeremiah addressed the people assembled at the temple and not its officiating priests underscores that he is speaking of the voluntary individual sacrifice and not the mandatory cultic sacrifices. In the only other passage in which Jeremiah scores the sacrificial system (6.8-20), he again refers to the *'ola* and *zaebaḥ* and here he explicitly rebukes the people (העם, cf. v. 19.21) (1977:274).

Milgrom observes that the individual character of the sacrifice is emphasized by the fact that Jeremiah commands the worshipper to eat the זבח, while 'the only mandatory *zaebaḥ* in the entire priestly sacrificial system, that of the Pentecost, is eaten by the priest and not the laity'.

> In sum, Jeremiah has nothing to say whatsoever concerning the fixed Temple sacrifices such as the *tamid*. Rather he turns to the people and urges them to renounce their individual offerings because their ritual piety is vitiated by their immoral behavior. He underscores his point with the claim that the wilderness covenant never enjoined upon the people to honor God with sacrifices. Thus Jeremiah does not contradict the Priestly Code which considers the *'ola* and *zaebaḥ* as individual, voluntary offerings.

Elsewhere Milgrom (1970:70) cogently remarks that

> Jeremiah can only be made over into an antagonist to the institution of the Temple, per se, by declaring spurious all contradictory verses in his book (e.g. 3.17; 14.21; 17.12; 31.5; 33.18-22) . . . The objections to the Temple in both Jeremiah and Isaiah are nothing more than variations on a ubiquitous prophetic theme: rite without ethics is worthless.

The verses surrounding 7.21-23 support Milgrom's position. The subject of vv. 16-20 is the offerings prepared by Judahite families for the worship of foreign deities. Verses 30-34 are also concerned with pagan worship as well as the ensuing pollution of the Temple (the phrase 'I have not commanded' occurs in both vv. 22 and 31; v. 32 is written in the Jeremianic style of thesis—antithesis). Thus Jeremiah's objection to voluntary offerings is conditional: how could God be appeased by voluntary offerings while the people are simultaneously voluntarily engaging in pagan worship? One must conclude that the contention that Jeremiah opposed the sacrificial system as such, and so could not have written 33.18-22, has no basis in the text.

Indeed, there is strong evidence that vv. 14-26 are authentic to Jeremiah. It has already been demonstrated (Chapter 3, above) that vv. 20-22, 25-26 are similar in style and content to the Jeremianic passage of 31.35-37. Additionally, just as 31.35-37 closes out the New Covenant prophecy by contributing the element of eternality, so too does 33.(14-16) 17-26 concerning the promises of physical and spiritual renewal in vv. 6-13.

The first part of Jeremiah 33 (vv. 1-13) has received ambiguous treatment at the hands of scholars.

> Volz sees it as a later addition with vv. 10-11 dependent upon Jer. 32.43; 16.9; 25.10; cp. 17.26; 30.19. To Rudolph, 33.1-13 is written in the first years following the destruction, but is not of Jeremiah since it has an apocalyptic nature. However, he holds that 33.4-6a, 7b, 12 and 13b perhaps derive from prophecies of Jeremiah on the rebuilding of Jerusalem. According to Hyatt (1956), vv. 1-13 shows dtr. influence, although the section as a whole is from a later editor. He considers vv. 4-5 to be 'a genuine historical fragment', but the promise in vv. 6-9 'is too vague and optimistic to be from Jeremiah, especially coming immediately after v. 5b' (similarly, Böhmer, 1976:44-45). Although Nicholson (1973) asserts that vv. 1-13 are probably from a dtr. editor, he states that 'what is herein contained must be seen as a development of Jeremiah's own belief in the restoration of the nation at God's hand' (similarly, Weiser and Bright 1965). Raitt (1977:112)[10] claims that from the perspectives of content and structure vv. 6-9 must be viewed as one of the six genuine 'pivotal oracles of deliverance'.

For the purposes of this study, vv. 6-9 carry the most import in the chapter. Following the description of the destruction wrought by the siege in vv. 4-5, YHWH promises to heal the people (cp. 30.17) and bring them peace (v. 6), to restore their fortunes and to rebuild them (v. 8; cp. 31.34), and thus to give YHWH a name of praise and glory among the nations (v. 9). Verse 9 has affinities with such verses in Psalms as 48.11 and 66.8, as well as Hab. 3.3. Its clearest parallels, though, are with Deut. 26.19; Jer. 13.11; Zeph. 3.19-20. Only in Zephaniah and Jer. 33.9 does this theme appear in relationship to the future restoration, except that in Zephaniah *Israel's* name will be praised. Jeremiah alone speaks of the restoration as resulting in the praise of *God's* name among the nations, a theme which will be picked up by Ezekiel, who will speak of the sanctification of God's name among the nations due to the restoration (Ezek. 26.23).[11]

In sum, 33.6-9 fits perfectly into the context given it by the book—the last days of Jerusalem when Jeremiah had already abandoned repentance as a possible motivation for redemption. The promise of eternality in 33.14-26 is an appropriate and compatible conclusion.

E. **42.9-12**

וַיֹּאמֶר
אֲלֵיהֶם כֹּה־אָמַר יְהוָה אֱלֹהֵי יִשְׂרָאֵל אֲשֶׁר שְׁלַחְתֶּם אֹתִי
אֵלָיו לְהַפִּיל תְּחִנַּתְכֶם לְפָנָיו׃ אִם־שׁוֹב תֵּשְׁבוּ בָּאָרֶץ
הַזֹּאת וּבָנִיתִי אֶתְכֶם וְלֹא אֶהֱרֹס וְנָטַעְתִּי אֶתְכֶם וְלֹא
אֶתּוֹשׁ כִּי נִחַמְתִּי אֶל־הָרָעָה אֲשֶׁר עָשִׂיתִי לָכֶם׃ אַל־ 11
תִּירְאוּ מִפְּנֵי מֶלֶךְ בָּבֶל אֲשֶׁר־אַתֶּם יְרֵאִים מִפָּנָיו אַל־
תִּירְאוּ מִמֶּנּוּ נְאֻם־יְהוָה כִּי־אִתְּכֶם אֲנִי לְהוֹשִׁיעַ אֶתְכֶם
וּלְהַצִּיל אֶתְכֶם מִיָּדוֹ׃ וְאֶתֵּן לָכֶם רַחֲמִים וְרִחַם אֶתְכֶם 12
וְהֵשִׁיב אֶתְכֶם אֶל־אַדְמַתְכֶם׃

> [9]and said to them, 'Thus says the LORD, the God of Israel, to whom you sent me to present your supplication before him: [10]If you will remain in this land, then I will build you up and not pull you down; I will plant you, and not pluck you up; for I repent of the evil which I did to you. [11]Do not fear the king of Babylon, of whom you are afraid; do not fear him, says the LORD, for I am with you, to save you and to deliver you from his hand. [12]I will grant you mercy, that he may have mercy on you and let you remain in your own land.

In 42.9-12 Jeremiah is depicted prophesying to the survivors of the

Mizpah massacre. God promises restoration if only the remnant remains in Judah. However, if they obstinately go down to Egypt they shall be destroyed (vv. 13-22). Thus, although the people are not required to repent, they are expected to accept the prophetic word concerning their destiny. Here an implicit condition of redemption is made explicit—the people must believe that YHWH's promise of restoration will come to pass and must act minimally in accordance with that belief. It is noteworthy that the portrayal of Jeremiah's last days (44.1-30) has him rebuking the people for their idolatrous worship. If one is not required to repent for past sins in order to benefit from the divine plan of redemption, neither is one permitted to disregard YHWH's torah.

The concept of restoration in 42.9-12 does not reflect the dtr. perspective (contra Nicholson [1973] and Hyatt [1956]), nor is it necessary to view it as a product of the Babylonian exiles (contra Carroll, 1981:236).[12] There is no reason to doubt Bright (1965) and Thompson,[13] who accept the historicity of the recorded events. The content of 42.9-12 is utterly consistent with the last stage of Jeremiah's prophecies of restoration.

F. The Prophecies of Redemption in Jer. 50–51

Most scholars deny the authenticity of the prophecies of redemption in Jer. 50–51, as well as the whole of those two chapters (e.g. Rudolph, Hyatt, Bright, Nicholson). The rejection of the restoration prophecies has recently been opposed by Hoffman (1977:128-29), who generally accepts the authenticity of both chapters. Hoffman, however, following Segal (1967:381-82), views the restoration prophecies as later additions. Hoffman particularly argues against Kaufmann (1967: III, 422). The latter contends that Jer. 50–51 was proclaimed during the reign of Zedekiah prior to the destruction of the Temple. Kaufmann points out that the Temple is not mentioned as destroyed, only ravaged (50.28; 51.5, 11, 34-35, 51). Hoffman (1977:127) counters that neither later prophecy (Ezek. 25.2; 26.2; 35.5; Obad. 11-15) nor Psalms (Ps. 137) mentions the burning of the Temple, so the argument from silence cannot be used. Further, the urgent command to flee Babylon in 50.8 and 51.6 assumes the catastrophe of 587, for how could Jeremiah make such a demand at the same time in which he was predicting a long exile, i.e. during the period between the exiles? Hoffman's point is well made, but it has been the contention throughout this study that each passage must be studied upon its own merits. The four relevant passages will now be encountered individually.

1. *50.4-7*

בַּיָּמִים הָהֵמָּה וּבָעֵת הַהִיא נְאֻם־ 4
יְהוָה יָבֹאוּ בְנֵי־יִשְׂרָאֵל הֵמָּה וּבְנֵי־יְהוּדָה יַחְדָּו הָלוֹךְ וּבָכוֹ
יֵלֵכוּ וְאֶת־יְהוָה אֱלֹהֵיהֶם יְבַקֵּשׁוּ׃ צִיּוֹן יִשְׁאָלוּ דֶּרֶךְ הֵנָּה ה
פְנֵיהֶם בֹּאוּ וְנִלְווּ אֶל־יְהוָה בְּרִית עוֹלָם לֹא תִשָּׁכֵחַ׃
צֹאן אֹבְדוֹת הָיוּ עַמִּי רֹעֵיהֶם הִתְעוּם הָרִים שׁוֹבְבוּם מֵהַר 6
אֶל־גִּבְעָה הָלָכוּ שָׁכְחוּ רִבְצָם׃ כָּל־מוֹצְאֵיהֶם אֲכָלוּם 7
וְצָרֵיהֶם אָמְרוּ לֹא נֶאְשָׁם תַּחַת אֲשֶׁר חָטְאוּ לַיהוָה נְוֵה־
צֶדֶק וּמִקְוֵה אֲבוֹתֵיהֶם יְהוָה׃

4 'In those days and in that time, says the LORD, the people of Israel and the people of Judah shall come together, weeping as they come; and they shall seek the LORD their God. 5They shall ask the way to Zion, with faces turned toward it, saying, "Come, let us join ourselves to the LORD in an everlasting covenant which will never be forgotten."

6 'My people have been lost sheep; their shepherds have led them astray, turning them away on the mountains; from mountain to hill they have gone, they have forgotten their fold. 7All who found them have devoured them, and their enemies have said, "We are not guilty, for they have sinned against the LORD, their true habitation, the LORD, the hope of their fathers".'

50.4-7 is separated at least from that which follows since in v. 8 the people are addressed in the second person while in the previous verses they are spoken of in the third person. Verse 4 alludes to the distant future, 'in those days and at that time', to a return of both Israel and Judah,[14], thus assuming minimally the Jehoiachin exile. The use of the roots הלך and בקש in connection with God is reminiscent of 29.12-13. The reference to 'the eternal covenant which will not be forgotten' in v. 5 does not indicate the new covenant (32.40) for that one will not be established until *after* the ingathering of the exiles (contra Nicholson). Rather it signifies the old covenant long ago established between God and Israel (cp. Gen. 17.7, 13, 19; Exod. 31.16; Lev. 24.8; Isa. 24.5; Ps. 105.8-10). It appears that, like 29.10-14, Jer. 50.4-5 draws from Deut. 4.29-31; cp. Jer. 50.4, ואת יהוה אלהיהם יבקשו, with Deut. 4.29, ובקשתם משם את יהוה אלהיך, and Jer. 50.5, ברית עולם לא תשכח, with Deut. 4.31, ולא ישכח את ברית אבתיך. The condemnation of the 'shepherds' in v. 6 has clear affinities with 23.1-4.

Although other language in 50.4-7 brings to mind a variety of passages in Jeremiah, these verses most nearly approximate to prophecies of redemption from the time just after the 597 exile.[15] In resemblance to 24.4-7 and 29.10-14, 50.4-7 emphasizes redemption while minimizing repentance. Kaufmann (1967: III, 422) has already noted that הנה of v. 5 is evidence that the author prophesied from Jerusalem. There is no reason to doubt that 50.4-7 is an authentic Jeremiah prophecy from the transition period in his thought concerning repentance and redemption—the years between the exiles. That it may have been inserted by a compiler into a prophecy against Babylon is no reflection on its originality.

2. *50.17-20*

שֶׂה פְזוּרָה יִשְׂרָאֵל אֲרָיוֹת הִדִּיחוּ
הָרִאשׁוֹן אֲכָלוֹ מֶלֶךְ אַשּׁוּר וְזֶה הָאַחֲרוֹן עִצְּמוֹ נְבוּכַדְרֶאצַּר
18 מֶלֶךְ בָּבֶל׃ לָכֵן כֹּה־אָמַר יְהוָה צְבָאוֹת אֱלֹהֵי
יִשְׂרָאֵל הִנְנִי פֹקֵד אֶל־מֶלֶךְ בָּבֶל וְאֶל־אַרְצוֹ כַּאֲשֶׁר
19 פָּקַדְתִּי אֶל־מֶלֶךְ אַשּׁוּר׃ וְשֹׁבַבְתִּי אֶת־יִשְׂרָאֵל אֶל־נָוֵהוּ
וְרָעָה הַכַּרְמֶל וְהַבָּשָׁן וּבְהַר אֶפְרַיִם וְהַגִּלְעָד תִּשְׂבַּע
כ נַפְשׁוֹ׃ בַּיָּמִים הָהֵם וּבָעֵת הַהִיא נְאֻם־יְהוָה יְבֻקַּשׁ אֶת־
עֲוֺן יִשְׂרָאֵל וְאֵינֶנּוּ וְאֶת־חַטֹּאת יְהוּדָה וְלֹא תִמָּצֶאינָה כִּי
אֶסְלַח לַאֲשֶׁר אַשְׁאִיר׃

17 'Israel is a hunted sheep driven away by lions. First the king of Assyria devoured him, and now at last Nebuchadrezzar king of Babylon has gnawed his bones. [18]Therefore, thus says the LORD of hosts, the God of Israel: Behold, I am bringing punishment on the king of Babylon and his land, as I punished the king of Assyria. [19]I will restore Israel to his pasture, and he shall feed on Carmel and in Bashan, and his desire shall be satisfied on the hills of Ephraim and in Gilead. [20]In those days and in that time, says the LORD, iniquity shall be sought in Israel, and there shall be none; and sin in Judah, and none shall be found; for I will pardon those whom I leave as a remnant.

Although some think vv. 17b-20 are an expansion upon v. 17a (Berridge, 1970:83, Bright, 1965), others (e.g. Thompson) regard them as a poetic piece. In any case, the style appears Jeremianic—note the comparison of two similar entities (cp. 3.6-11), and that of v. 18, . . . הנני פקד אל . . .כאשר פקדתי אל, to 31.28, והיה כאשר שקדתי עליהם כן אשקד עליהם. The passage predicts a restoration to both

Israel and Judah (v. 20, although the emphasis is upon the northern tribes—v. 19) based upon the wiping out of sins. It thus fits in well with 31.34 and 33.8. Verses 17-20 should therefore, be considered as a Jeremianic prophecy approximately from the time of the destruction of Jerusalem, despite the fact that it is an insertion.

3. *50.33-34*

33 כֹּה אָמַר יְהוָה צְבָאוֹת עֲשׁוּקִים בְּנֵי־
יִשְׂרָאֵל וּבְנֵי־יְהוּדָה יַחְדָּו וְכָל־שֹׁבֵיהֶם הֶחֱזִיקוּ בָם מֵאֲנוּ
34 שַׁלְּחָם׃ גֹּאֲלָם ׀ חָזָק יְהוָה צְבָאוֹת שְׁמוֹ רִיב יָרִיב אֶת־
רִיבָם לְמַעַן הִרְגִּיעַ אֶת־הָאָרֶץ וְהִרְגִּיז לְיֹשְׁבֵי בָבֶל׃

33 ‘Thus says the LORD of hosts: The people of Israel are oppressed, and the people of Judah with them; all who took them captive have held them fast, they refuse to let them go. 34Their Redeemer is strong; the LORD of hosts is his name. He will surely plead their cause, that he may give rest to the earth, but unrest to the inhabitants of Babylon.

Unlike the previous two prophecies, it is difficult to see how vv. 33-34 could be from Jeremiah. The problem centers on the final words of v. 33—Judah's and Israel's captors ‘refused to send them’ back to their land (implied). One cannot agree with Hoffman (above) that Jeremiah could have accused Babylon after 587 of extending the exile. Jeremiah's position that the restoration would only take place after seventy years was not appropriate only to the period before 587. Rather, it represented the essential difference between Jeremiah and the false prophets who disturbed him so greatly. Were Jeremiah after 587 to renege on his earlier position, he would quite possibly lose both his credibility and authority. Thus it is probable that vv. 33-34, heartfelt though they may be, emanate from an anonymous prophet of the exile.

4. *51.50-51*

פְּלֵטִים מֵחֶרֶב הִלְכוּ אַל־תַּעֲמֹדוּ
זִכְרוּ מֵרָחוֹק אֶת־יְהוָה וִירוּשָׁלַ͏ִם תַּעֲלֶה עַל־לְבַבְכֶם׃
בֹּשְׁנוּ כִּי־שָׁמַעְנוּ חֶרְפָּה כִּסְּתָה כְלִמָּה פָּנֵינוּ כִּי בָּאוּ זָרִים
עַל־מִקְדְּשֵׁי בֵּית יְהוָה׃

50 ‘You that have escaped from the sword,
go, stand not still!
Remember the LORD from afar,

and let Jerusalem come into your mind:
51 "We are put to shame, for we have heard reproach;
dishonor has covered our face,
for aliens have come
into the holy places of the LORD's house"'.

Both medieval and modern commentators are agreed that 51.50 exhorts the exiles to quickly return to their land. Verses 50-51 could not, then, be Jeremianic for the reasons given in the previous paragraph. Note also that the shame expressed by the people in v. 51 is not for past sins (cp. 3.25; 31.19), but for the destruction of the Temple. These verses come from an anonymous exile.

G. Conclusion

The above analysis reveals that the 'miscellaneous' prophecies of redemption in Jeremiah support, rather than contradict, the findings of our previous three chapters. Indeed, Jeremiah's thoughts on repentance and redemption have been further fleshed out and the harshness of Israel's treatment at the hands of its attackers has been shown to be a significant spur to divine mercy and, consequently, to redemption.

EXCURSUS I

Amos and Hosea

In order to place Jeremiah's thought on repentance and redemption in perspective, this excursus will analyse the positions of the first two classical prophets who speak to a positive future—Amos and Hosea. As will be seen, Hosea's perspectives are crucial to Jeremiah.

A. Amos 9.8-15

8 הִנֵּ֞ה עֵינֵ֣י ׀ אֲדֹנָ֣י יֱהֹוִ֗ה בַּמַּמְלָכָה֙
הַֽחַטָּאָ֔ה וְהִשְׁמַדְתִּ֣י אֹתָ֔הּ מֵעַ֖ל פְּנֵ֣י הָאֲדָמָ֑ה אֶ֗פֶס כִּ֠י לֹ֣א
9 הַשְׁמֵ֥יד אַשְׁמִ֛יד אֶת־בֵּ֥ית יַעֲקֹ֖ב נְאֻם־יְהוָֽה׃ כִּֽי־הִנֵּ֤ה אָנֹכִי֙
מְצַוֶּ֔ה וַהֲנִע֥וֹתִי בְכָֽל־הַגּוֹיִ֖ם אֶת־בֵּ֣ית יִשְׂרָאֵ֑ל כַּאֲשֶׁ֤ר יִנּ֨וֹעַ֙
י בַּכְּבָרָ֔ה וְלֹֽא־יִפּ֥וֹל צְר֖וֹר אָֽרֶץ׃ בַּחֶ֣רֶב יָמ֔וּתוּ כֹּ֖ל חַטָּאֵ֣י
11 עַמִּ֑י הָאֹמְרִ֕ים לֹֽא־תַגִּ֧ישׁ וְתַקְדִּ֛ים בַּעֲדֵ֖ינוּ הָרָעָֽה׃ בַּיּ֣וֹם
הַה֔וּא אָקִ֛ים אֶת־סֻכַּ֥ת דָּוִ֖יד הַנֹּפֶ֑לֶת וְגָדַרְתִּ֣י אֶת־פִּרְצֵיהֶ֗ן
12 וַהֲרִסֹתָיו֙ אָקִ֔ים וּבְנִיתִ֖יהָ כִּימֵ֥י עוֹלָֽם׃ לְמַ֨עַן יִֽירְשׁ֜וּ אֶת־
שְׁאֵרִ֤ית אֱדוֹם֙ וְכָל־הַגּוֹיִ֔ם אֲשֶׁר־נִקְרָ֥א שְׁמִ֖י עֲלֵיהֶ֑ם נְאֻם־
13 יְהוָ֖ה עֹ֥שֶׂה זֹּֽאת׃ הִנֵּ֨ה יָמִ֤ים בָּאִים֙ נְאֻם־יְהוָ֔ה וְנִגַּ֤שׁ
חוֹרֵשׁ֙ בַּקֹּצֵ֔ר וְדֹרֵ֥ךְ עֲנָבִ֖ים בְּמֹשֵׁ֣ךְ הַזָּ֑רַע וְהִטִּ֤יפוּ הֶֽהָרִים֙
14 עָסִ֔יס וְכָל־הַגְּבָע֖וֹת תִּתְמוֹגַֽגְנָה׃ וְשַׁבְתִּי֮ אֶת־שְׁב֣וּת עַמִּ֣י
יִשְׂרָאֵל֒ וּבָנ֞וּ עָרִ֤ים נְשַׁמּוֹת֙ וְיָשָׁ֔בוּ וְנָטְע֣וּ כְרָמִ֔ים וְשָׁת֖וּ אֶת־
טו יֵינָ֑ם וְעָשׂ֣וּ גַנּ֔וֹת וְאָכְל֖וּ אֶת־פְּרִיהֶֽם׃ וּנְטַעְתִּ֖ים עַל־אַדְמָתָ֑ם
וְלֹ֨א יִנָּתְשׁ֜וּ ע֗וֹד מֵעַ֤ל אַדְמָתָם֙ אֲשֶׁ֣ר נָתַ֣תִּי לָהֶ֔ם אָמַ֖ר
יְהוָ֥ה אֱלֹהֶֽיךָ׃

8Behold, the eyes of the LORD God
are upon the sinful kingdom,
and I will destroy it from the
surface of the ground;
except that I will not utterly

destroy the house of Jacob, says the LORD.

9'For lo, I will command,
and shake the house of Israel among all the nations
as one shakes with a sieve,
but no pebble shall fall upon the earth',

10All the sinners of my people shall die by the sword,
who say, "Evil shall not overtake or meet us".

11'In that day I will raise up
the booth of David that is fallen
and repair its breaches,
and raise up its ruins,
and rebuild it as in the days of old;

12that they may possess the remnant of Edom
and all the nations who are called by my name',
says the LORD who does this.

13'Behold, the days are coming', says the LORD,
'when the plowman shall overtake the reaper
and the treader of grapes him who sows the seed;
the mountains shall drip sweet wine,
and all the hills shall flow with it.

14I will restore the fortunes of my people Israel,
and they shall rebuild the ruined cities and inhabit them;
they shall plant vineyards and drink their wine,
and they shall make gardens and eat their fruit.

15I will plant them upon their land,
and they shall never again be plucked up
out of the land which I have given them', says the LORD your God.

The one eschatological passage in Amos, 9.8-15, does not envision repentance as part of the redemptive process. Scholarship over the past century has been divided on the question of the origin of these verses (and their unity). The last score of years has seen more and more scholars declare this passage to be inauthentic. Their primary argument is ideological, as rendered by the oft quoted comment of Wellhausen:[1]

> Roses and lavender instead of blood and iron . . . Amos . . . means what he says . . . After he has just before far surpassed all his earlier threats, he cannot suddenly blunt their sharpness, he cannot let milk and honey flow from the cup of Yahweh's wrath at the

> end . . . It is a later Jew who has appended this coda, and removed the genuine conclusion, because this sounded too harshly in his ears.

Harper (1953) lists ten objections in all, based upon thematic, historical, and linguistic grounds, and recently Wolff (1977) has found four reasons for disallowing vv. 11-15. Among others, able defenses of this passage have been made by Driver (1915) and Gordis (1940:246-47, 250)[2] on ideological grounds, and Kaufmann (1967: III, 88-89, and n. 45) on linguistic grounds.

Without reiterating all the arguments for and against, suffice it to say that the authenticity of this passage is supported in three main ways:

1. Ideologically, the assumption that Amos's mentality had to be conceptually monolithic and dogmatic flies in the face of (a) the psychological understanding of the human mind as complex and diverse, (b) the probability that Amos prophesied over a considerable number of years, thereby increasing his prophetic possibilities, (c) evidence from other prophets. In the words of Driver (1915),[3]

> For a prophet to close the entire volume of his prophecies without a single gleam of hope . . . is very much opposed to the analogy of prophecy; Jeremiah and Ezekiel, for instance, blame Judah not less unsparingly than Amos blames Israel, but both nevertheless draw ideal pictures of the restored nation's future felicity.

2. Historically, the depiction of 'the fallen hut of David' (v. 11) fits (a) the period of the divided kingdom of Amos' time (Gordis, 1940:246), and (b) the lack of a developed messianic figure such as that found in I Isaiah (Driver, 1915).

3. Philologically, the language of redemption reverses that of doom (Kaufmann, 1967:III, 88-89), a characteristic of prophecies of redemption (cp. e.g. Hos. 2.17, 20 with 2.14; 2.23-24 with 2.6, 11; 11.9 with 8.5; Jer. 33.11 with 7.34; 16.9; 25.10; etc.).

If the passage is indeed from Amos, in light of his frequent emphasis on the theme of repentance (4.6, 8, 9, 10; 5.4, 6, 14-15, 23-24; 6.6b) it seems initially surprising that repentance is not mentioned in 9.8-15.[4] However, this difficulty is eliminated when one realizes that the prophecy of redemption calls first for the precondition that all the sinners of Israel are to be destroyed (v. 10). The implication is that the righteous will be saved (v. 9), and since they *are* righteous, repentance is superfluous.

Amos, the first prophet to predict national destruction, becomes the first confronted with the need to explain the ensuing process of redemption. He interprets both calamity and restoration in terms of divine justice. Repentance, then, is only a factor involving the wicked prior to the fulfillment of the doom oracles.[5] Once the wicked majority have been properly punished, the righteous remnant will be redeemed.[6]

B. Hosea[7]

The clarification of the relationship of repentance to redemption in Hosea's prophecy is hardly a simple matter, for it depends upon the composition of the book—an issue of some controversy and complexity. Three prominent scholarly approaches follow:

1. Y. Kaufmann (1967:III, 99), succeeded by H.L. Ginsberg, has maintained that the authorship of chs. 1–3 derives from a prophet other than the author of Hos. 4–14, and that the former lived in the ninth century BCE. Kaufmann (1967:III, 95-97) claims that the two parts of the book differ in style, phraseology, use of symbols, objectivity and lyricism, ideology (and conception of the people's sin), and attitude toward Baalism. Ginsberg (1971:1012-16, 1018-19) agrees with Kaufmann in the main (Ginsberg, 1960:50 n. 1) but, among other comments, emphasizes the emotionality of Hosea II to the point of asserting that this prophet depicts God as restoring Israel unconditionally because of his 'unmerited love', while Hosea I 'does not speak at all of YHWH's love either with reference to the past, present, or to the future . . .' (1971:1022). That Ginsberg holds this position despite such verses as 2.20-25 is quite surprising and virtually untenable.

To discuss and attempt to refute the claims of these two scholars in a comprehensive fashion is beyond the purview of the present inquiry.[8] Suffice it to say that the entire book of Hosea contains 197 verses, and yet, according to the superscription of 1.1, Hosea prophesied from the reign of Jeroboam II through that of Hezekiah! Although the maximum number of years would surely be far too great (784-698 BCE), most scholars posit a term of 25 years for Hosea's prophecies (750-725). Even if the extreme view of H. Tadmor (1960:84-88) is accepted[9] (that the *terminus ante quem* of the book is 738), Hosea is still left with a dozen years of activity. Certainly, if chs. 1–3 are from Hosea's early prophecies and 4–14 from later ones, enough time can have elapsed to explain certain differences of style, phraseology, symbolism, and even development of ideology. To assume that Hosea, or any thinking human, must always be consistent and unchanging is (as stated above concerning Amos) psychologically unacceptable. Furthermore, elements of a relationship between chs. 1–3 and 4–14 exist: cp. 2.10 with 14.9d; 2.15 with

13.6 (the root שכח); 2.10 with 11.3 (the use of root ידע); דגן ותירוש in 2.10, 11, 24; 7.14; גפן and/or תאנה in 2.14; 9.10; 10.1; 14.8; etc. (Kaufmann, 1967:III, 95 n. 2, names a few others). These linguistic ties are strong witnesses against the division of the book.

2. As has just been noted, there are wide differences of opinion among scholars concerning the dates of Hosea's prophecies (although there is unanimous agreement that Hosea did not prophesy after the fall of Samaria). These divisions reflect the absence of clear indications of dates in the text. This reality, in turn, makes the sure reconstruction of an historical development of Hosea's ideology extremely difficult, if not impossible. Nonetheless, G. Fohrer (1967:222-41) attempts just such a reconstruction by rearranging the order of the prophecies, as follows: 5.15–6.6; 14.2-9; 3.1-5; 2.16-25. Thus he arrives at the convenient conclusion that after initially believing in repentance as a prelude to redemption, the prophet abandons that hope when his prophetic experience makes him realize that Israel is incapable of repenting. Hosea then turns to a belief in redemption which is effected solely through God's grace. J. Bright (1976:92-93) accepts this reconstruction.

3. Unlike Fohrer, H.W. Wolff (1974:xxvii-xxix) accepts the order of the prophecies in the book, but sees the one in ch. 2 as being built upon Israel's repentance (by placing 2.9 *after* 2.15). Later, he opines, Hosea understands God's love to be the only precondition to Israel's restoration. This stand forces him to view 14.2-4 as 'an invitation to return (which) already presupposes this love'. Thus, through arbitrary and illegitimate methods, Wolff and Fohrer arrive at the same (preconceived?) conclusions concerning the development of Hosea's ideology.

The four relevant passages promising redemption in Hosea will now be examined.

2.4-25[10]

רִיבוּ
בְאִמְּכֶם רִיבוּ כִּי־הִיא לֹא אִשְׁתִּי וְאָנֹכִי לֹא אִישָׁהּ וְתָסֵר
זְנוּנֶיהָ מִפָּנֶיהָ וְנַאֲפוּפֶיהָ מִבֵּין שָׁדֶיהָ׃ פֶּן־אַפְשִׁיטֶנָּה
עֲרֻמָּה וְהִצַּגְתִּיהָ כְּיוֹם הִוָּלְדָהּ וְשַׂמְתִּיהָ כַמִּדְבָּר וְשַׁתִּהָ
6 כְּאֶרֶץ צִיָּה וַהֲמִתִּיהָ בַּצָּמָא׃ וְאֶת־בָּנֶיהָ לֹא אֲרַחֵם כִּי־
7 בְנֵי זְנוּנִים הֵמָּה׃ כִּי זָנְתָה אִמָּם הֹבִישָׁה הוֹרָתָם כִּי
אָמְרָה אֵלְכָה אַחֲרֵי מְאַהֲבַי נֹתְנֵי לַחְמִי וּמֵימַי צַמְרִי
8 וּפִשְׁתִּי שַׁמְנִי וְשִׁקּוּיָי׃ לָכֵן הִנְנִי־שָׂךְ אֶת־דַּרְכֵּךְ בַּסִּירִים
9 וְגָדַרְתִּי אֶת־גְּדֵרָהּ וּנְתִיבוֹתֶיהָ לֹא תִמְצָא׃ וְרִדְּפָה אֶת־
מְאַהֲבֶיהָ וְלֹא־תַשִּׂיג אֹתָם וּבִקְשָׁתַם וְלֹא תִמְצָא וְאָמְרָה
אֵלְכָה וְאָשׁוּבָה אֶל־אִישִׁי הָרִאשׁוֹן כִּי טוֹב לִי אָז מֵעָתָּה׃

י וְהִיא לֹא יָדְעָה כִּי אָנֹכִי נָתַתִּי לָהּ הַדָּגָן וְהַתִּירוֹשׁ
11 וְהַיִּצְהָר וְכֶסֶף הִרְבֵּיתִי לָהּ וְזָהָב עָשׂוּ לַבָּעַל׃ לָכֵן אָשׁוּב
וְלָקַחְתִּי דְגָנִי בְּעִתּוֹ וְתִירוֹשִׁי בְּמוֹעֲדוֹ וְהִצַּלְתִּי צַמְרִי
12 וּפִשְׁתִּי לְכַסּוֹת אֶת־עֶרְוָתָהּ׃ וְעַתָּה אֲגַלֶּה אֶת־נַבְלֻתָהּ
13 לְעֵינֵי מְאַהֲבֶיהָ וְאִישׁ לֹא־יַצִּילֶנָּה מִיָּדִי׃ וְהִשְׁבַּתִּי כָּל־
14 מְשׂוֹשָׂהּ חַגָּהּ חָדְשָׁהּ וְשַׁבַּתָּהּ וְכֹל מוֹעֲדָהּ׃ וַהֲשִׁמֹּתִי
גַּפְנָהּ וּתְאֵנָתָהּ אֲשֶׁר אָמְרָה אֶתְנָה הֵמָּה לִי אֲשֶׁר נָתְנוּ־
טו לִי מְאַהֲבָי וְשַׂמְתִּים לְיַעַר וַאֲכָלָתַם חַיַּת הַשָּׂדֶה׃ וּפָקַדְתִּי
עָלֶיהָ אֶת־יְמֵי הַבְּעָלִים אֲשֶׁר תַּקְטִיר לָהֶם וַתַּעַד נִזְמָהּ
וְחֶלְיָתָהּ וַתֵּלֶךְ אַחֲרֵי מְאַהֲבֶיהָ וְאֹתִי שָׁכְחָה נְאֻם־יְהוָה׃
16 לָכֵן הִנֵּה אָנֹכִי מְפַתֶּיהָ וְהֹלַכְתִּיהָ הַמִּדְבָּר וְדִבַּרְתִּי עַל־
17 לִבָּהּ׃ וְנָתַתִּי לָהּ אֶת־כְּרָמֶיהָ מִשָּׁם וְאֶת־עֵמֶק עָכוֹר לְפֶתַח
תִּקְוָה וְעָנְתָה שָׁמָּה כִּימֵי נְעוּרֶיהָ וּכְיוֹם עֲלוֹתָהּ מֵאֶרֶץ־
18 מִצְרָיִם׃ וְהָיָה בַיּוֹם־הַהוּא נְאֻם־יְהוָה תִּקְרְאִי אִישִׁי
19 וְלֹא־תִקְרְאִי־לִי עוֹד בַּעְלִי׃ וַהֲסִרֹתִי אֶת־שְׁמוֹת הַבְּעָלִים
כ מִפִּיהָ וְלֹא־יִזָּכְרוּ עוֹד בִּשְׁמָם׃ וְכָרַתִּי לָהֶם בְּרִית בַּיּוֹם
הַהוּא עִם־חַיַּת הַשָּׂדֶה וְעִם־עוֹף הַשָּׁמַיִם וְרֶמֶשׂ הָאֲדָמָה
וְקֶשֶׁת וְחֶרֶב וּמִלְחָמָה אֶשְׁבּוֹר מִן־הָאָרֶץ וְהִשְׁכַּבְתִּים
21 לָבֶטַח׃ וְאֵרַשְׂתִּיךְ לִי לְעוֹלָם וְאֵרַשְׂתִּיךְ לִי בְּצֶדֶק
22 וּבְמִשְׁפָּט וּבְחֶסֶד וּבְרַחֲמִים׃ וְאֵרַשְׂתִּיךְ לִי בֶּאֱמוּנָה וְיָדַעַתְּ
23 אֶת־יְהוָה׃ וְהָיָה ׀ בַּיּוֹם הַהוּא אֶעֱנֶה נְאֻם־יְהוָה אֶעֱנֶה
24 אֶת־הַשָּׁמָיִם וְהֵם יַעֲנוּ אֶת־הָאָרֶץ׃ וְהָאָרֶץ תַּעֲנֶה אֶת־
הַדָּגָן וְאֶת־הַתִּירוֹשׁ וְאֶת־הַיִּצְהָר וְהֵם יַעֲנוּ אֶת־יִזְרְעֶאל׃
כה וּזְרַעְתִּיהָ לִּי בָּאָרֶץ וְרִחַמְתִּי אֶת־לֹא רֻחָמָה וְאָמַרְתִּי לְלֹא־
עַמִּי עַמִּי־אַתָּה וְהוּא יֹאמַר אֱלֹהָי׃

[4]"Plead with your mother, plead—
for she is not my wife,
and I am not her husband—
that she put away her harlotry from her face,
and her adultery from between her breasts;

[5]lest I strip her naked
and make her as in the day she was born,
and make her like a wilderness,
and set her like a parched land,
and slay her with thirst.

[6]Upon her children also I will have no pity,
because they are children of harlotry.

[7]For their mother has played the harlot;

she that conceived them has acted shamefully.
For she said, "I will go after my lovers,
who give me my bread and my water,
my wool and my flax, my oil and my drink."

8 Therefore I will hedge up her way with thorns;
and I will build a wall against her,
so that she cannot find her paths.

9 She shall pursue her lovers,
but not overtake them;
and she shall seek them,
but shall not find them.
Then she shall say, "I will go
and return to my first husband,
for it was better with me then than now".

10 And she did not know
that it was I who gave her
the grain, the wine, and the oil,
and who lavished upon her silver
and gold which they used for Baal.

11 Therefore I will take back
my grain in its time,
and my wine in its season; and I will take away my wool and my flax,
which were to cover her nakedness.

12 Now I will uncover her lewdness
in sight of her lovers,
and no one shall rescue her out of my hand.

13 And I will put an end to all her mirth,
her feasts, her new moons, her sabbaths,
and all her appointed feasts.

14 And I will lay waste her vines and her fig trees,
of which she said,
"These are my hire,
which my lovers have given me".
I will make them a forest,
and the beasts of the field shall devour them.

15 And I will punish her for the feast days of the Baals
when she burned incense to them
and decked herself with her ring and jewelry,
and went after her lovers,
and forgot me, says the LORD.

[16]‘Therefore, behold, I will allure her,
  and bring her into the wilderness,
  and speak tenderly to her.

[17]And there I will give her her vineyards,
  and make the Valley of Achor a door of hope.
And there she shall answer as in the days of her youth,
  as at the time when she came out of the land of Egypt.’

[18]‘And in that day, says the LORD, you will call me, “My husband”,
and no longer will you call me, “My Baal”. [19]For I will remove the
names of the Baals from her mouth, and they shall be mentioned
by name no more. [20]And I will make for you a covenant on that day
with the beasts of the field, the birds of the air, and the creeping
things of the ground; and I will abolish the bow, the sword, and war
from the land; and I will make you lie down in safety. [21]And I will
betroth you to me for ever; I will betroth you to me in
righteousness and in justice, in steadfast love, and in mercy. [22]I will
betroth you to me in faithfulness; and you shall know the LORD.

[23]‘And in that day, says the LORD,
  I will answer the heavens
  and they shall answer the earth;

[24]and the earth shall answer the grain, the wine, and the oil,
  and they shall answer Jezreel;

[25]and I will sow him for myself in the land.
And I will have pity on Not pitied,
  and I will say to Not my people, “You are my people”;
  and he shall say, “Thou art my God”.’

2.4-25 appears to be a continuous literary unit. Most commentators see 2.18-25 as a later addition (even if authentic to Hosea) by an editor (e.g. Wolff, 1974; Mays, 1969). However, the first words of v. 18, ‘and it shall be in that day’, assume some prelude! Furthermore, one would expect that a prophecy of redemption which succeeds a prophecy of punishment would contain references to, and a reversal of, that punishment. This is precisely the occurrence here: cp. v. 19 with v. 15; vv. 18-19 with v. 4; חית השדה in v. 20 and v. 14; √ידע in v. 22 and v. 10; v. 23 with v. 5; v. 24 with v. 11; √רחם in vv. 21, 25 and v. 6.

Although the root שוב does not appear, v. 4b contains an element of repentance: God calls for a cessation of sin, specifically idolatry, by Israel to avert the impending punishment of vv. 5-15. Some scholars (e.g. Procksch, 1910; Weiser, 1964; Rudolph, 1966) have sought the people's positive response in v. 9b, ואמרה אלכה ואשובה אל אישי הראשון כי טוב לי אז מעתה.[11] However, if this was, indeed, repentance then the following verses, 10-15, are anomalous and even paradoxical, for the punishment of vv. 5-8 continues and worsens (cp. מאתה of v. 9b with v. 12, ... ואתה). Additionally, the שוב of v. 11 seems to reflect in direct contrast the ואשובה of v. 9, for the immediately preceding לכן in v. 11, which introduces further punishment, is, by definition, consequential (cf. March, 1974:268-69). Thus, it appears that the statement placed in the mouth of the faithless mother Israel in v. 9b is only the expression of selfish concern, כי טוב לי אז מעתה.[12] The use of the comparative here ('for it was better for us/me x than y') is reminiscent of the type of amoral, physical gratification sought by the generation of the desert, who, also, longed for the comforts of a fertile land rather than desert-like desolation (Exod. 14.12, כי טוב לנו עבד את מצרים ממתינו במדבר; similarly, Num. 11.18; 14.3). At the best, then, the statement in v. 9b is false repentance, a theme which reoccurs in the book (5.6; 6.1-4).

It is only after punishment, not repentance, that the process of redemption is initiated. Verses 16-17 depict the renewal of the 'marriage' between God and Israel as reminiscent of the inception of the relationship as it occurred in the Sinai desert (17b, וענתה שמה כימי נעוריה וכיום עלתה מארץ מצרים). However, it may not be necessary to assume that this redemptive process is preceded by exile from the land. The punishment in vv. 5-15 explicitly indicates only drought and wild beasts (a sequence which also appears in Lev. 26.19-22). The 'desert' mentioned in v. 16 is, in reality, part of the Promised Land—v. 17a, ונתתי לה את כרמיה משם ואת עמק עכור לפתח תקוה. The site herein indicated is the Judean Desert since עמק עכור appears to be near Jericho (Josh. 7.1-26; 15.7). The words והשכבתים לבטח in v. 20 do not have to presuppose exile (cp. Job 11.18), but rather insecurity, and the same may be said for the expression וזרעתיה לי בארץ of v. 25 where the reference may be to agricultural increase (in agreement with vv. 23-24 and in reversal of the punishment of v. 11; cf. v. 10).

The reconstitution of a fertile agriculture is, thus, depicted in historical terms, since it was from the Valley of Achor that Joshua's armies are viewed rising to conquer the hill country. The renewed fertility will be magnified over that of pre-punishment days, for the Valley of Achor will become full of vineyards (see, similarly, Amos 9.13-14).

Thus, vv. 16-17a portray God wooing and giving a dowry to Israel, which result in a positive response (vv. 17b-18). It is God, too, not the people, who ensures their loyalty (v. 19). In other words, the people's acknowledgment of YHWH's lordship is preceded by actual divine acts of redemption. These acts continue in a new covenant, which differs from the Sinaitic one by guaranteeing a completely peaceful existence for Israel, and harmony with wild animals (v. 20, which harks back to Genesis 1–2; similarly, Isa. 11.6-9).[13] Additionally, the relationship between God and Israel will be eternal (v. 21a), of mutual correct behavior (v. 21b), and Israel's obedience is secured (v. 22). These sureties are accompanied by natural harmony and crop production.

Nowhere in the prophecy of redemption in vv. 16-25 is there any indication of Israel's confession of sin, or promise of the cessation of sin, or decision to return to God. Acceptance of YHWH (vv. 18, 25b) and obedience (v. 22b) are results of God's redemptive acts. It must be concluded that Hos. 2.4-25 demands sincere repentance to avoid divine punishment (vv. 4-5), but that once judgment has been executed, God will restore Israel, assuring the people's fealty, in a process in which repentance (or even confession) has no part.

3.4-5[14]

כִּ֣י ׀ יָמִ֣ים רַבִּ֗ים יֵֽשְׁבוּ֙ בְּנֵ֣י יִשְׂרָאֵ֔ל אֵ֥ין מֶ֙לֶךְ֙ וְאֵ֣ין שָׂ֔ר 4
וְאֵ֥ין זֶ֖בַח וְאֵ֣ין מַצֵּבָ֑ה וְאֵ֥ין אֵפ֖וֹד וּתְרָפִֽים׃ אַחַ֗ר יָשֻׁ֙בוּ֙ ה
בְּנֵ֣י יִשְׂרָאֵ֔ל וּבִקְשׁוּ֙ אֶת־יְהוָ֣ה אֱלֹהֵיהֶ֔ם וְאֵ֖ת דָּוִ֣יד מַלְכָּ֑ם
וּפָחֲד֧וּ אֶל־יְהוָ֛ה וְאֶל־טוּב֖וֹ בְּאַחֲרִ֥ית הַיָּמִֽים׃

> 4 For the children of Israel shall dwell many days without king or prince, without sacrifice or pillar, without ephod or teraphim. [5]Afterward the children of Israel shall return and seek the LORD their God, and David their king; and they shall come in fear to the LORD and to his goodness in the latter days.

Verse 3 symbolizes the coming isolation of the people Israel predicted in v. 4. Neither verse seems to imply exile, but rather a period when Israel will have neither government nor ritual. This end to local political and religious institutions indicates, perhaps, oppressive rule by foreigners. The words אין מלך of v. 4 appear to allude to the frequent אין מלך בישראל in Judges (17.6; 18.1; 21.25; cp. 19.1) in prophecy of a similar time of anarchy. On the other hand, the words כי ימים רבים ישבו seem to suggest the punishment of the generation of the desert (Deut. 1.46; Josh. 24.7). After this period of desolation, Israel will return to God and will come 'tremblingly' to the divine 'bounty'.[15] It is puzzling that this prophecy contains no description of divine acceptance of the people's repentance, other than the oblique טובו. Nonetheless, it seems clear[16] that repentance succeeds punishment and precedes restoration, in contradistinction to ch. 2. Neither chapter, though, indicates exile.

11.1-11

א 2 כִּי נַעַר יִשְׂרָאֵל וָאֹהֲבֵהוּ וּמִמִּצְרַיִם קָרָאתִי לִבְנִי׃ קָרְאוּ
לָהֶם כֵּן הָלְכוּ מִפְּנֵיהֶם לַבְּעָלִים יְזַבֵּחוּ וְלַפְּסִלִים יְקַטֵּרוּן׃
3 וְאָנֹכִי תִרְגַּלְתִּי לְאֶפְרַיִם קָחָם עַל־זְרוֹעֹתָיו וְלֹא יָדְעוּ כִּי
4 רְפָאתִים׃ בְּחַבְלֵי אָדָם אֶמְשְׁכֵם בַּעֲבֹתוֹת אַהֲבָה וָאֶהְיֶה
ה לָהֶם כִּמְרִימֵי עֹל עַל לְחֵיהֶם וְאַט אֵלָיו אוֹכִיל׃ לֹא יָשׁוּב
6 אֶל־אֶרֶץ מִצְרַיִם וְאַשּׁוּר הוּא מַלְכּוֹ כִּי מֵאֲנוּ לָשׁוּב׃ וְחָלָה
7 חֶרֶב בְּעָרָיו וְכִלְּתָה בַדָּיו וְאָכָלָה מִמֹּעֲצוֹתֵיהֶם׃ וְעַמִּי
8 תְלוּאִים לִמְשׁוּבָתִי וְאֶל־עַל יִקְרָאֻהוּ יַחַד לֹא יְרוֹמֵם׃ אֵיךְ
אֶתֶּנְךָ אֶפְרַיִם אֲמַגֶּנְךָ יִשְׂרָאֵל אֵיךְ אֶתֶּנְךָ כְאַדְמָה אֲשִׂימְךָ
9 כִּצְבֹאיִם נֶהְפַּךְ עָלַי לִבִּי יַחַד נִכְמְרוּ נִחוּמָי׃ לֹא אֶעֱשֶׂה
חֲרוֹן אַפִּי לֹא אָשׁוּב לְשַׁחֵת אֶפְרָיִם כִּי אֵל אָנֹכִי וְלֹא־
י אִישׁ בְּקִרְבְּךָ קָדוֹשׁ וְלֹא אָבוֹא בְּעִיר׃ אַחֲרֵי יְהוָה יֵלְכוּ
11 כְּאַרְיֵה יִשְׁאָג כִּי־הוּא יִשְׁאַג וְיֶחֶרְדוּ בָנִים מִיָּם׃ יֶחֶרְדוּ
כְצִפּוֹר מִמִּצְרַיִם וּכְיוֹנָה מֵאֶרֶץ אַשּׁוּר וְהוֹשַׁבְתִּים עַל־
בָּתֵּיהֶם נְאֻם־יְהוָה׃

1When Israel was a child, I loved him,
and out of Egypt I called my son.

2The more I called them,
the more they went from me;
they kept sacrificing to the Baals,
and burning incense to idols.

3Yet it was I who taught Ephraim to walk,
I took them up in my arms;
but they did not know that I healed them.

4I led them with cords of compassion,
with the bands of love,
and I became to them as one
who eases the yoke on their jaws,
and I bent down to them and fed them.

5 They shall return to the land of Egypt,
and Assyria shall be their king,
because they have refused to return to me.

6 The sword shall rage against their cities,
consume the bars of their gates,
and devour them in their fortresses.

7 My people are bent on turning away from me;
so they are appointed to the yoke,
and none shall remove it.

8 How can I give you up, O Ephraim!
How can I hand you over, O Israel!
How can I make you like Admah!
How can I treat you like Zeboiim!
My heart recoils within me,
my compassion grows warm and tender.

9 I will not execute my fierce anger,
I will not again destroy Ephraim;
for I am God and not man,
Holy One in your midst,
and I will not come to destroy.

10 They shall go after the LORD,
he will roar like a lion;
yea, he will roar,
and his sons shall come trembling from the west;

11 they shall come trembling like birds from Egypt,
and like doves from the land of Assyria;
and I will return them to their homes, says the LORD.

Despite the obscurity of the text of ch. 11, certain significant observations are possible. Israel has declined to repent—v. 5, כי מאנו לשוב. Verse 7 is, admittedly, a crux. Notwithstanding, it is exceedingly implausible that it implies the people's repentance.[17] Verse 8 relates the beginning of God's redemptive decision in words which underscore the fact that repentance is not a factor, but is rather a spontaneous act of divine mercy—נהפך עלי לבי יחד נכמרו נחומי. The expression נכמרו נחומי parallels נכמרו רחמים in Gen. 43.30; נכמרו רחמיה in 1 Kgs 3.26. The familial relationship underlying all three verses (cp. vv. 1, 3, 10) points to the instinctive flood of compassion and love.[18] God's promise not to eradicate Israel is delivered in v. 9.[19] Although the authenticity of vv. 10-11 has been questioned,[20] the return from exile and the obedience to God follow logically. Whether

אחר יהוה ילכו of v. 10 represents repentance after the fact of redemption, or is simply a description of Israel's future loyalty, is a moot point. In either case repentance did not lead to redemption.

14.2-9

שׁוּבָה יִשְׂרָאֵל עַד יְהוָה 2
אֱלֹהֶיךָ כִּי כָשַׁלְתָּ בַּעֲוֺנֶךָ׃ קְחוּ עִמָּכֶם דְּבָרִים וְשׁוּבוּ אֶל־ 3
יְהוָה אִמְרוּ אֵלָיו כָּל־תִּשָּׂא עָוֺן וְקַח־טוֹב וּנְשַׁלְּמָה פָרִים
שְׂפָתֵינוּ׃ אַשּׁוּר ׀ לֹא יוֹשִׁיעֵנוּ עַל־סוּס לֹא נִרְכָּב וְלֹא־ 4
נֹאמַר עוֹד אֱלֹהֵינוּ לְמַעֲשֵׂה יָדֵינוּ אֲשֶׁר־בְּךָ יְרֻחַם יָתוֹם׃
אֶרְפָּא מְשׁוּבָתָם אֹהֲבֵם נְדָבָה כִּי שָׁב אַפִּי מִמֶּנּוּ׃ אֶהְיֶה ה 6
כַטַּל לְיִשְׂרָאֵל יִפְרַח כַּשּׁוֹשַׁנָּה וְיַךְ שָׁרָשָׁיו כַּלְּבָנוֹן׃ יֵלְכוּ 7
יֹנְקוֹתָיו וִיהִי כַזַּיִת הוֹדוֹ וְרֵיחַ לוֹ כַּלְּבָנוֹן׃ יָשֻׁבוּ יֹשְׁבֵי 8
בְצִלּוֹ יְחַיּוּ דָגָן וְיִפְרְחוּ כַגָּפֶן זִכְרוֹ כְּיֵין לְבָנוֹן׃ אֶפְרַיִם 9
מַה־לִּי עוֹד לָעֲצַבִּים אֲנִי עָנִיתִי וַאֲשׁוּרֶנּוּ אֲנִי כִּבְרוֹשׁ רַעֲנָן
מִמֶּנִּי פֶּרְיְךָ נִמְצָא׃

[2]Return, O Israel, to the LORD
    your God,
for you have stumbled because
    of your iniquity.

[3]Take with you words
    and return to the LORD;
say to him,
    'take away all iniquity;
accept that which is good
    and we will render
    the fruit of our lips.

[4]Assyria shall not save us
    we will not ride upon horses;
and we will say no more, "Our God",
    to the work of our hands.
In thee the orphan finds mercy.'

[5]I will heal their faithlessness;
    I will love them freely,
    for my anger has turned from them.

[6]I will be as the dew to Israel;
    he shall blossom as the lily,
    he shall strike root as the poplar;

[7]his shoots shall spread out;

his beauty shall be like the olive,
and his fragrance Lebanon-like.

8They shall return and dwell beneath my shadow,
they shall flourish as a garden;
they shall blossom as the vine,
irtheir fragrance shall be like the wine of Lebanon.

9O Ephraim, what have I to do with idols?
It is I who answer and look after you.
I am like an evergreen cypress,
from me comes your fruit.[21]

Much of the wording of 14.2-9 is uncertain. Nevertheless, certain essentials are clear. 14.2 is a plea to Israel to return to YHWH, for it has already suffered punishment כי כשלת בעונך.[22] Verse 3a is a further exhortation to verbal repentance. Whatever the meaning of v. 3b,[23] v. 4 is a confession of the futility of disloyalty to God, a rejection of idolatry, and recognition of divine mercy. These words, placed in the mouth of the people by the prophet, contain none of the elements of false repentance previously expressed by the people. There is no refusal to accept responsibility for sin, nor any selfish preoccupation with material benefit. The earnest declaration elicits God's assurance of restoration.[24] He will heal and love them, for his anger is turned away (v. 5). The many metaphors of plant growth in vv. 6-9 promise Israel's reinvigoration and secure existence under YHWH's care. The reference to the striking of roots in v. 6 appears to point to a return from exile. Certainly, the placement of this passage at the end of the book denotes a redemption after all the predicted punishments have come to pass. Equally certain, the positive response of the people to the summons to repentance is an essential prelude to redemption.

C. **Conclusions**

Among the four passages discussed above, 2.16-25 and 11.8-11 depict redemption despite the people's lack of repentance while 3.5 and 14.5-9 portray redemption preceded by repentance. It should be noted that 3.5 *predicts* repentance whereas 14.5-9 is based on a *call* to repentance to which the people respond positively.

The similarities between passages found in diverse sections of the book[25] point to the improbability of delineating an historical pattern. It would be facile to claim that an editor arranged the materials improperly, and that a rearrangement would, indeed, bring a pattern to life. It seems much more probable that the inconsistency of the message of redemption reflects the inner turmoil of the prophet. Hosea is caught on a tension wire between two poles. On the one hand is judgment: Israel has sinned, suffers, and must repent or suffer further punishment. On the other hand is mercy: Israel seems incapable of repentance, but how can YHWH, who loves the people as a father/husband, annihilate them! So, Hosea vacillates between one pole and the other, sometimes prophesying redemption dependent upon repentance, sometimes not. Sometimes Hosea feels that Israel does not deserve the benefits of YHWH's love unless it repents, and sometimes YHWH's love overwhelms his senses. The prophet finds a rationale for the latter in the exodus traditions (2.16-17; 11.1),[26] but the tension is never resolved.

Hosea, more so than his predecessor Amos, is the first prophet to exist on the edge of national disaster, and, thus, the need to relate repentance and redemption is more critical with him than with Amos. Also, he has no prophetic models to follow, for he conceives of no innocent remnant, as does Amos.[27] Therefore it is not surprising that he has more than one view of the redemptive process, given the tempestuous times in which he lived and how they must have played upon his psyche. It is more than passing interest that Jeremiah, too, will, in his lifetime, have more than one view of redemption, and will go to Hosea for *his* models.

D. **Hosea and Jeremiah**

Extensive spadework on the literary relationship of Jeremiah to Hosea was done more than fifty years ago by Gros (1930). In redemption passages Gros (1930:1-14) noted connections between Hos. 2.1 and Jer. 33.22; Hos. 3.5b and Jer. 31.12a, 14; Hos. 14.2a, 5a and Jer. 3.22; Hos. 2.1b, 11.1 and Jer. 3.19c, 31.9, 20; Hos. 2.25 and Jer. 31.27; Hos. 11.8 and Jer. 31.20; Hos. 14.5-9 and Jer. 31.3-13; Hos. 2.2 and Jer. 3.18;[28] Hos. 11.11 and Jer. 32.37b.[29] Gros (1930:30-33) concluded that Jeremiah knew and was greatly influenced by Hosea's writings.

Additionally, Ginsberg has recognized the ideological influence of Hos. 2.21-22 on Jeremiah:

> YHWH will make a new God-and-people covenant with Israel and will obviate any occasion for dissolving it like the first by making Israel constitutionally incapable of breaking it. This idea was taken over from Hosea by Jeremiah (Jer. 31.30-33 [31-34]) . . .

From the study undertaken here, it is apparent that while Hosea was, as it were, a prophet on a pendulum, swinging back and forth between the views of redemption preceded by repentance or not, Jeremiah held the former perspective and gradually came to accept the latter. Nonetheless, it seems irrefutable that whichever position Jeremiah took, he looked to Hosea for his model. It has already been pointed out (Chapter 1 above) that the prophecy of repentance and redemption in Jer. 3.6-13, 19–4.2 imitates Hos. 14.2-9 in both structure and meaning. Similarly, Ginsberg appears to be correct in his understanding of Hosea 2 and the new covenant prophecy in Jeremiah. Note the following: (1) both Hos. 2.17 and Jer. 31:32 speak of the positive relationship between God and Israel on the 'day' they left 'the land of Egypt' (2) the root זכר in Hos. 2.19 and Jer. 31.34; (3) the phrase וכרתי... ברית in Hos. 2.20 and Jer. 31.31; (4) the idea of security at the end of Hos. 2.20 and Jer. 31.28b; (5) the assurance that the people will 'know' YHWH in Hos. 2.22 and Jer. 31.34; (6) the verbal use of the root זרע in Hos. 2.25 and Jer. 31.27; (7) the eternality of the relationship in Hos. 2.21a and Jer. 31.35-37.

It may be safely concluded, then, that the writings of Hosea were critical to Jeremiah's comprehension of the relationship of YHWH to His people. Even though Jeremiah's view on repentance and redemption changed with the course of his life and that of his people, he could always turn to Hosea for support and guidance in his prophecy. Although the relationship of Jeremiah to Hosea took place across the gap of a century and more, it can truly be called that of a student to a teacher.

EXCURSUS II

The Influence of Jeremiah upon Ezekiel

To date, the basic treatment of the relationship of Ezekiel to Jeremiah has been that of Miller (1955). In that comprehensive study, Miller (1955:90-107) notes the following connections between redemption passages (or segments from units which include words of redemption): Jer. 3.6-11—Ezek. 16.44-52 (23.1-35); Jer. 24—Ezek. 11.14-21; Jer. 24.7—Ezek. 11.19; 36.26; Jer. 31.31ff.—Ezek. 36.24ff.; Jer. 30.19 והרבתים (31.27)—Ezek. 37.26 והרבתי אותם (36.10. 37); Jer. 31.5—Ezek. 36.8; 34.27; Jer. 30.8—Ezek. 34.27; Jer. 30.18—Ezek. 36.33; 28.25; Jer. 30.10—Ezek. 34.28; the new covenant concept of Jer. 31.31-34 reflected in Ezek. 11.17-20; 36.24-27; בקרב in Jer. 31.33 and Ezek. 36.27; 11.19; חדש in Jer. 31.22, 31 and Ezek. 11.19; 18.31; 36.26; Jer. 31.34—Ezek. 36.25; Jer 31.33—Ezek. 11.20; ונתתי את תורתי in Jer. 31.33—ואתן את רוחי in Ezek. 36.27; Jer. 31.29—Ezek. 18.1ff.; Jer. 31.30—בעונו appears elsewhere in the Bible only in Ezek. 3.18, 19; 7.13, 16; 18.18; 33.6, 8, 9; Josh. 22.20; Jer. 23.1-2—Ezek. 34.1-16; Jer. 31.10, יקבצנו ושמרו כרעה עדרו—Ezek. 34.12, כבקרת הרעה עדרו; Jer. 30.11—Ezek. 11.13; Jer. 30.14—Ezek. 23.5; Jer. 31.19—Ezek. 21.17; Jer. 29.5—Ezek. 28.26; Jer. 23.1, הוי רעים—Ezek. 34; Jer. 23.1, אבר—Ezek. 34.4, 16; Jer. 23.1-2, פוץ—Ezek. 34.5; Jer. 23.2, נדח—Ezek. 34.4, 16; Jer. 23.2, על הרעים—Ezek. 34.10; Jer. 23.2, צאן -Ezek. 34.11, 12; Jer. 23.1, צאן מרעיתי—Ezek. 34.31; Jer. 23.5, והקמתי לדוד—Ezek. 34.23, והקמתי . . . עבדי דוד; Jer. 3.19, נחלת צבי צבאות—Ezek. 20.6, 15, צבי הוא לכל הארצות; Jer. 4.1, ואם תסיר שקוציך—Ezek. 11.18, והסירו את כל שקוציה.[1]

To the above linguistic and ideological links, Raitt (1977:204) adds the expression of divine forgiveness in Jer. 31.34; 33.8 and Ezek. 36.25, 29, 33; 37.23; and the phrase כרתי להם ברית עולם in Jer. 32.40 and Ezek. 37.26. However, Raitt's most significant contributions to the relationship of Ezekiel to Jeremiah lie in the realms of content and structure of the 'deliverance oracles' in both books. In regards to content, the redemption prophecies of Jeremiah and Ezekiel share in nine characteristics.[2] Additionally, (1) all these oracles are in prose, (2) they contain the covenant formula, (3) 'God endows the people with something to make them more able to live in relationship with him' (such as the new heart), (4) the covenant is reinitiated, and (5) 'there is some clear remembrance of the judgment and the implication that the deliverance is in tension with it' (1977:123-24). Most of these oracles have a two element structure—'God Intervenes to Deliver his People (from Exile)' and then 'God Reinitiates a Relationship with his People' (1977:132). Some oracles contain a third element which most often appears between the two just mentioned—'God Creates a Transformation' (1977:130-36).

Nor are the above comments exhaustive. Ezek. 16.51-63 is dependent upon a variety of verses in Jeremiah: the use of the root צדק in Jer. 3.11 and Ezek. 16.51, 52; the roots כלם, בוש, and נשא in Jer. 3.25; 31.19 and Ezek. 16.52, 54, 61, 63; the expressions על כל אשר עשו in Jer. 31.37 (cp. 3.7) and מ/לכל אשר עשית in Ezek. 16.54, 63; Jer. 2.2 (cp. Hos. 2.17) and Ezek. 16.60 (cp. vv. 22, 43[3]); ברית עולם in Jer. 32.40 and Ezek. 16.60. It thus appears (against most commentators)[4] that Ezek. 16.1-63 is one unit based not only upon Jer. 3.6-11, but also upon the rest of that chapter, as evidenced by the similarities with Jer. 3.25. Similarly, Ezekiel 18 is not only influenced by Jer. 31.29-30, but also by Jer. 31.32-33, as witnessed by Ezek. 18.31. This does not mean that Ezekiel simply imitates Jeremiah—unlike Jer. 3.12-13, 19–4.2, Ezek. 16.53-63 does not depict contrition and repentance preceding redemption, but predicts that God's redemptive acts will evoke the people's remorse. In like fashion, in Jer. 31.32-33 it is God who transforms the people's heart, while in Ezek. 18.30-31 it is an act which the people are called upon to do.

Thereby arises a crucial issue. Given that Ezekiel's 'new heart and new spirit' passages are dependent upon Jeremiah, do Ezekiel and Jeremiah have the same perceptions of the relationship of repentance to redemption? Are the changes in Jeremiah's thought matched by those in Ezekiel's?

Although there is an assumption in Ezekiel that repentance is required in order for the *individual* to survive (3.16-21; 18; 33.10-20), the concept of repentance as a necessary precondition for redemption is absent. There are only slight indications that if the people ceased their idolatrous acts, the way to redemption would be paved: 14.1-11 (note the covenant formula in v. 11); 18.30-32 (cp. מכשול עון in v. 30

with 14.3, 7; 44.12); 20.30ff. (particularly v. 39). This idea, though, is not essentially different from that found in Jer. 44.1-30 (Chapter 4, above). Indeed, in Ezekiel contrition and remorse do not precede but, rather, succeed redemption: 16.54, 63; 20.43; 36.31; 39.26. In 36.32 and 43.10-11, the very message of restoration is supposed to elicit remorse, but this is in no way critical.

Only in 11.18 does repentance appear to be an integral part of the redemption process.[5] There, after YHWH will have returned Israel to its land and before the giving of the new heart and spirit, the people will remove all their idolatrous abominations from the land. This statement is unique in the book and may well accurately reflect the date of 8.1—592 BCE. It will be recalled that although in Jer. 24.4-7 and 29.10-14 redemption is promised, repentance is predicted (not demanded) as part of the restoration process. This marks the transition stage in Jeremiah's thought on repentance and redemption. Ezek. 11.14-21 (written just shortly after the letter in Jeremiah 29?) may reproduce that thought. It may well be the case that Jeremiah 29 (and 24?) is a source for Ezekiel 8–11. Note that in both passages the inhabitants of Jerusalem are contrasted with the first exiles—the former are doomed and the latter are promised restoration (cp. Ezek. 11.16-17 with Jer. 29.10, 14). False advice is the subject of Ezek. 11.3 and Jer. 29.8-9 (though addressed to different situations). Ezek. 11.3, לא בקרוב בנו בתים, is contrasted to Jeremiah's message to the exiles, בנו בתים ושבו (Jer. 29.5)—in other words, the Jerusalemites claim that the prophetic warning of YHWH's judgment will not soon be crystallized[6] (cp. Jer. 16.1-3), so that one may securely plan for the future (cp. 11.15), while Jeremiah contends that YHWH's promise of restoration will not soon be fulfilled, so the exiles should wait patiently and build normal lives. The promise of God to be a 'small sanctuary' in Ezek. 11.16 echoes the assurance of Jer. 29.12-14a that God will hear their prayers (v. 12) and will be found by them (vv. 13, 14a) even in exile. It is not surprising, then, that the implicit repentance in Jer. 29.12-14a (and 24.7b?) is paralleled by Ezek. 11.18.[7] However, as mentioned above, in the later prophecies of redemption in Ezekiel repentance plays no part.

In conclusion, it cannot be demonstrated that Ezekiel ever prophesied that repentance was a determinant of national destiny. Even in Ezek. 11.18 repentance is a secondary factor to YHWH's redemptive acts. This accords well with Ezekiel's historical background as a prophet. For him, the destruction of Jerusalem is a foregone conclusion. Thus he enters into prophecy at Jeremiah's second stage of thought on repentance and redemption and follows his teacher into the third stage in which a passive Israel is redeemed by YHWH, cleansed of its sins, and transformed inwardly to insure the eternal certainty of its obedience and prosperity under YHWH's benevolence.

EXCURSUS III

Jeremiah and Isaiah (34-35) 40-66

Initial, albeit superficial, investigation on the influence of Jeremiah upon II Isaiah (Isa. 34–35, 40–66)[1] has been conducted by Cassuto (1973:141-77). If one culls from his study those passages concerning redemption in Jeremiah which affected II Isaiah, the following list evolves:[2] Jer. 30.5, ואין שלום, with Isa. 48.22; 57.21; Jer. 30.10-11, ואתה אל תירא עבדי יעקב... ישראל... כי אתך אני, with Isa. 41.8, 10, 13-14; 43.1, 5; 44.2; Jer. 30.14, 15, רב... עצמו, Isa. 47.9; Jer. 30.16, בשבי ילכו, with Isa. 46.2; the LXX of Jer. 30.16, κρέας αὐτῶν... ἔδονται, with Isa. 49.26; Jer. 30.17, כי נדחה קראו לך ציון, with its opposites in Isa. 60.14; 62.4, 12; Jer. 30.18, ומשכנתיו ארחם with Isa. 49.13; Jer. 30.19, תודה וקול, with Isa. 51.3; Jer. 31.7, רנו..., with Isa. 44.23; 49.13; 52.9; 54.1; Jer. 31.8 with Isa. 43.6; 49.12; Jer. 31.9, אובילם, with Isa. 55.12; Jer. 31.9 with Isa. 49.10; Jer. 31.10 with Isa. 40.11; 29.1; 42.12; 48.20; Jer. 31.12, והיתה... כגן רוה, with Isa. 58.11; Jer. 31.16, שכר לפעלתך, with Isa. 40.10; 62.11; Jer. 31.23, הר הקדש, with Isa. 56.7; 57.13; 65.11, 25; 66.20; Jer. 31.33, תורתי בקרבם, with Isa. 51.7; Jer. 31.34, ולחטאתם לא אזכר, with Isa. 43.25; Jer. 31.35 with Isa. 51.15; Jer. 50.34, גאלם... יהוה צבאות שמו, with Isa. 47.4: Jer. 33.2 with Isa. 45.18; Jer. 4.2 with its opposite in Isa. 48.1; Jer. 33.3 with Isa. 48.6; Jer. 3.8 with Isa. 50.1; Jer. 32.40 with Isa. 55.3; 61.8; Jer. 3.22, שובו... ארפה, with Isa. 57.17-18; Jer. 3.17, ונקוו..., with Isa. 60.9; Jer. 32.41, וששתי עליהם, with Isa. 62.5; 65.19; Jer. 32.18, ומשלם... אל חיק, with Isa. 65.6; Jer. 33.10-11, ישמע... קול, with Isa. 65.19; Jer. 29.5 with Isa. 65.21.

In light of the above, Cassuto's conclusion (1977:160) is not surprising:

> it is clear that the formal links between Deutero-Isaiah and Jeremiah are numerous and, at times, exceedingly close. Undoubtedly, the prophecies of the prophet of Anathoth were very

> familiar to the prophet of the Babylonian exile, for he often recalled them, and the words and expressions of the earlier prophet influenced his own utterances. The anonymous author of Isaiah xl–lxvi certainly studied . . . the writings of [Jeremiah] . . . The echo of Jeremiah's language in the prophecies of Deutero-Isaiah constitutes invaluable evidence of the importance attributed to Jeremiah's words in the days of the Babylonian exile.

To the above list, Paul (1969:118)[3] adds that the father-son image in Jer. 31.20 (19) as well as the words המו מעי לו רחם ארחמנו are echoed in Isa. 63.15-16, המון מעיך ורחמיך . . . כי אתה אבינו. Like Cassuto, Paul (1969:120) concludes that 'those passages which are clearly recognized as stemming from Jeremiah and which . . . were adapted by Second Isaiah, establish the writings of the former as a very important source for the literary creativity of the latter'.

In addition, in the present study it has already been illustrated that Isa. 35.3-10 reflects Jer. 31.7-14[4] and that Isa. 54.9-10; 66.22 are conscious developments of Jer. 31.35-37; 33.20-22, 25-26.[5] Furthermore, connecting threads are noticeable between: Isa. 40.2 and Jer. 50.20; Isa. 40.3 and Jer. 31.15 (the use of קול); Isa. 40.3 and Jer. 31.9 (the use of דרך); Isa. 48.19; 55.13; 56.5 and Jer. 33.18, לא יכרת . . ., Isa. 51.3 and Jer. 33.11 (ששון, שמחה, קול, תודה); Isa. 51.11=35.10 and Jer. 31.11, 12, 13;[6] Isa. 51.4 and Jer. 50.17; Isa. 55.2 and Jer. 31.14 (דשן, נפש); Isa. 55.6; 65.1 and Jer. 29.12-13; Isa. 58.9, אם תסיר . . ., and Jer. 4.1; Isa. 59.21 and Jer. 31.33, זאת הברית . . ., 36, ימשו . . . זרע; Isa. 60.19 and Jer. 31.35, שמש לאור יומם . . . ירח; Isa. 65.17 and Jer. 3.16, ולא יעלה על לב ולא יזכרו בו; Isa. 66.12-13 and Jer. 31.20.

Despite the influence of Jeremiah on II Isaiah in terms and concepts of redemption, it is exceedingly doubtful that II Isaiah reflects a transposed Jeremianic interpretation of the relationship between repentance and redemption. Rather, II Isaiah should be approached in consideration of the historical background of Isaiah (34–35) 40–66—the days encompassing the Persian conquest of Babylon (ca 540 BCE). This approach is complicated by the question of authorship. Most modern scholars are persuaded that Isa. 40–55 is, in the main, the product of one author and that Isa. 56–66 was produced later by another, or others.[7] The prevailing argument in favor of this opinion has been that whereas Isa. 40–55 was written from an exilic perspective, 56ff. originates among those who have returned from Babylon.[8]

A divergent view, whose adherents include Kaufmann (1970:73-94) and Haran (1963:73-102), holds that Isa. 40–66 belongs to only one prophet. Kaufmann (1970:69-73) maintains that these prophecies precede the building of the Second Temple and come from a Babylonian locale. Although Haran agrees that the prophecies were written before the rebuilding of the Temple, he (1963:29-32, 73-102) contends that chs. 40–48 were written in Babylon by the same hand that later, after 539 BCE, wrote 49–66 in Jerusalem. In other words, according to Haran, the differences between Isa. 40–48 and 49–66 are reasonably explainable by changes in environment and circumstances —the prophet speaks first in exile before the return, and then prophesies as a member of the restored community.

To detail the relative arguments between the two perspectives just cited is beyond the scope of the present study. Nonetheless, Kaufmann and Haran build their case for the single authorship of Isa. 40–66 convincingly. This view gains additional support from the logical relationship of 54.9-10 to 66.22 noted in Chapter 3 above. The idea that Isa. 40–66 is the work of one author is therefore herein accepted.

A scan of II Isaiah reveals that elements and hints of repentance are sparse in chs. 40–54, but increase dramatically from 55 on:

(1) confession appears in 42.24, הלוא יהוה זו חטאנו לו, followed in 43.1 by YHWH's assurance of Israel's redemption, אל תירא כי גאלתיך;
(2) 43.22-24, 26-27 is a rebuke which encircles a divine promise to forgive Israel for God's own sake, i.e. not for any repentant act—43.25, אנכי אנכי הוא מחה פשעיך למעני וחטאתיך לא אזכר;
(3) repentance *is* demanded in 44.22, but the effect is weakened by the presupposition of YHWH's forgiveness and redemption— מחיתי כאב פשעיך וכענן חטאתיך שובה אלי כי גאלתיך;
(4) 49.5 avows the goal of return to YHWH, לשובב יעקב אליו וישראל לו יאסף, but 49.6 uses the root שוב in an apparent reference to return from exile, ונצירי ישראל להשיב (cp. 51.11), as the root אסף is used in 52.12 (cp. 58.8; 62.9). So 49.5 may not refer to repentance at all, but, rather, to physical restoration;
(5) קוי יהוה (40.31) and קוי (49.23) are those who, it seems, trust in God's saving acts and not the penitent (cp. 51.5, אלי איים יקוו; 60.9). Similarly, 50.10 refers to those who depend upon God, ירא יהוה... יבטח בשם יהוה וישען באלהיו;
(6) 51.1, רדפי צדק מבקשי יהוה; 51.7, ידעי צדק עם תורתי בלבם; and 54.17, עבדי יהוה, may all speak of the righteous of Israel, but

again there is no indication that they are repentant, only a conviction that they will be redeemed (51.3, 5-6, 8, 11, etc.);

(7) 53.4-6 is another confession, but there is no evidence that this is an integral part of redemption;

(8) the first sign that repentance is a critical part in the redemption process is 55.6-7, דרשו ה׳ בהמצאו קראהו בהיותו קרוב יעזב רשע דרכו ואיש מחשבתיו וישב אל ה׳ וירחמהו ואל אלהינו כי ירבה לסלוח;

(9) a demand for righteous action, which resembles 55.6-7, appears in 56.1-2;

(10) 56.9–57.13 are reproofs;

(11) 57.20-21 promises the wicked no peace;

(12) 58.1-12 is a cry for moral behavior (vv. 2, 6-7, 9b, 10a) in order for the people's prayers to be accepted (v. 9a), for secure life (v. 11), and reconstruction, apparently, of ruined cities (v. 12);

(13) 58.13-14 promises that if the people will keep the Sabbath, they will enjoy the security and fruitfulness of the land;

(14) 59.1-8 is another rebuke followed by the people's confession in vv. 9-13. Verse 20 concludes that only those who repent from rebellious acts against God will be redeemed, ובא לציון גואל ולשבי פשע ביעקב;

(15) After several prophecies of comfort and redemption, the people's confession reappears in 64.4-6 as a prelude to a plea for the restoration of Jerusalem;

(16) Following a rebuke to idolaters (65.1-7), in 65.8–66.17, 22-24 God's servants are promised the heritage of the restored land and Jerusalem.

It is no secret that the dominant theme in chs. 40–54 is that of unconditional redemption. The only clear call for repentance is in 44.22c, but, as has been seen, it is mitigated by the surrounding phrases. Nonetheless, its appearance here, anomalous though it may be, testifies to II Isaiah's unwillingness to eliminate permanently every vestige of repentance from the redemption process. If chs. 40–54 belong to one period in the life of the prophet, it appears that it is a time when his attention is focused on the mercies of YHWH for His people. Little else is of significance.

On the other hand, fully half of Isa. 55–66 is devoted to the theme that complete restoration of Jerusalem and the land will come only to those who are obedient to God's commands. Repentance is explicitly mentioned in 55.6-7 and 59.20, the latter as a precondition for redemption. Confession occurs in 59.9-13 and 64.4-6.

It is now permissible to hazard a reconstruction of the relationship of repentance to redemption in II Isaiah. The significance of repentance in 44.22c is minimized in comparison to God's mercies. It probably reflects the prophet's mind and mood after Cyrus's conquest of Babylon. The call for repentance in 55.6-7 (cp. 56.1-2) may have been uttered on the eve of the return from exile, when the approaching hour of emigration from Babylon alerts the prophet to the need to make sure that all is in order, that 'all the bases are covered'. The reference to repentance in 59.20 along with the harsh words preceding it, were probably spoken in Jerusalem to a people whose expectations for rebuilding of the land had not been realized. Now that they are returned to their land, the old pre-exilic concept of obedience to God in order to ensure national success is again the standard of religion.

CONCLUSIONS

A. The Three Stages of Jeremiah's Thought

The in-depth analysis of the prophecies of redemption in Jeremiah presented here has revealed that the prophet's thoughts concerning the relationship of repentance to redemption progress through three stages.

The first stage takes place during the reign of Josiah and is evidenced by 3.6-13, 19–4.2; 31.2-9, 15-22. At that time, the young Jeremiah believed in the possibility of repentance and saw it, along with YHWH's mercy, as the determining condition for redemption. It is important to realize that Jeremiah did not stand only within the tradition of the Sinaitic covenant. In truth, the covenant is ultimately only a *symbol* of the relationship between God and Israel. It represents a dominant *image* in the Hebrew Bible—YHWH as suzerain and Israel as vassal—but certainly not the only one. A variety of images expressive of the bond between God and the people coexisted in the mind of the ancient Israelite, and Jeremiah was no exception. Note the significance of the husband-wife and father-son images in the book. If the covenant denotes a binding legal relationship viewed under the concept of justice, then the family relationship denotes love which results in acts of mercy. In the words of Heschel (1962:part 2, 10),

> The covenant is an extraordinary act, establishing a reciprocal relation between God and man; it is conceived as a juridical commitment. Pathos, on the other hand, implies a constant concern and involvement; it is conceived as an emotional engagement. From the point of view of the unequivocal covenant-idea, only two forms of relationship between God and people are possible: the maintenance or the dissolution of the covenant. This rigid either-or is replaced by a dynamic multiplicity of forms of relationship implied in pathos.

Thus Jeremiah, in his youth, may (like his predecessor, Hosea) have vacillated between the two concepts of justice and mercy in attempting to articulate the motivations for redemption (see the comments on 30.5-17 in Chapter 4, above).

The second stage emanates from the period between 597 and 587 and is represented in 3.14-18; 24.4-7; 29.10-14; 50.4-7. The prophet's constant calls for repentance went unheeded by the population, and punishment materialized in the form of the Jehoiachin exile. These exiles have suffered for their sins and are, therefore, now favored. A subtle shift occurs as the element of divine mercy outweighs that of human repentance in the mind of Jeremiah. The prophet has begun to despair of the people's ability to return of its own accord to its God.

The third and final stage belongs to the period of the destruction of Jerusalem, and is expressed in 31.27-37; 32.37-41; 33.1-26; 50.17-20 (23.1-8 may also belong here; 42.9-12 is contemporaneous). After a short period of calm, the full fury of the Babylonian storm broke upon Jerusalem; the Temple was razed and Judah exiled. During those horrible days of holocaust, the aged prophet again voiced his hope for the future restoration of his people. Now, on the basis of his tragic experience, yet consumed by his belief in YHWH's eternal commitment to Israel, Jeremiah abandons the principle of free will and the attendant demand for repentance. Redemption would be solely the work of God, who would establish a new covenant with Israel, as permanent and unshakable as creation itself.

B. The Character of the Redaction

The analysis of Jeremiah's prophecies of redemption reveals that in most of these passages not only is there the lack of a dtr. ideology, but rather there exists an *anti*-dtr. perspective—the absence or secondary nature of repentance. Indeed, the view of redemption in Deuteronomy and 1 Kings 8 reflects a pre-Jeremianic concept—one from the days of Hosea which was held by Jeremiah during the reign of Josiah (his initial stage). Thus, the claim of a dtr. redaction for these prophecies is invalid. How does one, then, explain existing similarities between the language of Deuteronomy and Jeremiah? It was Kaufmann (1967:III, 440) who suggested that Jeremiah was taught Deuteronomy at Anatoth. Jeremiah *was* a student of Deuteronomy, just as he was of Hosea, but he developed his thinking in his own way, based upon his own experiences. Clearly, the findings of this

study raise a challenge to the entire theory of a dtr. redaction of Jeremiah.

Is one then not allowed to speak of *any* redaction of Jeremiah? Not necessarily. The book itself testifies to the work of Baruch ben Neriah (36.1-32). It is conceivable that Baruch couched at least some of Jeremiah's words in his own phraseology. Certainly, the literature in the book serves witness to a biographer. Furthermore, additions have been noted in the passages under discussion (50.33-34; 51.50-51), although these are no evidence of a systematic redaction.

If the prophecies examined here are a representative sample, then it may be hypothesized that certain prophecies underwent a rewording by one or more disciples of Jeremiah, who, nonetheless, were faithful to the thought of the prophet. In any case, it is imperative that the investigator of a prophecy in Jeremiah, who believes that he has discovered the footsteps of a redactor, be very careful lest he limit the potential of the prophet himself to shade his own words and ideas.

C. The Prophet among his Peers

The material on repentance and redemption in Amos, Hosea, Ezekiel and II Isaiah places the thought of Jeremiah in historical perspective. Although unquestionably familiar with Hosea, Jeremiah was no imitator but a true student—one who used his mentor's teachings but extended them in directions and circumstances unforseeable by his precursor. As Jeremiah used the works of Hosea, so would Ezekiel and II Isaiah adopt and adapt Jeremiah's words—conscious of themes, motifs, and language they would yet strike out on their own paths, based upon their own perceptions.

If one takes Jeremiah, Ezekiel, and II Isaiah as forming a continuous line from the latter part of the seventh century BCE to the latter part of the sixth, a general pattern emerges. As long as destruction had not overtaken Judah, prophecies of redemption still contain the preconditional element of repentance (dovetailing with the standard prophetic calls for repentance to avoid divine punishment). However, once Jerusalem is destroyed and the full exile underway, redemption is seen as totally dependent upon God's beneficence. With the Persian defeat of Babylon and the advent of the actual restoration to the land, the requirement of repentance begins to reappear. Finally, when the people once again find themselves in their homeland, the demand to return to YHWH regains the prominence it had before the Jehoiachin exile.

It appears that the effect of the cruelty of destruction and the harshness of exile served in large measure to wipe out the need for repentance. The manifestation of the punishment is a motivation for divine forgiveness and purification of the people. In the exilic situation, the very demand to repent (in order to bring about national redemption) might have been more than the people could have borne. However, once the redemptive process had palpably begun, once YHWH had begun to respond to the prayers of Israel, the people could no longer remain passive, the concept of repentance was reactivated. Now, the gift of a new covenant and a new heart, which would have obviated the need for repentance since it would have eliminated sin, would withdraw in the consciousness of the people to await future needs.

In the final analysis, the essential factor in the mind of each of the three prophets of the exile was the unbreakable eternality of YHWH's love for Israel. Twenty-five centuries later, we, who have survived a different holocaust and who live in a still hostile world, find solace in that knowledge.

NOTES

Notes to Introduction

1. Petuchowski (1968:180), notes that the English word 'repent' is derived from the Latin, meaning 'to make sorry'.

2. For the explication of Jer. 3.12-13, see Chapter 1, below. All citations are from Kittel, 1968.

3. In connection with the expression והתודו את עונם, 'they shall confess their sin', in Lev. 26.40, there appears יכנע לבבם הערל, 'their uncircumcised heart shall be humbled', in v. 41. The latter expression apparently denotes confession accompanied by prayer and acts of contrition, cp. 1 Kgs 21.27-29; 2 Kgs 22.11, 19; 2 Chron. 12.6-7; 32.20, 24-26; 33.12-13, 19 (only in 2 Chron. 7.14 is √כנע mentioned together with prayer *and* repentance). Thus this phrase does not testify to obedience to God's commands. Similarly, the idiom ירצו את עונם, 'they will accept (the punishment for) their sins' (vv. 41, 43) does not denote a return to God but only that the sins of the people have been expiated through the sufferings of destruction and exile—cp. v. 43 with Isa. 40.2 (see Hoffman, 1972 on Lev. 26.41; cp. Ehrlich, 1899 on Lev. 1.4). Despite the fact that refusal to obey God is mentioned explicitly in vv. 14, 15, 18, 21, 27, repentance in the prophetic sense is lacking in Leviticus 26 (and see Milgrom, 1976a:121-23).

4. Synonyms of שוב may be סוג and סור, in the negative sense (cp. Ps. 80.19; Jer. 32.40). See, further, Holladay, 1958:155-56.

5. Holladay (1958:117-18), notes that approximately 30% of all instances of covenantal שוב occur in Jeremiah.

6. The emphases are Eichrodt's. Cp. Petuchowski's criticism (1968:176).

7. Similarly, see von Rad, II, 1965: 215-16.

8. The emphases are Kaufmann's. The brackets are added here.

9. These works are significant contributions in both content and methodology to the study of Jeremiah.

10. See also Raitt, 1971; 1974.

11. See also the general remarks of Alter, 1981:14-15.

12. Two methodological aids in this task are Greenberg, 1978 and Tov, 1981.

13. See J. Berridge's book review (1982:114) of Carroll. Carroll never comes to grips, for example, with Raitt's evidence.

14. So, for example, Jeremiah scholarship is much the poorer because of the ignorance of Kaufmann in Hebrew. Greenberg's translation and abridgment (1961) of Kaufmann encapsulates the latter's 81-page Hebrew section on Jeremiah in a mere 18 pages (pp. 409-26). Similarly, A. Rofe's punctilious work (1975) on parallel passages in Jeremiah appears to be unknown to non-Jewish scholars of Jeremiah.

15. A translation and revision of Weiss, 1967 (Hebrew). Weiss kindly allowed the present author to photocopy portions of the manuscript before publication, for which he is thanked.

16. Greenberg (1980:164) acknowledges his debt to Weiss.

17. This work had its origins in an M.A. thesis in the Bible Department at the Hebrew University of Jerusalem. Professor Greenberg was the thesis director. This book is primarily a stylistic revision of a doctoral dissertation written at the University of California, Berkeley, accepted in 1983.

Notes to Chapter 1

1. The practice of some scholars of citing page numbers in reference to commentaries has been eschewed here, except when the reference is to be found outside the verse under discussion.

Translations of Biblical texts within the chapter narratives are paraphrases by the author of May, 1973.

2. In his earlier composition (1914), Mowinckel had referred to a dtr. *source*.

3. Hyatt believes that the dates of 1.2; 25.3 and 36.2 are also imaginary.

4. Holladay is referring to Hyatt's commentary.

5. Thiel owes much to Hermann (1965), although the former's work is more comprehensive than the latter's. McKane (1981:231) expands upon Thiel's view, but his article suffers from two flaws: lack of references to relevant secondary sources, and many methodologically problematic assumptions. The latter criticism is justified when one considers the assumption that 'it is unlikely that the interpretation of vv. 1-5 which is assumed by vv. 6-11 is the right one . . .' (p. 230). How does McKane know that vv. 6-11 are not connected *associatively* to vv. 1-5, and, therefore, the passage is *not* an interpretation? This question is not even considered.

6. Holladay and Jobling are only recent representatives of a commonly held view.

7. Hobbs (1974:23-29) concludes that Jer. 3.1-5 and Deut. 24.1-4 were independent developments of an earlier law. It seems probable, though, that to a deuteronomist, Jer. 3.1 would appear to be based upon Deuteronomy. See also Long, 1976:386-90.

8. Morag defines משבה as a 'sharp deviation from the straight path, a type of sickness—its correction is done by healing', as in Jer. 3.22 and 8.5.

9. Examples of the repetitions in ch. 2 are: 'they did not say "where is YHWH"'—vv. 6, 8; 'they followed (vanity, worthlessness)'—vv. 5, 8; 'your abandoning YHWH your God'—vv. 17, 19.
10. Mowinckel states that the prose speech of 3.6-12a, 14-18 is parallel to, and breaks the original continuity of, 3.1-5, 12b-13, 19-20.
11. The authenticity of v. 12a may be indicated by the fact that the words 'Go and call' are found elsewhere only in 2.2. Cp. 13.1; 19.1—'Go and buy'; 28.13; 34.2; 35.13; 39.16—'Go and say'; 17.19—'Go and stand'.
12. Cf. the comments of Rashi, Joseph Kara, and Bright (1965).
13. Böhmer follows Weiser (1960).
14. The sections are: 3.1-5, 12b-14a, 19-20, and 21-25.
15. Thus, Holladay's structure (see note 14 above) is also faulty.
16. Verse 19 is influenced by the language and sound of Hos. 11.8:

Hos. 11.8	*Jer. 3.19*
אין אתנך אפרים אמגנך ישראל	איך אשיתך בבנים
איך אתנך כאדמה אשימך כצבאים	ואתן לך ארץ חמדה
	נחלת צבי צבאות גוים

(in opposition to Talmon [1969:128-29], who thinks that the *Vorlage* of the MT to Jer. 3.19 had אמן יהוה כי or אמנה כי instead of איך).

It is possible that Jeremiah borrowed here from this prophecy of Hosea due to the similar context—prophecies of redemption to Ephraim.

17. One should not assume that the use of the verbs בגדה and בגדתם בי ('faithless') in v. 20, which are from the same root as the words used to describe Judah in vv. 7, 10 and 11 (בגודה... בגדה), indicates that the reference here is to Judah. The usage of the verbs in v. 20 is analogous to the use in 5.11, where betrayal describes both halves of the people: כי בגוד בגדו בי בית ישראל ובית יהודה נאם יהוה, 'for the house of Israel and the house of Judah have surely been faithless to me, the speech of YHWH'.
18. Thus, vv. 19-20 are an even later addition.
19. Weinfeld (p. 33), though, believes that 3.19–4.4 is 'a prophecy joined to the section containing the prophet's words on the ark of the covenant (3.16-18)'.
20. Holladay neither attempts to describe nor refute the arguments for the attachment of 4.1-2 to the previous verses.
21. The speech of YHWH begins with the interrogative הראית 'have you seen', which appears in the Bible only in prophetic speech where God addresses the prophet—1 Kgs 20.13; 21.29; Ezek. 8.12, 15, 17; 47.6. This is further evidence of Jeremianic authorship of this passage.
22. A reference to vv. 4-5?
23. The form Y מ X צדקה is reminiscent of Gen. 38.26, where, similarly, the behavior of Judah (!) was more reprehensible than that of Tamar. It is conceivable that Jeremiah was influenced by this passage.
24. The words הצפון, מצפון, צפונה, צפון are found 25 times in the book,

and, without exception, they refer to either a geogaphical direction or a boundary found *outside* the borders of the Promised Land (e.g.: 1.13, 14, 15; 3.18; 16.15; 25.26; 46.6). Nonetheless, it is not impossible that the call to turn back to YHWH is extended to all the remnants of the Northern Kingdom, whether they have been exiled or have remained upon the land, for the prophet is interested in the redemption of all the ten tribes.

25. There is no reason to assume (as do Rashi, Joseph Kara, Kimḥi, and later, Duhm and Volz) that the imperative שובה refers to return from exile, for there is no evidence for this in vv. 6-13. The verse itself is concerned with God's relationship to His people and not with the triangular identification of God, people, and land. The Septuagint reads ἐπιστραφητι πρός με =return to me. Similarly, cf. Welch (1928:84); Heschel (1962: I, 104); Raitt (1971:34, 37). Holladay (1958:133-34), who tends to understand שובה as meaning 'repentance', is undecided and admits the possibility that the term refers to return from exile to the land. As evidence for this meaning, he brings the imperative in Jer. 31.21b—שובי בתולת ישראל שבי אל עריך אלה, 'return Virgin of Israel, return to these your cities'. However, in contradistinction to 3.12, in ch. 31 the promise of God to return His people from exile *precedes* the imperative—ושבו בנים לגבולם 'your children shall return to their border' (31.17). Hyatt, in his commentary, defends both approaches—Jeremiah intended שובה to refer to repentance, but an editor misunderstood it as indicating return from exile, and therefore placed v. 14, which begins with שובו and refers to return from exile, after v. 13.

26. אכן לשקר מגבעות makes no grammatical sense; a verb is missing and the most common one that goes with לשקר is שבע (cp. Jer. 5.2; 7.9). Thus, v. 23a is a fitting counterpart to 4.2, ונשבעת... באמת, 'and if you swear... in truth'.

27. המון may mean either multitude (cf. Gen. 17.4) or tumult (cf. 1 Sam. 4.14).

28. בשת means Baal; cp. Jer. 11.13.

29. Kimḥi; Luzzato (1876); Yellin (1939:I, 116-17), all interpret the second appearance of תשוב as 'rest' by reference to Isa. 30.15 בשובה ונחת תושעון.

30. Rashi, Joseph Kara, Kimḥi, Abarbanel (1955), and, among the moderns, von Orelli and others all understand ולא תנוד as the apodosis. Streane sees it as the end of the condition.

31. In reality, there is a fourth choice—'If you return, the speech of YHWH, to me, then you shall return (from exile)'. While this has the advantage of agreeing with ולא תנוד, it does not take into account the phrase 'the speech of YHWH' which seems situated purposely to divide אלי from the condition. Additionally, see the comments in the text rejecting the first choice.

32. Cf. Orelli.

33. Similarly, Abarbanel.

34. Skinner (1922:86-87) suggests a similar structure, but without extensive detail.

35. Also, cf. note 16 above and Gros, p. 6.

36. In certain regards, our reconstruction resembles Holladay's (see p. 29 above). Holladay (1976:30ff.) breaks up the blocks as follows: 2.5-37 (the first half of the Harlotry Cycle); 3.1-5, 12b-14a, 19-25 (the second half of the Harlotry Cycle); 4.1-4 (prelude to the Foe Cycle); 4.5-6.30 (the Foe Cycle). He views 2.2-3 as foreshadowing this whole complex.

37. Most recent scholarship interprets ושוב אלי as a question, 'and would you return to me?', implying that this is impossible—cf. Bright (1965); Nicholson (1973); Lundbom (1975:37); Long (1976:26). The logic behind this interpretation is drawn out by Nicholson: 'The point being made here is that Israel . . . is even worse than a divorced woman who could not be remarried to her first husband: for Israel . . . had played the harlot with many lovers, thus rendering her uncleanness even more intense'. However, grammatically the infinitive absolute may be used as an imperative, as Henderson pointed out in 1851 (cp. 2 Kgs 4.43; Isa. 21.5; Jer. 3.12). Additionally, there are good ideological reasons for the imperative, as illustrated by Hos. 11.8-9:

> 'How shall I place you Ephraim, give you up Israel, how shall I place you as Admah, put you as Zeboim! My heart is over-turned within me, together My compassions are stirred. I shall not vent My anger, I shall not return to destroy Ephraim, *for I am God and not man*, holy in your midst, and I shall not come upon the city'.

The familial relationship of father and son, expressed in vv. 1-4, evokes YHWH's mercies in v. 8, resulting in the promise of v. 9 not to punish Ephraim according to the measure of strict justice, 'for I am God not Man'. As seen in note 16, Jeremiah has been influenced by v. 8. It is not far-fetched to posit that he was also influenced by v. 9 and that Jer. 3.1 may be interpreted accordingly—if God's familial relationship with Israel (husband-wife) evokes His mercies, it might cause Him to override strict justice and call for Israel to return (and cp. v. 4, where the father image is represented).

38. 4.5-31 and the following chapters all deal with the threat of punishment.

39. Similarly, cf. Holladay (1976:172).

40. Carroll (1981:15-16) argues vociferously against the accuracy of this account, as is his wont vis-à-vis the prose passages of *Jeremiah*: 'It is a story created to legitimate the role of the scribe in the creation and transmission of the Jeremiah tradition, just as the finding of the lawbook in the temple in Josiah's time . . . is an attempt to legitimate Deuteronomy by the deuteronomistic historians'.

41. Concerning חסיד (v. 12), Sakenfeld (1978:194-96) has shown convincingly that חסד refers to covenant faithfulness.

42. For example, McKenzie (1968:xviii-xx and commentary) attaches Isaiah 35 to Deutero-Isaiah, whom he dates to 550-540 BCE.

43. Cf. Henderson and Orelli. Volz claims that v. 14 is an addition either

and from the hand of a priest or a supporter of the cult. However, the mention in both vv. 14 and 12 of טוב as well as the roots רוח and נפש runs counter to that possibility.

44. Cf. also Weiser and Martens, pp. 73-74. The latter discusses thematic contacts but misinterprets the connection.

45. For another study which illustrates how one literary unit was dependent in its composition on two others, see Unterman, 1980:161-66.

46. Cf. also Holladay, 1966:238-39.

47. Cf. the similar language in 2.2; cp. e.g. the Targum, the medieval rabbinic commentators, Holladay (1964:164) and Bright (1965). The rabbinic commentators (as does Nicholson, 1973, today) understand 'from afar' in v. 3 as a reference to the *time* of the Exodus, but it is almost certain that geographic distance is meant, since מרחוק never refers to time in the Bible. The Septuagint rendering, that God appeared 'to him' from afar, seems preferable to MT 'to me', so that מרחוק should be understood as referring to the place of exile, the במדבר 'wilderness' of v. 2. Kimḥi, also, understands 'to me' as referring to the exiles.

48. For חסד here as God's persistent covenant faithfulness, see Sakenfeld (1978:195).

49. The roots בנה 'build' and נטע 'plant' appear frequently side-by-side in Jeremiah (1.10; 18.9; 24.6; 29.5, 8; 31.28; 42.10; 45.4). Their purpose is to symbolize the opposite of destruction and exile. Cf. Bach (1961:7-32). Cf. also Martens's comprehensive critique of Bach (more positive than negative; 1972:208-27).

50. The expression נטעו נטעים וחללו, 'the planters shall plant and enjoy the fruit' in v. 5 is an apparent reversal of the curse of Deut. 28.30 (cp. Deut. 20.6). Similarly, Amos 9.14 reverses 5.11 (cp. Zeph. 1.13).

51. Kara, Luzzatto, Henderson, and Orelli hold that the call of the 'watchers' is their announcement of the beginning of the harvest festivals.

52. The Septuagint reads 'for thus says God *to Jacob*'; similarly, Kimḥi who explains that רנו and ליעקב must be understood in the reverse order. However, the plural inidication of the verbs militates against this view.

53. Streane, Hyatt (1956), and Bright (1965), for example, translate 'for Jacob', and Nicholson (1973) 'for Jacob's sake', but 'to Jacob', although awkward in English, may be not inapplicable since Jacob is addressed later on in the verse (see in the text). Also, בראש הגוים is unclear (cf. Brown, 1966:90b, definition IV)—does the ב mean 'because of', 'in front of', 'with'?

54. Cp. e.g. Pss. 111; 117; 135.1-4.

55. As opposed to 'his people' in the Septuagint and the vast majority of commentators and translators.

56. The exact expression בכי ותחנונים appears only in these two verses in the entire Bible.

57. שמוע שמעתי, 'I have surely heard', is reminiscent of Exod. 3.7; 22.22;

1 Sam. 1.11—in each instance God will act of behalf of the oppressed. יסרתני ואוסר כעגל לא למד, 'you have chastened me and I was chastened like an untrained calf' may have been written under the influence of Hos. 10.10-11, באותי ואסרם ואספו עליהם עמים באסרם לשתי עינתם ואפרים עגלה מלמדה אהבתי לדוש..., 'In my desire I will chastise them and nations shall be gathered against them when they are chastised for their double iniquity and Ephraim is an untrained calf that loves to thresh' (cf. Gros. 1930:12); Deut. 8.5, וידעת עם לבבך כי כאשר ייסר איש את בנו יהוה אלהיך מיסרך, 'Know in your heart that, as a man chastises his son, YHWH your God chastises you', or the wisdom tradition: Prov. 19.18, 20, יסר בנך כי יש תקוה... שמע עצה וקבל מוסר למען תחכם באחריתך, 'chastise your son while there is hope... listen to advice and accept chastisement that you may gain wisdom for your future' (cp. Prov. 29.17, 19), and, perhaps, even religious confessions: Ps. 118.18, יסר יסרני יה ולמות לא נתנני 'YH has surely chastised me but He has not given me over to death'. השיבני ואשובה (cp. Jer. 15.19, אם תשוב ואשיבך; Zech. 1.3, שובו אלי ואשוב אליכם; Mal. 3.7, שובו אלי ואשובה אליכם; Lam. 5.1 השיבני יהוה אליך ונשובה) indicates that אחרי שובי means 'after I turned away (from You)' (cp. 8.4, היפלו ולא יקומו אם ישוב, 'will they fall and not rise—will he turn away', ולא ישוב 'and not turn back'), in agreement with Orelli, Volz, Rudolph, and Bright (1965), and against Levinger (1962:167). ואחרי הודעי means 'after my sin was made known to me', like דעי עונך in 3.13 (cp. p. 32 above), as opposed to Baar (1968:21), who understands the root ידע here and in Prov. 10.9; 14.33 to mean 'make submissive', 'humiliate', and 'chastise'.

58. The interpretation of this verse was arrived at independently, although Trible (1976-77:275) has an identical understanding of the mother image here, and for the same reasons. See also Trible, 1976:368-69.

59. Cp. Gen. 1.2; the only other appearance of the root רחף is in Deut. 32.11, where God is compared to an eagle hovering over its young. Perhaps motherly care is alluded to at the start of creation; cp. Cassuto, 1961:24-25.

60. Cp. Isa. 35.8. Ps. 48.12-15 seems to have more than just a passing connection with Jeremiah 31. Note the similar language—ישמח, סבו, שיתו לבכם, and the references to Zion, the rejoicing daughters, and God leading the people (and God's saving acts?—משפטיך). If this is a pilgrim's psalm, then did Jeremiah draw upon it? (There does not appear to be any cogent reason to date it after Jeremiah's time.)

61. עד מתי used in terms of repentance is found in Hos. 8.5 and Jer. 4.14.

62. In agreement with Kaufmann (1967:III, 466), except that he accepts vv. 10-14 as from the period of Josiah.

63. Similar confessions which the prophet places in the mouths of the people are found in 14.7-9, 20-22, but they result in a negative response from God (14.10-12; 15.1). Cf. Hyatt (1956); Blank (1961:98, 104); Eissfeldt

(1966:113-14); Berridge (1970:158). Since these confessions do result in a negative response by God, they may have been written somewhat later than the prophecies of redemption to Ephraim, for they may indicate that Jeremiah has serious doubts about the people's willingness to repent.

Notes to Chapter 2

1. Cp. Hyatt (1951:74).
2. There he cites Brueggemann (1968:387-402).
3. Raitt first stated this discovery in 1974:180.
4. The LXX version of vv. 10-14 will be examined in the text below.
5. Verses 8-10 are the organic continuation of 24.4-7.
6. Contra Weinfeld (1972:348).
7. Cp. Weinfeld (1972:334).
8. Hoffmann (1961) refers to this prediction as a 'promise'.
9. Kaufmann's view; see above.
10. The German original appeared in 1943.
11. Originally published in 1947.
12. For a survey of the position of scholarship on the two editions of the dtr. history, see Nelson (1981). This study, though, predates the most recent articles of Levenson and R.E. Friedman mentioned below. Nelson, also, shows no familiarity with the theological observations of Raitt.
13. Following N. Lohfink.
14. Noted by Weinfeld (1972:369).
15. I thank R.E. Friedman for bringing this to my attention.
16. Cp. 2 Kgs 25.22 with Jer. 40.5-7; 2 Kgs 25.23 with Jer. 40.7-8; 2 Kgs 25.24 with Jer. 40.9; 2 Kgs 25.25 with Jer. 41.1-3; 2 Kgs 25.26 with Jer. 41.17–42.1, 8, 11, 14, 15, 17, 19; 43.1-5, 7.
17. E.g. Kuenen (1886:270-71).
18. For similar sentiments see Rowley (1963:192).
19. On the relationship of repentance to redemption in Hosea, see Excursus I, below.
20. For other arguments suggesting the early date of 1 Kings 8, see Kaufmann (1967:II, 261, 267-68). There is no evidence that these arguments have been considered by the scholars cited in this section.
21. As mentioned earlier, Berridge (1970:63-68) singles out 24.1-10 as the pure form of the prophetic-literary pattern—the vision and its explanation.
22. As Volz, Rudolph, Hyatt (1956), Bright (1965), and others translate. It should be remembered that the subject under discussion is human 'knowledge' concerning God, and neither divine nor human 'knowledge' concerning man. Therefore, despite the similar verb, the following verses are not comparable: Exod. 32.22; 2 Sam. 3.25; 1 Kgs 5.17; Ps. 94.11.
23. For this view, see Streane and Hyatt (1941:386). Also, see the

discussion in Chapter 3 below on the meaning of the word 'torah'.

24. Similarly, see McKenzie (1955:22-27) and Mays (1969).

25. Likewise, the *New English Bible* translates '*for* I am the Lord' (NEB, 1970). Also, Martens (1972:53).

26. For broader discussions of 'love of YHWH', see Moran (1963:77-87); McCarthy (1965:144-147); Weinfeld (1972:81-83, 333, 368); McKay (1972:426-35).

27. For אהב see the previous note. For ידע see Huffmon (1966:31-37).

28. See Weinfeld (1972:274).

29. According to Bultmann (1965:I, 698), in the Bible 'Knowledge is not thought of in terms of the possession of information. It is possessed only in its exercise or actualization'. Similarly, see Driver (1966:xv); Heinemann (1973:697-700); Scott (1969:212-13).

30. The appearances of the formula in 30.22 and 31.1 are not included in this survey since the context there does not contribute to its understanding.

31. 31.33 and the surrounding verses will be examined in detail in Chapter 3. Suffice it to say that YHWH's beneficent actions are found in 31.27-28, 35-37.

32. Cp. Martens (1972:323). 'Being God's people is possible only within the relationship of a wholehearted returning to Yahweh. This turning is not so much a precondition of being God's people as it is the evidence for it'.

33. This view is held by Volz; Dietrich (1936:122-24); Eichrodt (1967:II, 468-69); Nicholson (1970:81); von Rad (1965:216); Wolff (1951:142); Raitt (1977:178); Martens (1972:52). Raitt (1971:32-33) points out the Protestant belief which is mirrored in this interpretation (!).

34. Of course, it is *possible* that Deut. 30.8 refers to Israel's return to God *after* YHWH has 'circumcised their heart', but this seems unlikely, for what would be the need of repentance *then*? It is also possible that 30.8-10 are a later addition to 30.1-7, but that is not a necessary interpretation.

35. Naḥmanides' commentary to Deut. 30.6. He also suggests the first answer.

36. Herein lies the explanation for the ideological difference between 24.4-7 and 18.7-10 (against Nicholson, p. 57 above). Chapter 18 is concerned with a sinning people which has not yet suffered divine punishment. In such a condition it is still possible to hope for repentance. However, in 24.4-7 divine punishment has already broken forth.

37. Thus the relationship of Jeremiah to either Jehoiachin or Zedekiah is not at issue (against Hyatt, p. 56 above).

38. Verses 16-20 may well be an organic part of the letter. Note also that vv. 16, 20 are addressed directly to the exiles, while vv. 17-19, 21-23 speak of those who remained in the land and the false prophets in the third person. Thus, the word אל in vv. 16 and 21 should be translated 'on' and not 'to' (see particularly v. 16, אל כסא דוד, 'on the throne of David'). Compare the verses cited in Brown *et al.* (1966:41). Interestingly, Hyatt (1956) has

proposed that vv. 16-20 were not recorded by the Septuagint due to a homoioteleuton—both vv. 15 and 20 end with the word בבלה, 'to Babylon'.

39. See Driver (1906) and Streane.

40. These verses will be investigated in Chapter 4.

41. Neither this list nor the one concerning the root בקש is exhaustive.

Notes to Chapter 3

1. The term 'night' is used here as a counterpart to 'eve' and in the sense of Wiesel's soul-shattering work, *Night* (1960). One who wishes to understand the effect of the destruction of Jerusalem on the people of Judah must appreciate both the physical horror and the resulting devastating despair which, together, threatened to crush completely their religious spirit.

2. For example, Skinner (1922:332), on his interpretation of v. 32, 'I hazard the suggestion that this is closely analogous to the manner in which Jesus speaks of the law...'; Smith (1929:280), 'This is, as has been said (Giesebrecht), a prophecy of Christianity which has hardly its equal in the Old Testament. It is the Covenant which Jesus Christ the Son of God accepted for Himself and all men and sealed with His own blood'; Hyatt (1958:106-107), 'Jeremiah... first enunciated... what has come to be a central principle of Protestantism'; Böhmer (1976:79), in his closing comment on vv. 31-34, 'Die Einheit von Gottes Zorn und Gnade wird erst das Kreuz Jesu Christi offenbaren'. More subtle is the comment by Clements (1965:113): 'Whilst Jeremiah knew that the law was a gift of Yahweh's grace, *he knew also that it was the curse of the law that had brought disaster on the nation* in his own lifetime' (emphasis added).

3. See also Hertzberg (1952:74).

4. *Ibid*. For Carroll's specious, antiquated comments on the post-exilic Jewish community, see pp. 224-25. One can only wonder how Carroll views Christianity with its doctrine of original sin which requires the blood sacrifice of a god to effect human salvation.

5. See note 1, above.

6. Martens (1972:213-14) agrees with this assessment.

7. See Cassuto (1973:149-52) and Bright (1951:22), who assert Jeremiah's authorship over these verse.

8. רגע הים appears elsewhere in Job 26.12.

9. For similar verses, cp. 9.24; 23.5; 30.3; 33.14-15; 48.12; 49.2; 51.47, 52; 1 Sam. 2.31; 2 Kgs 20.17 // Isa. 39.6; Amos 8.11; 9.13-14.

10. This formula is also found in Jer. 3.16-17; 7.32 // 19.6; 16.14-15 // 23.7-8. Weiss (1962:256) and Weinfeld (1976:17-19) noted the affinity between the verses but did not relate their observation to the question of literary unity.

11. The word זרע appears in a similar context in prophecies of

redemption in 23.8; 30.10; 33.22, 26 (a parallel prophecy to 31.35-37). In 31.36, 37 'Israel' symbolizes both parts of the nation; see Gelin (1950:163). The words of the prophet appear to stand here in opposition to the words of retribution in 7.15 (cp. 2 Kgs 17.20). זרע of Israel in a liturgical context appears in Pss. 22.24; 105.6 // 1 Chron. 16.13. The appearance of זרע of Israel in a prophecy of redemption is understandable and even expected when one considers its usage in the promises to the patriarchs: Gen. 12.7; 13.15-16; 15.5; 16.10; 17.7-8; 22.17; 26.4; 28.14; 32.13, etc.

12. Cp. the distinctive comments of Weiss (1962:258).

13. Rudolph and Hyatt (1956) noticed this contradiction, which led them to opt for the possibility that vv. 29-30 were borrowed from Ezekiel 18, and are thus inauthentic.

14. Weiss (1962:258) understands vv. 29-30 to be directed by Jeremiah to the people in their present situation:

> At the time when the individual denies personal responsibility because of resignation or lethargy (caused by the general situation) or due to some other reason, the prophet will not subject his listeners to the truth that the individual is chained within the links of the tradition of his ancestors and is entrapped in the net of the fate of his surroundings, his city and his people. Rather he will place before the eyes of his flock the truth that the individual is indeed a free person and his fate is in his own hands, therefore he will not speak of collective retribution but of individual retribution.

Weiss, therefore, is of the opinion that it is impossible to learn from the words of the prophet his doctrine of retribution concerning the exiles in the future. Thus it should not be assumed that Weiss, who does not posit an organic connection between vv. 29-30 and vv. 31-34, would point here to a real contradiction.

15. The phrase בימים ההם/הימים ההם appears another 44 times in the Bible. It always refers to an event that will take place in the future, or one that has already taken place in the past and has not been continued into the present. Additionally, 'ביום that I held their hand to take them out of the land of Egypt' refers only to the period of the exodus. Similarly, see 7.22; 11.4, 7; 34.13. It is therefore impossible to claim that 'those days' in v. 33 signify the period which includes the 'day' of v. 32 and all succeeding days from the exodus until the day of exile or the day of the establishment of the new covenant.

16. Abarbanel interprets 'after those days': 'after their redemption and ingathering I will put my torah within them . . .'; similarly, Altschuler, *Metẓudat David*, 'after they return from exile'. Cp. the attempts of Rudolph and Coppens (1963:14) to come to grips with these words. In opposition, Weiss (1962:256) contendes that both vv. 27-30 and vv. 31-34 are divided 'into two primary units . . . by two indications of time' (v. 27, הנה ימים באים, as opposed to v. 29, בימים ההם, and v. 31, הנה ימים באים, as against v. 33, אחרי הימים ההם). However, Weiss did not consider the essential difference

between '*after* those days' and '*in* those days'. Similarly, Bright (1965) translates, '*when* that time comes' (!).

17. Weippert (1979:338, 346) notes that the new covenant is conditional upon the forgiveness of sins.

18. Weiss (1962:254-55) is correct in his argument that a comparison of vv. 29-30 with 16.14-15 proves that the people *shall say* 'Each one . . .'

19. The same is true of 16.14-15 // 23.7-8, 'It shall no longer be said, "YHWH lives who has brought up the children of Israel from the land of Egypt", but "YHWH lives who has brought up the children of Israel from the land of the North"'.

Despite the connection between Jer. 31.29-30 and Deut. 24.16, 'Fathers shall not be put to death for sons, and sons shall not be put to death for fathers, each man shall die for his own sin (בחטאו)' (and compare the parallel verse in 2 Kgs 14.6), this does not indicate the hand of the dtr. redactor: the noun עון is never used by the dtr. editor of Kings and appears in Deut. only in 5.9 and 19.15! It does appear in Jeremiah 24 times (and the verb twice). עון, which refers to the fathers' act of breaking the covenant with God, appears in 11.10; 14.20; 16.10-12; 32.18.

20. See Kimḥi, 'for I shall forgive their sins that they transgressed while they were still in exile and I will give them a heart to know me'.

21. See Jer. 33.8, 'And I shall purify them from all their sins . . . and I shall forgive . . .' (cp. 50.20). See also Ezek. 36.25-26, which is influenced by Jer. 31.33-34, 'I will sprinkle purifying water upon you and you shall be purified, from all your impurities . . . I will purify you and I shall give you a new heart . . .'

22. Carroll does not cite Duhm in this regard. For a negation of this view, see Kaufmann's polemic (1967:III, 471 n. 65).

23. For the relationship of these verses to Deuteronomy, see Weinfeld (1972:299-303).

24. For similar understandings, see Harrelson (1962:673b); Lindars (1968:131); Mays (1969) on Hos. 4.6.

25. Compare Ostborn (1945:89-111) on the priest as the teacher of the torah. Also, de Vaux (1965:353-55). Weinfeld (1976:28-29) thinks that v. 34 is written on the background of the demand in Deuteronomy that the parents teach the torah to the children.

26. Independently arrived at, but noted also by Long (1976:386-90), who, however, remarked only concerning the opening word הן.

27. The pattern . . . ה . . . אם, which appears in Hag. 2.13, is found elsewhere in Job 14.14.

28. Isa. 11.3 should also be included among these verses. In place of MT, והריחו ביראת יהוה, 'and his delight (?) shall be in the fear of YHWH', one should read והרהו, 'and he shall teach him'. Two reasons militate against the acceptance of והריחו: (1) the context cannot tolerate a verb derived from the root ריח, 'smell', for what can it conceivably mean to 'smell' ביראת יהוה? (2)

there is no Hebrew verb derived from the root רוח 'wind, spirit'. On the other hand, several passages testify on behalf of the reconstruction והרהו:

(a) Isa. 11.3 appears to be dependent upon the passage concerning Bezalel in Exod. 35.31-35, particularly vv. 31, 34.

Exod. 35.31, 34	*Isa. 11.2-3*
וימלא אתו רוח אלהים בחכמה בתבונה ובדעת...ולהורת נתן בלבו	ונחה עליו רוח ה׳ רוח חכמה ובינה... רוח דעת ויראת ה׳ והריחו ביראת ה׳
and he has filled him with the spirit of God with wisdom, with understanding and with knowledge... and he has placed in his heart the ability to teach	and the spirit of YHWH shall rest upon him, a spirit of wisdom and understanding, a spirit of knowledge and fear of YHWH, והריחו in the fear of YHWH

(b) Compare 2 Kgs 17.28, an example of a priest teaching others how to fear God, והיה מורה אותם איך יראו את יהוה, 'and he taught them how to fear YHWH'.

(c) The word הורהו appears in 2 Kgs 12.3 in a similar context, 'and Jehoash did that which was right in the eyes of God all his days which Jehoiada the priest taught him (הורהו)'.

Thus, in Isa. 11.3 'the spirit of YHWH' will instruct the 'shoot' in the 'fear of YHWH' (and contrast the seductive 'spirit' of 2 Kgs 22.21).

It is possible to reconstruct the steps which led to the corruption in the following manner: the second ה in והרהו was accidentally rendered ח by a copyist (interchanges between ה and ח in Qere and Kethib are well known, e.g. 1QIsa. חוברי in place of MT הברו in 47.13). This mistake created an incomprehensible word. A later copyist who saw before him והרחו added the י, and so formed a word which is suitable at least in sound to the many occurrences of the word רוח in the passage. It is also possible that this copyist was influenced by reference to the senses of sight and hearing in v. 3, מראה עיניו, 'the sight of his eyes' and משמע אזניו, 'the hearing of his ears', and so formed the word והריחו as an indication of the sense of smell.

29. It is not inconceivable that ימושו in Isa. 54.10 is borrowed from Jer. 31.36 and that תמוט was influenced by Ps. 125.1, כהר ציון לא ימוט לעולם ישב, 'like Mt Zion which cannot be moved but abides forever'. Concerning the root מוט see also Isa. 24.19; Ps. 46.3, and elsewhere in Psalms.

30. The idea of eternality appears in 13.15, כי את כל הארץ אשר אתה ראה לך אתננה ולזרעך עד עולם 'for all the land which you see I will give to you and your descendants *forever*'.

31. For similar views, see Lofthouse (1925:89-90); Rudolph; von Rad (1965:216-17); Bright (1966:197).

32. Contra Kaufmann (1967:III, 471) and Levinger (1962:184).

33. This fortuitous image is borrowed from my teacher, J. Milgrom.

34. Similarly, see Ezek. 18.31, 'make yourselves a new heart and a new spirit', contrasted with 36.26 (//11.19), 'I will give them a new heart and a new spirit'.

35. For similar perspectives concerning the new covenant, see Kimḥi to v. 30, 33, 35; Naḥmanides to Deut. 30.6; Altschuler, *Metẓudat David* to v. 32; Kaufmann (1967:III, 470); Heaton (1968:381-83); and particularly the enlightening analysis of von Rad (1965:II, 213-14),

> The content of the Sinai covenant was the revelation of the torah . . . the revelation of Israel's election . . . by Jahweh and his will as expressed in law. This torah is also to stand in the centre of the new covenant . . . The reason why a new covenant is to ensue on the old is not that the regulations revealed in the latter proved inadequate, but that the covenant has been broken because Israel had refused to obey it . . . the new factor . . . is . . . a change in the way in which the divine will is to be conveyed to men . . . the new thing is to be that the whole process of God's speaking and man's listening is to be dropped . . . Jahweh is . . . to put his will straight into Israel's heart . . . We should completely ignore the distinction between outward obedience and obedience of the heart, for it scarcely touches the antithesis in Jeremiah's mind . . . Deuteronomy, too, insists on an obedience which springs from the heart and conscience . . . however, Jeremiah goes far beyond Deuteronomy, for in the new covenant the doubtful element of human obedience . . . drops out completely. If God puts his will directly into their hearts, then . . . the rendering of obedience is completely done away with, for the problem of obedience only arises when man's will is confronted by an alien will. Now however the possibility of such a confrontation has ceased to exist for men are to have the will of God in their heart, and are only to will God's will. What is here outlined is the picture of a new man, a man who is able to obey perfectly because of a miraculous change of his nature.

36. Volz, Welch (1928:218-19), Rudolph, and Carroll (1981:215), also, claim these verses as a late addition.

37. Yet this expression is already attested in Arslan Tash in the 7th cent. BCE. See Zevit (1977:110-18).

38. For example, Weippert (1973:23) notes that the phrase בכל לבי ובכל נפשי in Jer. 32.41 refers to God, unlike the occurrences in dtr. where it refers to Israelites. In many ways, Weippert's work parallels this one, even though she deals with other material.

39. Cp. Raitt's position presented in Chapter 2 above.

40. On ירא, see Bamberger (1924:39-53). Lists of verses may be found in Weinfeld (1972:332-33). For the Near Eastern background, see Weinfeld (1976:30 n. 49).

41. Note the comment by Altschuler, *Metẓudat David* to v. 39, 'i.e. I shall bend the heart so that they shall have one heart and they shall no longer be doubtful and hopping upon two branches and they shall not turn from walking on one path to fear YHWH all the days'.

42. On p. 214 von Rad compares 32.37-41 with 31.31-34.

43. With Raitt, and against Hyatt, Nicholson, *et al.*

44. The disappearance of the element of repentance may also be reflected in Jeremiah's perception of the generation of the desert. 'To return to YHWH'

assumes that at some point in history the ideal relationship between God and Israel was a reality, but in the course of time, due to the people's bad behavior, it became corrupted (see Holladay, 1958:53).

It is possible that Jeremiah, early in his life, believed that this harmonious existence occurred after the exodus from Egypt (2.2). Eventually, though, Jeremiah dropped this view and came to believe that during the period of the desert wandering YHWH's faithfulness to Israel was not reciprocated (7.24-25; 31.32; 32.30). The new covenant prophecy does not acknowledge a period during which Israel was fully obedient to YHWH's torah.

Notes to Chapter 4

1. In addition to prophecies of redemption, there exist prophecies of comfort of the type which predicts the destruction of nations which have harmed Israel: cp. 2.1-3; 10.25; 25.12-14; 46–51.

2. On שרירות see now Spencer (1981:247-48).

3. On Hos. 11.8-11, see Excursus I.

4. Ish-Shalom (1904:541-49) contends that Josiah had the ark hidden because it was becoming a fetish for the masses. Weinfeld (1976:23) agrees with this view. The idea that Josiah hid the ark goes back to the Talmud (*b. Yoma* 52b; cp. *Shekalim* 6.1-2) on the basis of 2 Chron. 35.3. Haran (1963:46-58) discounts 2 Chron. 35.3 as biased, and suggests that the ark was removed when the image of Asherah was placed in the holy of holies by Manasseh (pp. 50-51). As Weinfeld (1976:24) notes, this was already suggested by Rashi and Kimḥi to 2 Chron. 35.3. Haran (1963:51) terms Jer. 3.16 'Decisive evidence as to the disappearance of the ark after Manasseh', since he believes that verse (as well as the surrounding ones) to be from Jeremiah's early prophecies.

5. פקד here may also have a cultic sense; cp. Exod. 38.21, פקודי המשכן אשר פקד על פי משה... The same may well be true of ולא יעשה עוד which, instead of meaning 'it shall not be made any more' (Streane), possibly refers to worship cp. 2 Kgs 17.29, 30, 31 (cp. Talmon, 1981:64-65).

6. Weinfeld delineates the influence of Lev. 26.4-13 upon Ezek. 34.25-30.

7. The authenticity of Hos. 3.5 has been questioned. For the different scholarly treatments, see Ward (1966). Recently, the verse has been ably defended by Andersen and Freedman (1980).

8. For similar sentiments, see Greenberg (1978:144).

9. Tov (1981:296) takes a different view of the LXX of *Jeremiah*: 'it now has to be recognized that the LXX and 4QJer[b] reflect not a different *textual* form (recension) of Jer., but an earlier *edition* of the book'. Nonetheless, Tov does not indicate that he considers complete passages absent in the LXX, such as 33.14-26, to be of a later date than that of the 'earlier edition'.

10. Cp. pp. 116, 132.

11. Nor may it be coincidental that Ezekiel uses the root טהר as does Jer. 33.8—cp. Ezek. 36.25, 33; 37.23.

12. Carroll relies heavily on Pohlmann. The latter (1978:129-33, 225), however, accepts 42.9-10 and possibly v. 11 as belonging to the original kernel of the story.

13. For the varying viewpoints on the formation of the biographical material in Jeremiah, see Thompson, 1980:38-43 (47-50).

14. Note particularly v. 4, יבאו . . . יחדו, and 3.18, ויבאו יחדו.

15. See the previous footnote and cp. v. 5, ונלוו, with 3.17, ונקוו. Other parallels: v. 5—the desire to return to Zion, with 31.6; v. 7 with 2.3; 30.16; 17.13; 14.8; 31.23, etc.; v. 4, √בכה with 3.21; 31.8.

16. Similarly, Segal (1967:382). Segal, as in the present study, accepts the authenticity of 50.17-20 and rejects 50.33-34; 51.50-51 'due to several reasons which cannot be elaborated here'.

Notes to Excursus I

1. As quoted in Eissfeldt (1966:401). The original German may be found in Wellhausen (1963:96).

2. See his review of literature on p. 245.

3. Cf. Gordis's analogy of Amos and Isaiah (1940:250).

4. See the comment of Smith (1896:195).

5. In accordance with Milgrom's scheme (1964:170).

6. In this regard it may be noteworthy that Lev. 26.5, which has such obvious similarities to 9.13-15, is a reward not to the repentant, but to the consistently obedient to the divine laws (v. 3).

7. The following is a condensed and edited version of Unterman, 1982:540-50. In addition to the passages discussed here, that article deals also with 5.4-7; 5.14–6.4; 6.11b–7.2; 7.10, 13-16; 10.3; 10.12; 12.7-10; 13.14. None of those passages contains a promise of redemption.

8. On the relationship of 2.16-25 to the rest of the book, see Biram (1955:124-39). On the matter of Baalism, see Halpern (1976:11-13).

9. For a review of the controversy, see Halpern (1976:9-12). Ginsberg (1971:1018) lowers the *terminus ante quem* to 734. The authenticity of 1.1 has also been debated (cp. Isa. 1.1; Mic. 1.1, and the works cited here).

10. 2.1-3 appears out of context. Wolff (1974), Ward (1966) and others have placed these verses at the end of the chapter, and, indeed, they have no continuity with the surrounding verses. Ideationally, they discuss the effects of redemption. Once removed, 1.9 flows smoothly into 2.4 and creates a larger unit starting with 1.2: cp. ופקדתי in v. 4 and 2.15; והשבתי in v. 4 and 2.13; √זנה in v. 2 and 2.4, 6, 7; √שבר in v. 5 and 2.20; vv. 4, 6, 8 with 2.24-25. 1.7 has long been considered a Judahite interpolation (cf. the com-

mentaries), but the succession חרב, קשת, מלחמה appears only here and 2.20 in the entire Bible! The verse itself predicts God's mercies and salvation to Judah.

11. However, in order for them to hold this opinion they have been forced to place vv. 8-9 after v. 15. Kaufmann (1967:III, 107), Wolff (1974), and Ginsberg (1971:1011), too, see this as genuine repentance.

12. Cheyne (1897) comments, 'it is not so much the expression of penitence, as of a longing to escape from the sense of misery'. Von Rad (1965:II, 142) adds, 'Israel . . . failed to see that she had been brought into a *status confessionis* before Jahweh because of these gifts; rather, she fell victim to a mythic divinisation of husbandry and of its numinous, chthonic origins'. Ward feels that because Israel 'has not changed her means or goals, she has not changed at all'. Cassuto, (1973:I, 124) argues that 'she designated the Lord "my first Husband", and thus showed that she did not yet realize who and what He was to her . . . the implication is that she thinks that others like Him exist'.

13. J. Milgrom (private communication) holds that Lev. 26.6 is the real source of Hos. 2.20. Note that Lev. 26.6, 20 present a similar contrast to Hos. 2.20, 14!

14. Modern scholarship has concerned itself with the authenticity of 3.1-5 as well as its relationship to the previous chapters, and the dating of these verses (for treatments of the text, see Ward). For an unusual approach, see Halpern, who claims that vv. 4-5 refer back to the period of the Judges as a symbolic lesson for Hosea's personal life.

15. Ginsberg's definition (1971:1013), cp. Jer. 31.12, 14.

16. Contra F.I. Andersen and D.N. Freedman, who refer to v. 5 as 'cryptic remarks'.

17. Logically, repentance in v.7 would be incongruous after v. 5. ואל על is interpreted as a reference to Baal by Wolff (1974) and Ward. Others (Cheyne and Halpern) were preceded by Rashi and Abarbanel (cp. Ehrlich to the latter).

18. Cp. also Kaufmann, 1967:III, 145 n. 75. Contra Andersen and Freedman.

19. One must take exception to the reading and translation by Andersen and Freedman of v. 9, 'I will certainly act out my burning anger. I will certainly come back to destroy Ephraim. For I am a god and not a human. I, the Holy One, will certainly come into the midst of your city'. Despite their acknowledgment of the 'sentiment' of v. 8, Andersen and Freedman maintain that for YHWH not to act with strict justice would be deceitful. How do they explain the (now) paradoxical depiction of restoration that appears immediately in vv. 10-11? They give no explanation. All they say is 'There is an abrupt change at this point'. Such sophism is hardly worthy of these two excellent scholars. The compassionate content of vv. 8 and 10 necessitates the negative לא in v. 9 and not the asseverative. Furthermore,

they ignore the fact that v. 9b is a parallelism:

כי אל אנכי ולא איש
בקרבך קדוש ולא אבוא בעיר

Thus, if YHWH comes into the city, according to Andersen and Freedman, then He also claims that He is a man.

20. For a review of scholarship see Ward.

21. These verses appear as vv. 1-8 in the RSV.

22. Cp. 5.5. The reference is apparently to destruction of some type (cf. Abarbanel) for in 4.5 כשל is paralleled to דמה, which indicates death (cp. 10.7, 15 and the contexts there). Also, cp. Wolff.

23. Cp. the commentaries and Gordis (1955:88-90).

24. Contra Wolff.

25. Calls to repentance which are in reality parts of prophecies of judgment, and, consequently, express the refusal of Israel to repent, are found in 2.4 and 12.7 (with vv. 8-10; v. 9 is the people's response to the call in v. 7). False or insincere repentance appears in 2.10; 5.6; 6.1-3; 7.14 and 8.2 (10.3 has not been included here because it appears to contain words of mourning which the prophet predicts the people will utter, rather than repentance). Refusal to repent is found in 7.2, 14, 16; 8.10; 11.5; 12.9. 5.4 and 7.2 hint at the inability of Israel to repent due to their habitual sins.

26. 1.7 is incongruous. On 2.1-3 see note 10 above.

27. Amos 9.8-10 is perfectly consistent with Amos 2.6-7, 12; 3.9; 4.1; 5.11-12.

28. Gros (1930:23-24) sees Jer. 3.18 as a later addition.

29. Gros (1930:24) sees Jer. 32.37ff. as a later addition.

Notes to Excursus II

1. It has been observed, also (Chapter 4 above), that Jer. 23.8 is expanded by Ezek. 34.8, 12-13, 25, 27.

2. See the list in 1977:115-17.

3. Noted by Miller (1955:107).

4. E.g. Eichrodt (1970); Wevers (1969); Carley (1974); Zimmerli (1979).

5. Ezek. 11.1-21 is seen by Zimmerli as an addition, as two additions (vv. 1-13, 14-21) by Wevers, Carley, and Cooke (1936), and vv. 14-21 as an addition by Eichrodt. Greenberg (1980), while envisioning the possibility of the integrity of vv. 14-21 (p. 153) casts doubt on vv. 17-20 as 'suspicious' due to their similarity to 36.24-28 (1980:163). In laying out his very proper methodology, Greenberg ignores one of the questions which he himself says should be asked of a passage: 'To what extent are themes, peculiarities or difficulties recurrent elsewhere? In identical or variant form?' (p. 146). This issue is dealt with in the text below. On the meaning and significance of vv. 14-21, Greenberg comments (p. 153),

due weight must be given, however, to the incidental nature of the consolation: what consoles the exiles is the prediction of Jerusalem's destruction. Whether this would have been regarded by the audience as a happy ending is itself a question.

How Greenberg could posit that even the speaker might have considered the destruction of Jerusalem as a consolation for the exiles is incomprehensible. See below.

6. The interpretation of Rashi, Kimḥi, and Abarbanel.

7. As mentioned earlier, Miller noted the relationship between Jer. 4.1 and Ezek. 11.18. However, Jer. 4.1 is conditional where Ezek. 11.18 is assured. It may very well be that Ezek. 11.18 draws also, but not solely, on Jer. 4.1.

Notes to Excursus III

1. Although it is common today in scholarship to designate Isa. (34–35) 40–55 as Deutero-Isaiah and Isa. 56–66 as Trito-Isaiah, for the purposes of this study the entire compilation will be referred to as II Isaiah (and see below in the text).

2. Cassuto indicates that these are 'parallels of *form* and . . . not . . . of *thought*' (1977:150). The list here is taken from pp. 149-60.

3. Paul did not know of Cassuto's Italian articles when he wrote his, and therefore unconsciously repeats many of Cassuto's observations.

4. Chapter 1, above.

5. Chapter 3, above. It is quite possible, too, that Isa. 66.21 draws upon Jer. 33.26 for the use of the verb לקח.

6. Chapter 1, above.

7. Duhm (1892) was the first to express this notion. More recently, see Muilenburg (1956:384-86, 397-98, 414); McKenzie (1968:xviii-xxiii); Westermann (1969:6-9).

8. See the recent commentaries cited in the previous note.

Note to Conclusions

1. Similarly, Bright (1951:27; 1966:30).

BIBLIOGRAPHY

Rabbinic Commentaries

Rashi (Solomon ben Isaac), David Kimḥi, Naḥmanides, David Altschuler (*Meẓudat David, Meẓudat Zion*), *Mikraot Gedolot* (corrected edn; Tel-Aviv: Am-Olam, 1961).

Kara, Joseph, פירוש ירמיה (Paris: A. Durlacher, 1881).

Abarbanel, Isaac, פירוש על נביאים אחרונים (Amsterdam, 1640; reprinted Jerusalem: Torah Vedaat, 1955).

Modern Scholarship

Alter, R., *The Art of Biblical Narrative* (New York: Basic Books, 1981).

Andersen, F.I. and D.N. Freedman, *Hosea* (Anchor Bible; Garden City, N.Y.: Doubleday, 1980).

Anderson, B.W., '"The Lord Has Created Something New": A Stylistic Study of Jer. 31.15-22', *CBQ* 40 (1978), pp. 463-78.

Avishur, Y., 'דגמי השאלה הכפולה והמשולשת במקרא (ובאוגריתית) להסתעפויותיהם' (M.A. thesis, Hebrew University, Jerusalem, 1970).

Barr, J., *Comparative Philology and the Text of the Old Testament* (Oxford: Clarendon Press, 1968).

Bach, R., 'Bauen und Pflanzen', *Studien zur Theologie der alttestamentlichen Überlieferungen* (ed. by R. Rendtorff and Klaus Koch; Neukirchen: Neukirchener Verlag, 1961), pp. 7-32.

Baltzer, K., *The Covenant Formulary* (trans. D.E. Green; Philadelphia: Fortress, 1971).

Bamberger, B.J., 'Fear and Love of God in the Old Testament', *HUCA* 6 (1924), pp. 39-53.

Berridge, J.M., *Prophet, People and the Word of Yahweh* (Basel Studies of Theology 4; Zurich: EVZ, 1970).

Binns, L.E., *The Book of the Prophet Jeremiah* (Westminster Commentaries; London: Methuen, 1919).

Biram, A., 'הושע ב 16-25', *E. Urbach Jubilee Volume* (Jerusalem: Israel Bible Society, 1955), pp. 116-39.

Blank, S.H., *Jeremiah: Man and Prophet* (Cincinnati: Hebrew Union College, 1961).

Böhmer, S., *Heimkehr und neuer Bund* (Göttingen: Vandenhoeck & Ruprecht, 1976).

Bright, J., 'An Exercise in Hermeneutics: Jer. 31.31-34', *Interpretation* 20 (1966), pp. 188-210.

—*Covenant and Promise* (Philadelphia: Westminster, 1976).

—*Jeremiah* (AB; Garden City, N.Y.: Doubleday, 1965).

—'The Date of the Prose Sermons in Jeremiah', *JBL* 70 (1951), pp. 15-35.

—'The Prophetic Reminiscence: Its Place and Function in the Book of Jeremiah', *Biblical Essays* (Proceedings: Die Ou-Testamentiese Werkgemeenskap; Stellenbosch: 1966), pp. 11-30.

Brown, F., S.R. Driver, and C.A. Briggs, *A Hebrew and English Lexicon of the Old Testament* (London: Oxford, 1966).

Brueggemann, W.A., 'Israel's Sense of Place in Jeremiah', *Rhetorical Criticism* (ed. J.J. Jackson and M. Kessler; Pittsburgh: Pickwick, 1974), pp. 149-65.

—'Jeremiah's Use of Rhetorical Questions', *JBL* 92 (1973), pp. 358-74.

—'The Kerygma of the Deuteronomistic Historian', *Interpretation* 22 (1968), pp. 387-402.

Buber, M., *The Prophetic Faith* (trans. by C. Witton-Davies; New York: Harper & Row, 1960).

Bultmann, R., 'γιγνώσκω', *TDOT* (ed. G. Kittel, trans. G.W. Bromley; Grand Rapids: W.B. Eerdmans, 1965), vol. I, pp. 689-719.

Calkins, R., *Jeremiah the Prophet* (New York: Macmillan, 1930).

Carley, K.W., *Ezekiel* (The Cambridge Bible Commentary; Cambridge: Cambridge University Press, 1974).

Carroll, R.P. *From Chaos to Covenant* (London: SCM, 1981).

Cassuto, U., 'On the Formal and Stylistic Relationship between Deutero-Isaiah and Other Biblical Writers', *Biblical & Oriental Studies*, vol. I (trans. and ed. I. Abrahams; Jerusalem: Magnes Press, 1973), pp. 141-77.

—*From Adam to Noah* (trans. I. Abrahams; Jerusalem: Magnes Press, 1961, reprinted 1972).

—'The Second Chapter of Hosea', *Biblical and Oriental Studies*, vol. I, pp. 101-40.

Cazelles, H., 'Israel du Nord et Arche d'Alliance', *VT* 18 (1968), pp. 149-58.

Cheyne, T.K., *Hosea* (CBSC; Cambridge University, 1897).

Clements, R.E., *Prophecy and Covenant* (London: SCM, 1965).

Cooke, G.A., *The Book of Ezekiel* (ICC; Edinburgh: T. & T. Clark, 1936).

Coppens, J., 'La Nouvelle Alliance en Jer. 31, 31-34', *CBQ* 25 (1963), pp. 12-21.

—'L'Espérance messianique royale à la veille et au lendemain de l'exil', *Studia Biblica et Semitica* (ed. W.C. van Unnik and A.S. van der Woude; Wageningen: H. Veenan & Zonen, 1966), pp. 46-61.

Cross, F.M., *Canaanite Myth and Hebrew Epic* (Cambridge, Mass.: Harvard, 1973).

Davies, W.D., *Torah in the Messianic Age and/or the World to Come* (JBL Monograph Series [1952]), pp. 26-28.

Dietrich, E.K., *Die Umkehr im Alten Testament und im Judentum* (Stuttgart: W. Kohlhammer, 1936).

Driver, S.R., *An Introduction to the Literature of the Old Testament* (New York: Meridian Books, 1967, 9th printing).

—*Joel and Amos* (CBSC; 2nd edn; Cambridge: Cambridge University Press, 1915).

—*The Book of the Prophet Jeremiah* (London: Hodder & Stoughton, 1906).

Duhm, B., *Das Buch Jeremia* (KHAT; Leipzig: J.C.B. Mohr, 1901).

—*Das Buch Jesaia* (Göttingen: Vandenhoeck & Ruprecht, 1892).

Ehrlich, A.B., המקרא כפשוטו, vol. I (Berlin: M. Poppelauer, 1899).

Eichrodt, W. *Ezekiel* (OTL; trans. C. Quin; Philadelphia: Westminster, 1970).

—*Theology of the Old Testament*, vol. II (trans. J.A. Baker; London: SCM, 1967).

Eissfeldt, O., *The Old Testament: An Introduction* (trans. P.R. Ackroyd; Oxford: Basil Blackwell, 1966).

Fohrer, G., *History of Israelite Religion* (trans. D.E. Green; Nashville: Abingdon, 1972).

—'Umkehr und Erlösung beim Propheten Hosea', *Studien zur alttestamentlichen*

Prophetie (BZAW, 99; 1967), pp. 222-41.

Friedman, R.E., 'From Egypt to Egypt: Dtr^1 and Dtr^2', *Traditions in Transformation* (ed. B. Halpern and J.D. Levenson; Indiana: Eisenbrauns, 1981), pp. 167-92.

—*The Exile and Biblical Narrative* (Harvard Semitic Monograpahs, 22; Scholars Press, 1981).

Gelin, A., 'Le sens du mot "Israel" en Jérémie 30–31', *Mémorial J. Chaine* (1950), pp. 161-68.

Giesebrecht, F., *Das Buch Jeremia* (HAT; Göttingen: Vandenhoeck & Ruprecht, 1894).

Ginsberg, H.L., 'Hosea', *Encyclopedia Judaica*, vol. VIII (Jerusalem: Keter, 1971), pp. 1010-24.

—'Studies in Hosea 1–3', *Yehezkel Kaufmann Jubilee Volume* (Jerusalem: Magnes Press, 1960), pp. 50-69.

Goldman, M.D. 'The Authorship of Jeremiah, chap. xxxi', *Australian Biblical Review* 2 (1952), p. 109.

Gordis, R., 'The Composition and Structure of Amos', *HThR* 33 (1940), pp. 239-51.

—'The Text and Meaning of Hosea 14.3', *VT* 5 (1955), pp. 88-90.

Gray, J., *I & II Kings* (OTL; 2nd edn; Philadelphia: Westminster, 1970).

Greenberg, M., 'Ezekiel', *Encyclopedia Judaica*, vol. VI (Jerusalem: Keter, 1971), pp. 1078-95.

—'Prolegomenon', *Pseudo Ezekiel and the Original Prophecy*, by C.C. Torrey (New York: KTAV, 1970), pp. xi-xxxv.

—'Some Postulates of Biblical Criminal Law', *Yehezkel Kaufmann Jubilee Volume* (ed. M. Haran; Jerusalem: Magnes Press, 1960), pp. 5-28.

—'The Use of the Ancient Versions for Interpreting the Hebrew Text', *SVT* 29 (1978), pp. 131-48.

—*Ezekiel, 1–20* (Anchor Bible; Garden City, N.Y.: Doubleday, 1983).

—'The Vision of Jerusalem in Ezekiel 8–11: A Holistic Interpretation', *The Divine Helmsman* (ed. J.L. Crenshaw and S. Sandmel; New York: KTAV, 1980), pp. 143-64.

Gros K., *Die literarische Verwandtschaft Jeremias mit Hosea* (Borna-Leipzig: Universitätsverlag von Robert Noske, 1930).

Halpern, E., הושע (Jerusalem: The Israel Society for Biblical Research, 1976).

Haran, M., בין ראשונות לחדשות (Jerusalem: Magnes Press, 1963).

—'The Disappearance of the Ark', *IEJ* 13 (1963), pp. 46-58.

Harper, W.R., *A Critical and Exegetical Commentary on Amos and Hosea* (ICC; reprinted Edinburgh: T. & T. Clark, 1953).

Harrelson, W.J., 'Torah', *IDB* (Nashville: Abingdon, 1962), vol. IV, p. 673b.

Heaton, E.W., *The Hebrew Kingdoms* (London: Oxford University Press, 1968).

Heinemann, I., 'דעת אלהים', *Encyclopedia Mikrait*, vol. II (Jerusalem: Bialik, 1973), cols. 697-700.

Held, M., 'Rhetorical Questions in Ugaritic and Biblical Review', *Eretz-Israel*, IX (1969), pp. 71-77.

Henderson, E., *Jeremiah and Lamentations* (London: Hamilton, Adam & Co., 1851).

Hermann, S., *Die prophetischen Heilserwartungen im Alten Testament* (BWANT, 85; Stuttgart, 1965).

Hertzberg, H.W., 'Jeremia und das Nordreich Israel', *ThLZ* 77 (1952), pp. 91-100.

Heschel, A.J., *The Prophets, I & II* (Philadelphia: JPS, 1962).

Hobbs, T.R., 'Jeremiah 3^{1-5} and Deuteronomy 24^{1-4}', *ZAW* 86 (1974), pp. 23-29.

Hoffman, Y., הנבואות על הגויים במקרא (Tel-Aviv University, Kibbutz Meuchad, 1977).
Hoffmann, D.Z. ספר דברים (trans. Z. Har-Shefer; Tel-Aviv: Hezach, 1961).
—ספר ויקרא, vol. II (trans. Z. Har-Shefer and A. Liebermann; Jerusalem: Mossad Harav Kook, 1972, 4th reprint).
Holladay, W.L., 'A Fresh Look at "Source B" and "Source C" in Jeremiah', *VT* 25 (1975), pp. 394-412.
—'Jer. xxxi 22B Reconsidered: "The Woman Encompasses the Man"', *VT* 16 (1966), pp. 236-39.
—'Jeremiah and Women's Liberation', *Andover Newton Quarterly* 12 (1971-1972), pp. 213-23.
—'Protypes and Copies: A new Approach to the Poetry-Prose Problem in the Book of Jeremiah', *JBL* 79 (1960), pp. 351-67.
—'Style, Irony and Authenticity in the Book of Jeremiah', *JBL* 81 (1962), pp. 44-54.
—*The Architecture of Jeremiah 1–20* (Cranbury, N.J.: Associated University Presses, 1976).
—'The Background of Jeremiah's Self-Understanding', *JBL* 83 (1964), pp. 153-64.
—'The Recovery of Poetic Passages of Jeremiah', *JBL* 85 (1966), pp. 401-35.
—*The Root ŠÛBH in the Old Testament* (Leiden: E.J. Brill, 1958).
Huffmon, H.B., 'The Treaty Background of Yada', *BASOR* 181 (1966), pp. 31-37.
Hyatt, J.P. 'Jeremiah and Deuteronomy', *JNES* 1 (1942), pp. 156-73.
—*Jeremiah: Prophet of Courage and Hope* (Nashville: Abingdon, 1958).
—*Jeremiah* (IB; Nashville, Abingdon, 1956).
—'The Deuteronomic Edition of Jeremiah', *Vanderbilt Studies in the Humanities* 1 (1951), pp. 71-95.
—'Torah in the Book of Jeremiah', *JBL* 60 (1941), pp. 381-96.
Ish-Shalom (Friedman), M., 'היכן הוא הארון', השילוח 13 (1904), pp. 541-49.
Jacob, E. 'Féminisme ou Messianisme? A propos de Jérémie 31, 22', *Beiträge zur alttestamentlichen Theologie* (ed. H. Donner, R. Hanhart and R. Smend; Göttingen: Vandenhoeck & Ruprecht, 1977), pp. 179-84.
Jobling, D., 'Jeremiah's Poem in III 1–IV 2', *VT* 28 (1978), pp. 45-55.
Kaufmann, Y., תולדות האמונה הישראלית, vols. II, III (Jerusalem: Bialik, 1967).
—*The Babylonian Captivity and Deutero-Isaiah* (originally published 1956, Hebrew; trans. C.W. Efroymson; New York: Union of American Hebrew Congregations, 1970).
—*The Religion of Israel* (trans. and abridged M. Greenberg; London: George Allen & Unwin, 1961).
Kuenen, A., *An Historico-Critical Inquiry into the Origin and Composition of the Hexateuch* (trans. P.H. Wicksteed; London: Macmillan, 1886).
Kugel, J.L., *The Idea of Biblical Poetry* (New Haven: Yale, 1981).
Leslie, E.A., *Jeremiah* (Nashville: Abingdon, 1954).
Levenson, J.D., 'From Temple to Synagogue: I Kings 8', *Traditions in Transformation* (ed. B. Halpern and J.D. Levenson; Indiana: Eisenbrauns, 1981), pp. 143-67.
—'Who Inserted the Book of the Torah?', *HThR* 68 (1975), pp. 203-33.
Levinger, J., 'רעיון התשונה בספר ירמיהו', *Zeidel Volume* (Jerusalem: The Israel Society for Biblical Research, 1962), pp. 165-85.
Lindars, B., '"Rachel Weeping for Her Children"—Jeremiah 31.15-22', *JSOT* 12 (1979), pp. 47-62.
—'Torah in Deuteronomy', *Words and Meanings* (ed. P.R. Ackroyd and B. Lindars; Cambridge: Cambridge University Press, 1968), pp. 117-36.

Lipinski, E., 'Jeremiah', *Encyclopedia Judaica*, vol. IX (Jerusalem: Keter, 1972), pp. 1345-61.

Lofthouse, W.F., *Jeremiah and the New Covenant* (London: SCM, 1925).

Long, B.O., 'The Stylistic Components of Jeremiah 3^{1-5}', *ZAW* 88 (1976), pp. 386-90.

Lundbom, J.R., *Jeremiah: A Study in Ancient Hebrew Rhetoric* (SBL Dissertation Series 18, 1975), p. 37.

Luzzato, S.D., פירושי שד״ל על ירמיה יחזקאל משלי ואיוב (Lemberg: A. Isaak Menkes, 1876; Jeremiah Commentary, reprinted Jerusalem: Hebrew University, 1973).

March, W.E., '*Laken*: Its Functions and Meanings', *Rhetorical Criticism* (ed. J.J. Jackson and M. Kessler; Pittsburgh: Pickwick, 1974), pp. 256-84.

Martens, E.Z. 'Motivations for the Promise of Israel's Restoration to the Land in Jeremiah and Ezekiel' (Ph.D. Dissertation; Claremont Graduate School, 1972).

May, H.G., 'The Chronology of Jeremiah's Oracles', *JNES* 4 (1945), pp. 217-27.

—'Towards an Objective Approach to the Book of Jeremiah: The Biographer', *JBL* 61 (1942), pp. 139-55.

May, J.L., *Hosea* (OTL; London: SCM, 1969).

McCarthy, D.J., 'Notes on the Love of God in Deuteronomy and the Father-Son Relationship between Yahweh and Israel', *CBQ* 27 (1965), pp. 144-47.

McKane, W., 'Relations between Poetry and Prose in the Book of Jeremiah with Special Reference to Jeremiah III 6-11 and XII 14-17', *SVT* 32 (1981), pp. 220-37.

McKay, J.W., 'Man's Love for God in Deuteronomy and the Father/Teacher—Son/Pupil Relationship', *VT* 22 (1972), pp. 426-35.

McKenzie, J.L., 'Knowledge of God in Hosea', *JBL* 74 (1955), pp. 22-27.

—*Second Isaiah* (Anchor Bible; Garden City, N.Y.: Doubleday, 1968).

Milgrom, J., 'Concerning Jeremiah's Repudiation of Sacrifice', *ZAW* 89 (1977), pp. 273-75.

—*Cult and Conscience* (Leiden: E.J. Brill, 1976).

— Did Isaiah Prophesy during the Reign of Uzziah?', *VT* 14 (1964), pp. 164-82.

—'Postscript on Eschatological Repentance' (unpublished).

—'Repentance in the Old Testament', *IDBS* (Nashville: Abingdon, 1976), pp. 736-38.

—*Studies in Levitical Terminology, I* (Berkeley: Univ. of California, 1970).

—'The Priestly Doctrine of Repentance', *Revue Biblique* 82 (1975), pp. 187-205.

Miller, J.W., *Das Verhältnis Jeremias und Heschiels sprachlich und theologisch untersucht* (Assen: van Gorcum, 1955).

Morag, S., 'על "מלות מפתח" ו"מלות עדות" בלשונו של ירמיהו', *Rozen Volume* (ed. U. Ornan and B.Z. Fischler; Israel: Council on the teaching of Hebrew, 1975), pp. 64-73.

Moran, W.L., 'The Ancient Near Eastern Background of the Love of God in Deuteronomy', *CBQ* 25 (1963), pp. 77-87.

Mowinckel, S., *Prophecy and Tradition* (Oslo: Dybwad, 1946).

—*Zur Komposition des Buches Jeremia* (Kristiania: Dybwad, 1914).

Muffs, Y., *Studies in Biblical Law IV (The Antiquity of P)* (Lectures in the Jewish Theological Seminary; New York: 1965).

Muilenburg, J., *The Book of Isaiah* (IB, V; Nashville: Abingdon, 1956).

Nelson, R.E. *The Double Redaction of the Deuteronomistic History* (JSOTS, 18; Sheffield: JSOT, 1981).

Nicholson, E.W., *Preaching to the Exiles* (New York: Schocken; 1970)
—*The Book of the Prophet Jeremiah 1–25* (Cambridge: Cambridge University Press, 1973).
Noth, M., *The Deuteronomistic History* (ET: JSOTS, 15; Sheffield: JSOT, 1981).
von Orelli, K., *The Prophecies of Jeremiah* (trans. J.S. Banks; Edinburgh: T. & T. Clark, 1889).
Ostborn, G., *Torah in the Old Testament* (Lund, 1945).
Paul, S., 'Literary and Ideological Echoes of Jeremiah in Deutero-Isaiah', *Proceedings of the Fifth World Congress of Jewish Studies 1* (1969), pp. 102-20.
Petuchowski, J.J., 'The Concept of "Teshuvah" in the Bible and Talmud', *Judaism* 17 (1968), pp. 175-85.
Pfeiffer, R.H., *Introduction to the Old Testament* (New York: Harper & Bros., 1941).
Pohlmann, K.-F., *Studien zum Jeremiabuch* (Göttingen: Vandenhoeck & Ruprecht, 1978).
Procksch, O., *Die kleinen prophetischen Schriften vor dem Exil* (Erläuterungen zum Alten Testament 3; Stuttgart: 1910).
von Rad, G., *Old Testament Theology*, vol. II (trans. D.M.G. Stalker; London: Oliver & Boyd, 1965).
—'The Deuteronomistic Theology of History in I and II Kings', *The Problem of the Hexateuch* (trans. E.W. Trueman Dicken; New York: McGraw-Hill, 1966; originally published in 1947), pp. 205-21.
Raitt, T.M., *A Theology of Exile: Judgment/Deliverance in Jeremiah and Ezekiel* (Philadelphia: Fortress, 1977).
—'Jeremiah's Deliverance Message to Judah', *Rhetorical Criticism* (ed. J.J. Jackson and M. Kessler; Pittsburgh: Pickwick, 1974), pp. 166-85.
—'The Prophetic Summons to Repentance', *ZAW* 83 (1971), pp. 30-48.
Rofe, A., 'עיונים בשאלת חיבורו של ספר ירמיהו', *Tarbiz* 44 (1975), pp. 1-29.
Rowley, H.H., 'The Prophet Jeremiah and the Book of Deuteronomy', *From Moses to Qumran* (London: Lutterworth, 1963), pp. 187-208.
Rudolph, W., *Hosea* (KAT; Gütersloh: Gerd Mohn, 1966).
—*Jeremiah* (HAT, 12; Tübingen: J.C.B. Mohr, 1947; 2nd edn, 1958).
Sakenfeld, K., *The Meaning of Hesed in the Hebrew Bible*: *A New Inquiry* (Missoula, Montana: Scholars Press, 1978).
Scott, R.B.Y., *The Relevance of the Prophets* (rev. edn; London: Macmillan, 1969).
Segal, M.Z., מבוא למקרא (Jerusalem: Kiryat Sepher, 1967).
Seidl, T., *Texte und Einheiten in Jeremia 27–29* (St. Ottilien: Eos Verlag, 1977).
Skinner, J., *Prophecy and Religion* (Cambridge: Cambridge University Press, 1922).
Smend, R., *Die Bundesformel* (Theologische Studien, 68; Zurich: EVZ, 1963).
Smith, G.A., *Jeremiah* (4th edn; New York: Harper & Bros., 1929).
—*The Book of the Twelve Prophets*, vol. I (The Expositor's Bible; London: Hodder & Stoughton, 1896).
Spencer, A.B., 'שרירות as Self-Reliance', *JBL* 100 (1981), pp. 147-48.
Streane, A.W., *The Book of the Prophet Jeremiah* (CBSC; Cambridge: Cambridge University Press, 1913).
Tadmor, H., 'הרקע ההיסטורי של נבואת הושע', *Yehezkel Kaufmann Jubilee Volume* (Jerusalem: Magnes Press, 1960), pp. פר—פח.
Talmon, S., '*Amen* as an Introductory Oath Formula', *Textus* 7 (1969), pp. 124-29.
—'Polemics and Apology in Biblical Historiography—2 Kings 17.24-41', *The Creation of Sacred Literature* (ed. R.E. Friedman; Berkeley: Univ. of California, 1981), pp. 64-65.

Thiel, W., *Die deuteronomische Redaktion von Jeremia 1–25* (WMANT, 41; Neukirchen-Vluyn: Neukirchener Verlag, 1973).
Thompson, J.A., *The Book of Jeremiah* (Grand Rapids: Eerdmans, 1980),
Torrey, C.C., 'The Background of Jeremiah 1–10', *JBL* 56 (1937), pp. 206-208.
Tov, E., *The Text-Critical Use of the Septuagint in Biblical Research* (Jerusalem: Simor, 1981).
Trible, P. 'God, Nature of, in the OT', *IDBS* (Nashville: Abingdon, 1976), pp. 368-69.
—'The Gift of a Poem: A Rhetorical Study of Jeremiah 31.15-22', *Andover Newton Quarterly* 17 (1976-77), pp. 271-80.
Tur-Sinai, N.H., הלשון והספר, vol. I (rev. edn; Jerusalem: Bialik, 1954).
Unterman, J., 'מגלות לגאלה בדברי ירמיהו' (M.A. Thesis, Hebrew University, 1975).
—'Repentance and Redemption in Hosea', *SBL Seminar Papers* (1982), pp. 541-50.
—'The Literary Influence of "The Binding of Isaac" (Genesis 22) on "The Outrage at Gibeah" (Judges 19)', *Hebrew Annual Review* 4 (1980), pp. 161-66.
de Vaux, R., *Ancient Israel*, vol. II (New York: McGraw-Hill, 1965).
Volz, P., *Der Prophet Jeremia* (KAT; Leipzig: 1928).
Wagner, S., 'בקש biqqesh; בקשה', *TDOT*, vol. II (ed. G.J. Botterweck and H. Ringgren; trans. J.T. Willis; rev. edn; Grand Rapids: Eerdmans, 1977), pp. 229-41.
—'דרש darash; מדרש', *TDOT*, vol. III (1978), pp. 293-307.
Ward, J.M., *Hosea* (New York: Harper & Row, 1966).
Weinfeld, M., *Deuteronomy and the Deuteronomic School* (Oxford: Oxford University Press, 1972).
—'Jeremiah and the Spiritual Metamorphosis of Israel', *ZAW* 88 (1976), pp. 2-56.
Weippert, H., 'Das Wort vom neuen Bund in Jeremia XXXI 31-34', *VT* 29 (1979), pp. 336-51.
—*Die Prosareden des Jeremiabuches* (BZAW, 32; 1973).
Weiser, A., *Das Buch der zwölf kleinen Propheten* (ATD 24; Göttingen: Vandenhoeck & Ruprecht, 1964).
—*Das Buch Jeremia* (ATD; Göttingen: Vandenhoeck & Ruprecht, 1960).
Weiss, M., *The Bible from Within* (Jerusalem: Magnes Press, 1984).
—המקרא כדמותו (Jerusalem: Bialik, 1967).
—'מבעיות תורת הגמול המקראית', Part I, *Tarbiz* 31 (1962), pp. 236-63.
Welch, A.C., *Jeremiah: His Time and His Work* (Oxford: Basil Blackwell, 1928).
Wellhausen, J., *Die kleinen Propheten* (4th edn; reprinted; Berlin: De Gruyter, 1963).
Westermann, C., *Isaiah 40–66* (OTL; Philadelphia: Westminster, 1969).
Wevers, J.W., *Ezekiel* (The Century Bible; London: Nelson, 1969).
Wiesel, E., *Night* (New York: Avon Books, 1960).
Wolff, H.W., 'Das Thema "Umkehr" in der alttestamentlichen Prophetie', *ZThk* 48 (1951), pp. 129-48.
—*Hosea* (Hermeneia; trans. G. Stansell; Philadelphia: Fortress, 1974).
—*Joel and Amos* (Hermeneia; trans. W. Janzen, S.D. McBride, Jr; and C.A. Muenchow; ed. S.D. McBride, Jr; Philadelphia: Fortress, 1977).
—'The Kerygma of the Deuteronomic Historical Work' (trans. F.L. Prussner; *The Vitality of Old Testament Traditions*; ed. W. Brueggemann and H.W. Wolff; Atlanta: John Knox, 1978), pp. 83-100.
Yellin, D., כתבים נבחרים vol. II (Jerusalem: Kiryat-Sepher, 1939).
Zeiner, G., '"Femina circumdabit virum" (Jer. 31, 22) eine Dittographie?', *BZ* 1

(1957), pp. 282-83.

Zevit, Z., 'A Phoenician Inscription and Biblical Covenant Theology', *IEJ* 27 (1977), pp. 110-18.

Zimmerli, W., *Ezekiel 1* (Hermeneia; trans. R.E. Clements; Philadelphia: Fortress, 1979).

SUPPLEMENTARY BIBLIOGRAPHY

The publication of this book has been delayed by a variety of administrative and technical exigencies. During this time three major commentaries were published as well as other significant works of a less comprehensive but nonetheless relevant nature. Unfortunately, it is impossible to do these studies justice within the body of this book. They will only be mentioned in passing here. Suffice it to say that none of these works adds any new substantial challenges to the arguments of this book.

The list below is not exhaustive.

Commentaries

R.P. Carroll, *Jeremiah* (OTL; Philadelphia: Westminster, 1986) is a consistent sequel to Carroll, 1981, with all the presumptions of that older work.

W. McKane, *Jeremiah* (I–XXV) (ICC; Edinburgh: T. & T. Clark, 1986) contains (pp. xli-xlvii) a valuable comparison of the approaches of Theil and Weippert, and a complex understanding of the development of the text (pp. xlvii-lxxxviii). Refreshingly, McKane makes use of Rashi, Kimḥi, and Luzatto (but not modern Hebrew scholarship).

W.L. Holladay, *Jeremiah 1* (1–25) (Hermeneia; Philadelphia: Fortress, 1986) lacks a significant introduction, other than an historical sketch based on Holladay's late dating of Jeremiah's call. A proper introduction will appear in Vol. 2. Holladay is one of the most original thinkers on Jeremiah, and this is reflected in the commentary.

Articles

An important volume of articles which came to my attention too late to include herein is P.M. Bogaert, ed., *Le Livre de Jérémie* (Leuven, Belgium: Leuven University, 1981):

W.L. Holladay, 'A Chronology of Jeremiah's Early Career', pp. 58-73, is self-explanatory.

J.A. Soggin, 'The Ark of the Covenant, Jeremiah 3,16', pp. 215-21, is a good survey of current opinion.

N. Lohfink, 'Der junge Jeremia als Propagandist und Poet: Zum Grundstock von Jer 30-31', pp. 351-68, attempts a reconstruction of the original text of Jer. 30-31 in seven stanzas: 30.5-7, 12-15, 18-21; 31.2-6, 15-17, 18-20, 21-22. Although he recognizes a male-female oscillation, even involving Jacob and Rachel, his rejection of 31.7-9 as late prevents him from arriving at the analysis presented here (in Chapter 1).

J. Lust, '"Gathering and Return" in Jeremiah and Ezekiel', pp. 119-42, deals with a theme which relates closely to the one under discussion here. However, on evidence so flimsy that it should have been given almost no weight at all (pp. 123-27), he rejects the whole concept of physical return in Jeremiah (!) and, thus, many significant verses as editorial additions (p. 136). Lust's conclusions concerning Ezekiel are similar (pp. 141-42).

E. Tov, 'Some Aspects of the Textual and Literary History of the Book of Jeremiah', pp. 145-67, has been revised as 'The Literary History of the Book of Jeremiah in Light of its Textual History', in J. Tigay, ed., *Empirical Models of Biblical Criticism* (Philadelphia: University of Pennsylvania, 1985), pp. 212-37. Tov makes an extremely strong case for viewing the LXX as based on a first edition of Jeremiah, while the MT reflects the second edition. The second editor's 'sources for his additions are the context, his own imgination, but also genuine Jeremianic material which somehow found its way into edition II' (p. 237). Therefore, Tov can conclude concerning 33.14-26 (p. 220).

> Although this section has often been denied to Jeremiah because it is absent from the LXX... there is no sound reason for this skepticism. On the contrary,... there are several Jeremianic expressions in this section reminiscent of other passages in the book, and the argument that these reflect a glossator's imitation is artificial. The burden of proof is on those who would deny the section to the prophet in whose name it has been transmitted.

See also note 9 to Chapter 4, above.

INDEXES

INDEX OF BIBLICAL REFERENCES

Genesis

1–2	160
1.2	187
3.16	93
12.2-3	35
12.7	191
13.15-16	191
13.16	103, 110
15.5	191
16.10	191
17.4	184
17.7-8	191
17.7	147
17.13	147
17.19	147
18.18	35
22.17	191
22.18	31, 35
25.23	49
26.4	35, 191
28.14	35, 191
28.30	186
32.13	191
38.26	183
43.30	162

Exodus

3.7	186
4.22	49
6.7	80
7.5	76
7.17	76
10.2	76
14.12	159
16.28	100
19.5-6	80
19.10-11	108
22.22	186
24.12	100, 102
29.46	76
31.13	76
31.16	147
32.22	188
35.31	193
35.34	193
38.21	195

Leviticus

1.4	181
10.11	100
14.54-57	100
14.57	100
20.8	79
24.8	147
25.17	79
26	12, 181
26.4-13	195
26.5	196
26.6	197
26.12	80
26.13	129
26.16	45
26.19-22	159
26.20	197
26.40-41	12
26.40	11, 181

Numbers

11.18	159
11.23	85
14.3	159

Deuteronomy

1–3	68
1–3.28	70
1.38	119
1.46	161
3.28	119
4.1	100
4.5	100
4.10	114
4.14	100
4.26-31	61, 121
4.29-40	68
4.29-31	12, 55, 67-74, 86, 147
4.29	50, 63, 111
4.31	66
5.9	192
5.26	113, 114
5.29	113
5.30	113
6.5	111
6.7	101
6.24	111, 114
8.5	187
8.6	111, 113, 114
10.12-13	113
10.12	111, 114
10.16	31
10.20	111
11.13	79, 101
11.16	101
11.18-19	101
11.22	79, 113
11.28	113
12.10	119
13.5	111
14.23	111, 114
17.8-11	100
17.18-19	68, 100
17.19	114
19.3	119
19.9	79, 113
19.15	192
20.6	186
24.8	100
24.16	192
26.16-19	80
26.16	111
26.17	113
26.19	145
27–28	70
28	68
28.9	113
28.11	66
28.30	186
28.36-37	69

(Deuteronomy cont.)
28.50 114
28.63-68 69
28.63 111
28.65 45
28.68 72
29.3 59
29.5 76
29.7 111
29.8 78
29.12 80
29.16 70
29.18 119
29.21-28 70
29.27 69
30–34 68
30 70
30.1-10 12, 55, 57, 61, 64-67, 68, 69, 70, 72, 73, 74, 81, 121
30.1-7 189
30.1-6 59
30.1-2 66
30.2-20 68-74
30.2 58, 61, 66, 111
30.3 63
30.5 60, 63
30.6 31, 66, 79, 92, 111
30.8-10 189
30.9 60
30.10 58, 61, 66, 111
30.16 79, 113
30.20 79
31.1-2 70
31.3 70
31.4-6 70
31.7 70, 119
31.12-13 100, 114
31.16-22 70
31.24-29 70
32.8-9 119
32.10 47
32.11 187
33.8-10 100
33.10 100

Joshua
1.7 77
7.1-26 159
9.9 120
15.7 159
21.45 85
22.5 79, 100
22.20 167
23.11 79
23.15 85
24.7 160
24.20 111

Judges
3.2 102
3.7-12 82
13.8 102
17.6 160
18.1 160
19.1 160
21.19-23 50
21.25 160

Ruth
1.11 49

1 Samuel
1.11 187
2.31 190
4.14 184
7.3 58

2 Samuel
3.25 188
7 69
7.14 49, 80
7.24 80
14.14 63

1 Kings
2.3-4 68
2.3 78
2.4 111
3.2 120
3.26 162
5.17 120, 188
5.19 120
6.12 85
8 12, 68, 73-74, 177, 188
8.17 120
8.20 120
8.23-53 71
8.33-53 73
8.33 66
8.34 66
8.36 102
8.43 72
8.44-53 12
8.44 72
8.46-53 61, 69, 72, 121
8.47-50 86
8.47-48 66
8.48 58, 63, 71, 72, 111
8.49-50 66
8.56 85
9.5-7 68
9.6-9 70
10.1 120
11.12 69
11.13 69
11.32 69
11.34 69
11.36 69
18.24 78
20.13 183
21.27-29 181
21.29 183
22 59
24.4 69

2 Kings
4.43 185
8.19 69
12.3 100, 193
14.6 192
17–19 69
17.7-40 27
17.7-23 26
17.18 38
17.20 191
17.27-28 100
17.28 193
17.29 195
17.30 195
17.31 195
18.6 68
19.34 69

(2 Kings cont.)

20.6	69
20.17-18	69
20.17	190
21.2-15	69
21.8-9	68
21.10-15	70
22.8	73
22.10	73
22.11	181
22.13	73
22.15-20	69, 70
22.19	181
22.21	193
23.2	73
23.15-20	28, 51
23.25-27	69
23.25	68, 111
23.26–25.30	69
24.2-4	70
24.2	72
24.20	73
25.22-26	72
25.22	188
25.23	188
25.24	188
25.25	188
25.26	72, 188
25.27-30	68, 73
26.26	72

1 Chronicles

16.8	78
16.13	191
17.22	80
25.8	100, 101

2 Chronicles

6.27	102
7.14	86, 181
12.6-7	181
15.3	100
15.4	86
17.9	100
32.20	181
32.24-26	181
33.12-13	181
33.19	181
35.3	101, 195

Ezra

1.1	62
1.4	62
2.59	62
7.10	100

Nehemiah

8.3-9	101

Job

11.8	159
14.14	192
26.12	190
34.32	102
41.14	45

Psalms

2.7	49
14.1-3	86
20.8	126
22.24	191
25.4	102
25.5	102
25.8	102
25.9	102
25.12	102
27.10	49
27.11	102
45.18	126
46.3	193
48.11	145
48.12-15	187
53.2-4	86
54.5	136
66.8	145
68.30	124
71.6	49
71.17	102
72.8-11	124
78.34	86
79.6-7	78
80.19	181
86.11	102, 114
88.10	45
89.27-28	49
90.10	108
94.10	102
94.11	188
94.12	100, 102
105.1	78
105.6	191
105.8-10	147
111	186
114.1	102
117	186
118.18	187
119.12	102
119.26	102
119.33-34	100
119.33	102
119.54	102
119.66	102
119.68	102
119.71-73	100
119.71	102
119.73	102
119.102	102
119.108	102
119.124	102
119.135	102
119.171	102
122.4	120
125.1	193
132.12	102
135	186
137	146
143.10	102

Proverbs

5.10	136
6.20-21	99
7.1-3	100
10.9	187
14.33	187
19.18	187
19.20	187
29.17	187
29.19	187
30.19	51

Canticles

1.6	50
1.7	50
1.14	50
2.15	50
2.17	50
3.2	46
5.4	49
5.6	50
7.2	50
7.13	50
8.11-12	50

Isaiah

1.1	196
1.7	136

(Isaiah cont.)
2.2-4 125
2.2-3 124
2.3 100
2.4 102
5.1-2 50
8.16 100
9.12 71, 86
9.14 100
10.24-26 72
11.2-3 114, 193
11.3 192
11.6-9 160
11.11-16 122
11.11 72
11.13 193
12–14 119
12.4 78
13 135
18.7 120, 124
19.22 71
21.5 185
24.5 147
24.19 193
25.6 124
26.20–27.1 135
27.12 135
27.13 135
28.26 102
29.13 114
30.15 184
31.1 86
34–35 171-75, 199
35 185
35.2 44
35.3-10 42-46
35.8 187
39.6 190
40–66 171-75
40–55 71, 199
40.2 181
41.8-10 136
41.8-9 93
41.9 93
41.13-14 136
43.1 136
43.5 136
44.1-2 136
44.19 70
46.8 70
48.17 102
49.1 49
49.14-15 49
49.15 103
49.25 103
50.4 102
51.6 103
51.8 103
51.15 93
54.6 93
54.10 103, 193
54.13 102
55.3 112
55.6-8 63, 85
55.6 86
56–66 199
59.11 93
60.9 120, 125
61.8 112
63.16 49
65.1 86
65.17 122
66.12 49
66.21 199
66.22 103

Jeremiah
1.4-19 59
1.8 136
1.10 92, 94, 117, 186
1.11-12 75
1.12 85, 92
1.13-15 184
1.13-14 75
1.14 92
1.17 136
2 27
2.1-3 195
2.1-2 60
2.2-3 185
2.2 168, 183, 186, 195
2.3 138, 196
2.4-37 36-37
2.4 45
2.5-37 29, 187
2.5 27
2.6 76
2.7 101
2.8 76, 79, 100, 101, 121
2.11 101
2.13 101
2.14 138
2.19-27 101
2.19 32, 136
2.20 136
2.23 29, 32, 113
2.25 29, 32
2.33-37 30
2.33 113
2.44-46 59
3.1–4.2 29
3 12, 67
3.1-5 28, 29, 36-37, 183, 185
3.1-3 101
3.1 26, 101
3.3-18 28
3.4 31, 85
3.5-11 26
3.6-18 124, 183
3.6-13 23-38, 53, 71, 74, 166, 176-77
3.6-12 183
3.6-11 30, 148, 167, 168
3.6-8 59, 83
3.6 187
3.7 34
3.8 171
3.11-20 124
3.11-13 83
3.11 168
3.12-14 185
3.12-13 11, 119, 121, 168, 181, 183
3.12 184, 185
3.14-22 121
3.14-18 28, 37, 118-32, 183
3.14 123, 127
3.15 77, 113, 123, 127
3.16-21 168
3.16-17 123, 124, 128, 190
3.16 126, 172
3.17 113, 127, 144, 171,

(Jeremiah cont.)
196
3.18 126, 128, 165, 168, 184, 196, 198
3.19–4.4 183
3.19–4.2 23-38, 53, 71, 74, 168, 176-77
3.19-25 184
3.19-21 82, 120
3.19-20 183
3.19 85, 165, 167, 183
3.21-25 183
3.21 48, 113, 196
3.22 125, 138, 171, 182
3.25 150, 168
4.1-4 31, 185
4.1-2 121
4.1 109, 167, 172, 199
4.2 171, 184
4.3-5 83
4.3-4 30, 31, 37, 38
4.3 30
4.4 109, 110
4.5–6.30 31, 185
4.5-31 185
4.5-7 37, 38
4.14 187
4.22 26-27, 79
4.27 117, 136
5 56
5.1-9 101
5.1-6 83, 107
5.2-3 31
5.2 32, 110, 184
5.3 31, 77
5.4-7 196
5.5 136
5.6 159
5.7 101
5.10 117, 136
5.11 27
5.14–6.4 196
5.18 117, 136
5.20-29 101
5.20 183
5.21 113
5.22-24 114
5.22 93, 111, 126
5.24 111
5.31 93, 111, 126
6.1-4 159
6.11–7.2 196
6.12-20 143
6.13 101
6.23 93
6.27 113
7.2 45
7.3-7 109
7.3 113
7.4 126
7.5 113
7.9 184
7.10 196
7.13-16 196
7.5 191
7.16-18 101
7.18 101
7.21-23 143, 144
7.22 143, 191
7.23 33, 80
7.24-25 195
7.24 113, 126
7.26 101
7.31 101, 126
7.32 124, 190
7.34 153
8.4-10 31
8.4 34, 184
8.5 77, 182
8.7 101
8.8-10 101
8.13 31
8.15 60
8.22 138
9.1-8 101
9.2 77, 79
9.3 45
9.5 77, 79
9.11-13 101
9.12-13 100, 101
9.12 33
9.13 126
9.23 77-78, 79
9.24 190
10.2 113, 136
10.3 196
10.12 196
10.21 86, 101, 126
10.24 136
10.25 78, 79, 195
11.3 81
11.4 80, 191
11.5 80
11.7-10 101
11.7 191
11.8 126
11.10 77, 192
11.13 184
11.15 169
11.19 126
12.3 113
12.7-10 196
12.11 113
12.14-17 117
12.14 126
13.1-11 59
13.1-8 56
13.1-3 59
13.1 183
13.9-11 56
13.10 77, 126
13.11 145
13.14 126, 196
13.15 193
13.23 107
14.7-9 187
14.8 196
14.10-12 187
14.10 126
14.14 101, 126
14.20-22 187
14.20 32, 101, 192
14.21 126, 144
15.1 187
15.9 109
15.13 138
15.15 126
15.18 138
15.19 13, 34, 82, 187
15.20 136
16.1-3 169
16.6 126
16.9 144, 153
16.10-12 192
16.11 101

(*Jeremiah cont.*)
16.12 101, 126
16.14-15 63, 108, 121, 190, 192
16.15 123, 126, 184
16.17 113
16.19 101, 124, 126
16.21 79
16.25 138
17.1 107, 110, 113
17.3 138
17.9 107
17.10 113
17.12 126, 144
17.13 196
17.18 136
17.19-27 83
17.20 45
17.26 113, 144
17.33 13
18.1-12 59
18.1-4 56
18.5-12 56
18.7-12 57
18.7-10 189
18.7-8 109
18.8 63
18.9 186
18.11 63, 109, 113
18.12 107, 126
18.15 113
18.18 101
19.1-13 59
19.1 183
19.6 124, 190
19.15 126
19.27 59
20.13 48
21 130
21.1-10 75
21.7 126
21.10 66
21.11-14 83
21.11 45
21.12 129
22 130
22.1-7 83
22.13-19 119
22.15-16 78
22.16 79
22.24-30 128
22.30 128
23 75
23.1-8 12, 126-30, 177
23.1-4 83, 119, 147
23.1-2 101, 123, 167
23.1 167
23.2-3 137
23.2 167
23.3-8 123
23.3-4 1121
23.3 125, 126, 127
23.4-6 123
23.4 126, 127, 131, 136,
23.5-6 83, 121
23.5 77, 94, 126, 167, 190
23.6 126, 127
23.7-8 63, 108, 124, 128, 190, 192
23.8 125, 126, 128, 136, 191, 198
23.9 128
23.11 101
23.13-17 101
23.17 126
23.21 101
23.22 113
23.25-32 101
23.27 101
23.36 126
24 56, 75-76, 138, 167, 169
24.1-10 17, 26, 83, 132, 188
24.1-3 56
24.4-10 56
24.4-7 12, 55-87, 97, 112, 121, 148, 169, 177, 188, 189
24.6-7 109
24.6 94, 123, 186
24.7 13, 14, 112, 113, 167, 161
24.8 85
24.9-10 84
24.9 66
25 75
25.1 125
25.3 87
25.5 87, 113
25.7 87
25.9 125
25.10 144, 153
25.12-14 195
25.12 108
25.26 184
25.29 136
25.33 126
25.34-36 119
26.1-6 126
26.3 63, 109, 113
26.13 109, 113
26.20-23 60
27 136
27.7 108
27.9-10 101
27.16 101
27.21-22 117
28 83, 136
28.1-17 123
28.2 84, 85
28.3-4 84
28.4 64, 85
28.6 63
28.11 84
28.13 183
29 56, 83-84, 138, 169
29.4-7 60, 112, 121
29.5 167, 169, 171, 186
29.6 108
29.8-9 101, 169
29.8 186
29.10-14 12, 14, 17, 55-87, 112, 117, 121, 123, 147, 148, 169,

(*Jeremiah cont.*)
177
29.10 108, 123, 169
29.12-14 169
29.12-13 50, 147, 172
29.13 68
29.14 112, 123, 169
29.32 117
30–31 16, 41, 83, 93
30.1–31.1 135
30 12, 135
30.1-17 132-39
30.1-10 61
30.2-3 121
30.3 126, 190
30.5-17 177
30.5-7 47
30.5 171
30.8-9 121
30.8 34, 123, 167
30.9 123
30.10-11 34, 171
30.10 167, 191
30.11 167
30.12-18 109
30.14 167, 171
30.15 171
30.16-17 18
30.16 171, 196
30.17-18 125
30.17 145, 171
30.18-22 117, 122
30.18 167, 171
30.19 144, 167, 171
30.22 80, 189
30.23-24 117
31 187
31.1 80, 189
31.2-26 92
31.2-14 42-46
31.2-9 38-53, 83, 176-77
31.2-6 122
31.2 27
31.3-13 165
31.3 136
31.4 27
31.5 144, 167
31.6 71, 120, 125, 196
31.7-14 172
31.7-9 120, 136
31.7 27, 125, 171
31.8 125, 126, 171, 196
31.9 27, 165, 171, 172
31.10-14 41-42, 45, 46, 94, 117
31.10 167, 171
31.11 172
31.12 165, 171, 172, 197
31.13 172
31.14-18 177
31.14 165, 172, 197
31.15-22 12, 18, 38-53, 74, 83, 176-77
31.15 33, 172
31.16 171
31.18-22 91
31.18-20 92
31.18 34, 82
31.19 11, 32, 150, 167, 168
31.20 34, 61, 165, 172
31.21 132
31.22 94, 167
31.23-26 94, 117, 184
31.23-25 45, 83
31.23 196
31.27-40 94
31.27-37 89-110, 114-16, 177
31.27-37 131, 189
31.27 165, 166
31.28 120, 148, 166, 186
31.29-30 192
31.29 124, 167
31.30-33 14, 165
31.30 124, 167
31.31-34 12, 14, 60, 112, 121, 124, 126, 128, 130, 167, 194
31.31-33 13, 167
31.31 166, 167, 184
31.32-33 168
31.32 125, 166, 195
31.33-34 78, 80, 192
31.33 57, 80, 81, 82, 112, 113, 167, 171, 172, 189
31.34 79, 131, 145, 149, 166, 167, 171
31.35-37 18, 144, 166, 172, 189, 191
31.35 171
31.36 192
31.37 168
31.38-40 83, 117, 121
31.40 123
32–33 41, 106
32 122
32.1-3 115
32.1-2 106
32.5 117
32.6-16 121, 123
32.6-15 59, 60, 112, 115
32.15-16 123
32.15 123
32.17-44 111-12
32.17-25 59
32.18 171, 192
32.19 113
32.23-25 112
32.25-36 83
32.30 195
32.35 59, 126
32.36-44 12, 83, 110-16
32.36-41 60
32.36-39 121
32.37-47 177
32.37-41 194, 198
32.37 85, 123, 165
32.38-40 80
32.38-39 57

(Jeremiah cont.)

32.38 80
32.39-41 80
32.39 14, 79, 82
32.40 81, 147, 167, 168, 171, 181
32.41 64, 85, 171, 194
32.42-44 60, 123
32.43-44 123, 131
32.43 137, 144
33 12
33.1-26 139-45, 177
33.1 106
33.2 171
33.3 171
33.6-11 109
33.6-9 60, 112, 121
33.6 138
33.7 123
33.8 149, 167, 192, 196
33.10-20 168
33.10-11 171
33.10 137
33.11-12 113
33.11 153, 172
33.13 113
33.14-26 18, 83, 195
33.14-16 121
33.14-15 190
33.14 85, 94
33.16 123, 126
33.17-18 121
33.18 172
33.19-22 121
33.20-22 103, 172
33.20-21 93, 103
33.22 165, 191
33.23-26 121
33.24-26 93
33.24 123
33.25-26 93, 103, 172
33.26 61, 109, 191, 199
34 129
34.2 183
34.13 191
34.14 101
35.7 126
35.13 183
35.15 113
36 37
36.1-32 178
36.3 113
36.7 113
39.8 71
39.16 66, 183
40.5-7 188
40.7–43.7 72
40.7-8 188
40.9 188
41.1-3 188
41.5 71
41.17–42.1 188
42 72
42.8 188
42.9-12 145-46, 177
42.9-10 196
42.10 94, 186
42.11 188
42.14 126, 188
42.15 45, 188
42.17 188
42.19 188
43.1-5 188
43.7 188
44.1-30 146, 169
44.10 126
44.21 126
44.24 45
44.27 66
45.1-5 117
45.4 94, 186
46–51 195
46.6 184
46.26 117
46.27-28 136
48.12 190
48.47 117
49.2 190
49.4 132
49.6 117
49.11 117
49.12 136
49.39 117
50–51 146-50
50.4-7 177
50.4-5 86
50.4 126
50.5 125
50.6 101
50.17-20 109, 177, 196
50.17 172
50.18-20 121
50.20 123, 125, 172, 192
50.33-34 178, 196
50.34 171
50.42 93
51.45 117
51.47 190
51.50-51 178, 196
51.50 120, 126
51.52 190
51.55 93

Lamentations

3.21 70
5.1 187

Ezekiel

3.16-21 168
3.18-19 167
4.13 66
7.13 167
7.16 167
7.26 101
8–11 169
8.1 169
8.5 72
8.12 183
8.15 183
8.17 183
11.1-21 198
11.3 169
11.13 167
11.14-21 167
11.16-17 169
11.16 169
11.17-20 167
11.18 167, 169, 199
11.19-20 80
11.19 167, 193
11.20 80, 167
14.1-11 12, 168
14.3 120, 169
14.7 169
14.11 80
14.14-21 169

(*Ezekiel cont.*)

16.44-63	25, 27
16.44-52	167
16.51-63	168
16.54	12, 169
16.63	12, 169
18	168, 191
18.1-3	167
18.18	167
18.30-32	12
18.31	167, 193
20.6	167
20.15	167
20.30-32	12, 169
20.39	169
20.43	12, 169
21.2	72
21.17	167
23	25, 27
23.1-35	167
23.5	167
23.46	138
25.2	146
26.2	146
26.23	145
28.25	167
28.26	167
33.6	167
33.8	167
33.9	167
33.10-20	168
34	130, 167
34.1-16	129, 167
34.4	137, 167
34.5	167
34.6	137
34.8	198
34.10	167
34.11	137, 167
34.12-13	198
34.12	167
34.16	137, 167
34.23	129, 167
34.25-30	195
34.25	129, 198
34.27	129, 167, 198
34.28	167
34.31	167
35.5	146
36.8	167
36.10	167
36.22	64, 85
36.24-28	198
36.24-27	167
36.24-26	167
36.25-26	192
36.25	167, 196
36.26	80, 167, 193
36.27	167
36.28	80
36.29	167
36.31	12, 169
36.32	169
36.33	167, 196
36.36	85
36.37	167
37.16-28	119
37.23	80, 167, 196
37.26	167
37.27	80
38.10	120
39.26	12, 169
43.10-11	169
44.12	169
44.23-24	100
44.23	100
47.6	183

Hosea

1-3	12, 154-55
1.1	196
1.2	196
1.7	196, 198
1.9	80, 196
2	12, 161, 166
2.1-3	196
2.1	165
2.2	165
2.4-35	12
2.4-25	155-60
2.4	80, 196, 198
2.6	153, 196
2.7	196
2.10	198
2.11	153
2.13	196
2.14	153, 197
2.16-25	164, 196
2.16-17	165
2.16	50
2.17	50, 153, 168
2.19	126
2.20-25	154
2.20	153, 196, 197
2.21-22	78, 165
2.21	50
2.23-24	153
2.24-25	196
2.25	92, 165
3.1-5	12, 197
3.4-5	12, 160-61, 197
3.5	68, 74, 86, 136, 164, 165, 195
4-14	154, 155
4.5	198
4.6	192
5.4-7	196
5.4	198
5.5	198
5.6	50, 198
5.11	186
5.14-6.4	196
5.15-6.1	71, 74, 86
5.15	50, 68
6.1-3	198
6.3	110
6.6	78
6.11-7.2	196
7.2	198
7.9	136
7.10	86, 196
7.13-16	196
7.14	198
7.16	198
8.2	198
8.5	153, 187
8.7	136
8.10	198
8.13	72
9.5-6	72
10.3	114, 196, 198
10.7	198
10.10-11	187
10.12	31, 86
10.15	198
11.1-11	12, 161-63
11.1	34, 165
11.5	72, 198

(Hosea cont.)
11.8-11 122, 164, 195
11.8-9 34, 185
11.9 153
11.11 72, 165
11.8 165, 183
12.7-10 196
12.7 198
12.9 198
13.4-5 34
13.14 196
14.2-9 12, 35, 74, 163-64, 166
14.2 71, 165
14.5-9 164, 165
14.5 165
14.6-9 34

Joel
2 135

Amos
2.6-7 198
2.12 198
3.9 198
4 74
4.1 198
4.6 71, 153
4.8 71, 153
4.9 71, 153
4.10 71, 153
4.11 71
5.4 77, 86, 153
5.6 77, 86, 153
5.11-12 198
5.14-15 153
5.14 77
5.23-24 153
6.6 153
6.10 126
7.1–9.4 59
7.1-3 75
7.4-6 75
7.7-9 75
8.1-3 75
8.11 190
9.1-4 75
9.2 74
9.3-4 74
9.4 60, 66
9.8-15 12, 151-54
9.8-10 198
9.11-15 123
9.11-12 122
9.13-15 122
9.13-14 159, 190
9.14 186

Obadiah
11-15 146
17 117

Micah
1.1 196
1.12 60
3.11 100
4.1-4 124
4.2 102
4.6 66, 100

Nahum
1.13 186

Habakkuk
3.3 145

Zephaniah
1.6 86
1.13 186
3.9 78
3.19-20 145

Haggai
2.3 125
2.9 125
2.11-13 101
2.13 192
2.23 130

Zechariah
1.3 187
3.1-6 130
4.1-14 130
6.9-15 130
8.8 80
13.9 80

Malachi
2.1-9 101
3.7 187

Matthew
26.28 91

Mark
14.24 91

Luke
22.20 91

John
13.34-35 91

1 Corinthians
11.25 91

2 Corinthians
3.1-18 91

Hebrews
8.6-13 91
9.15 91
12.24 91

1 John
2.8-11 91

INDEX OF AUTHORS

Alter, R. 181
Altschuler, D. 46, 191, 194
Andersen, F.I. 195, 197
Anderson, B.W. 47
Avishur, Y. 131

Bach, R. 92, 186
Baltzer, K. 81
Bamberger, B.J. 194
Barr, J. 187
Berridge, J.M. 28, 60, 136, 148, 181, 188
Binns, L.E. 96
Biram, A. 196
Blank, S.H. 94, 187
Böhmer, S. 16, 17, 29, 41, 58, 63, 93, 111-12, 120, 128, 131, 137, 144, 183, 190
Bright, J. 26, 27, 28, 30, 41, 47, 59-60, 64, 121, 128, 131, 136, 142, 144, 146, 148, 155, 183, 185-88, 190, 193, 199
Brueggemann, W.A. 28, 93, 188
Buber, M. 96
Bultmann, R. 189

Catkins, R. 28, 30
Carley, K.W. 198
Carroll, R.P. 17, 18, 29, 41, 47, 56, 58, 92, 93, 99, 112, 128-29, 136, 137, 146, 181, 185, 190, 192, 194, 196
Cassuto, U. 42, 136, 172, 171-72, 187, 190, 197, 199
Cazelles, H. 124
Cheyne, T.K. 197
Clements, R.E. 190
Cooke, G.A. 198
Coppens, J. 119, 128, 191
Cross, F.M. 69-70

Davies, W.D. 99
Dietrich, E.K. 14, 189
Driver, S.R. 26, 28, 62, 84, 96, 124, 153, 186, 189, 190
Duhm, B. 16, 17, 25, 27, 28, 41, 92, 93, 94, 99, 137, 184, 192, 199

Eichrodt, W. 13-14, 181, 189, 198
Eissfeldt, O. 187-88, 196
Ehrlich, A.B. 181, 197

Fohrer, G. 14, 15, 155
Freedman, D.N. 195, 197
Friedman, R.E. 72, 188

Gelin, A. 191
Giesebrecht, F. 29, 80, 120, 190
Ginsberg, H.L. 154, 165, 166, 196, 197
Goldman, M.D. 41
Gordis, R. 153, 196, 198
Gray, J. 71
Greenberg, M. 18-20, 96, 130, 182, 195, 198-99
Gros, K. 32, 165, 185, 187, 198

Halpern, E. 196, 197
Haran, M. 172-73, 195
Harper, W.R. 153
Harrelson, W.J. 192
Heaton, E.W. 194
Heinemann, I. 189
Held, M. 93
Henderson, E. 30, 185, 186
Hermann, S. 16, 29, 91, 92, 111, 182
Hertzberg, H.W. 28, 30, 135, 136, 190
Heschel, A.J. 176, 184
Hobbs, T.R. 182
Hoffman, Y. 146, 149
Hoffmann, D.Z. 181, 188
Holladay, W.L. 11, 15, 26, 27, 29, 31, 31-32, 47, 56, 119, 128, 135, 181-186, 195
Huffmon, H.B. 189
Hyatt, J.P. 17, 18, 26, 27, 41, 56, 63, 91, 93, 99, 111, 112, 119, 131, 135, 136, 137, 142, 144, 182, 184, 186, 188, 189, 190, 191, 194

Ish-Shalom, M. 195

Jacob, E. 47
Jobling, D. 26, 28-29, 30, 31, 32, 182

Kara, J. 46, 183, 184, 186
Kaufmann, Y. 14, 59, 123-24, 129, 146, 148, 153, 154, 155, 172-73, 177, 181, 182, 187, 188, 192, 193, 194, 197
Kimhi, D. 46, 184, 186, 192, 194, 195, 199
Kuenen, A. 188
Kugel, J.L. 17

Leslie, E.A. 30, 121, 142-43
Levenson, J.D. 70-72, 188
Levinger, J. 15, 187, 193
Lindars, B. 41, 47, 192
Lipinski, E. 46
Lofthouse, W.F. 94, 193
Lohfink, N. 188
Long, B.O. 182, 185, 192
Lundbom, J.R. 47, 185
Luzzatto, S.D. 47, 184, 186

March, W.E. 137-38, 159
Maetens, E.Z. 15, 29, 42, 64, 85, 112, 124, 128, 129, 131, 136, 137, 186, 189, 190
May, H.G. 26, 56
Mays, J.L. 158, 189, 192
McCarthy, D.J. 189
McKane, W. 17, 182
McKay, J.W. 189
McKenzie, J.L. 128, 185, 189, 199
Milgrom, J. 15, 16, 20, 143-44, 181, 193, 196, 197
Miller, J.W. 26, 129, 167, 198, 199
Morag, S. 131, 182
Moran, W.L. 189
Mowinckel, S. 16, 26, 27, 30, 41, 59, 91, 120, 182, 183
Muilenburg, J. 199
Muffs, Y. 80

Nelson, R.E. 205
Nicholson, E.W. 16, 17, 47, 56-58, 63, 91-93, 111, 112, 119, 128, 131, 135, 136, 137, 142, 144, 146, 147, 185, 186, 189, 194
Noth, M. 68

Orelli, K. von 47, 184, 185, 187
Ostborn, G. 99, 192

Paul, S. 42, 172, 199
Petuchowski, J.J. 181
Pfeiffer, R.H. 29
Pohlmann, K.-F. 58, 196
Procksch, O. 158

Rad, G. von 14, 68, 69, 73, 112, 115, 181, 189, 193, 194, 197
Raitt, T.M. 16, 18, 60-61, 64, 66, 80, 93, 112, 121-23, 128, 131, 144, 167-68, 181, 184, 188, 189, 194
Rofe, A. 182
Rowley, H.H. 188
Rudolph, W. 27-31, 41, 47, 59, 75, 84, 91, 92, 112, 121, 128, 131, 135, 136, 137, 142, 144, 146, 158, 187, 188, 191, 193, 194

Sakenfeld, K. 185, 186
Segal, M.Z. 146, 196
Scott, R.B.Y. 189
Seidl, T. 63
Skinner, J. 25, 26, 27, 30, 41, 58, 91, 99, 120, 184, 190
Smend, R. 80
Smith, G.A. 190, 196
Spencer, A.B. 195
Streane, A.W. 27, 31, 62, 84, 99, 120, 126, 128, 184, 186, 188, 190, 195

Tadmor, H. 154
Talmon, S. 183, 195
Thiel, W. 16, 17, 26, 27, 28, 29, 58, 120, 128, 182
Thompson, J.A. 16, 125, 131, 136, 146, 148, 196
Torrey, C.C. 31
Tov, E. 46, 195
Trible, P. 47, 187
Tur-Sinai, N.H. 96

Unterman, J. 61, 110, 186, 196

de Vaux, R. 192
Volz, P. 26, 27, 28, 30, 31, 62, 91, 112, 120-21, 128, 135, 137, 142, 144, 184, 185, 187, 188, 189, 194

Wagner, S. 86
Ward, J.M. 195, 196, 197, 198

Weinfeld, M. 26, 30, 63, 77, 80, 124-25, 126, 129, 130, 143, 183, 188, 189, 190, 192, 194, 195
Weippert, H. 192, 194
Weiser, A. 29, 47, 124, 128, 136, 144, 158, 183, 186
Weiss, M. 19, 20, 96, 182, 190, 191-192
Welch, A.C. 26, 28, 30, 58-59, 62-63, 91, 93, 120, 137, 142-43, 184, 194
Wellhausen, J. 71, 152-53, 196
Westermann, C. 199
Wevers, J.W. 198
Weisel, E. 190
Wolff, H.W. 14-15, 68-69, 153, 155, 158, 189, 196, 197, 198

Yellin, D. 184

Zeiner, G. 47
Zevit, Z. 194
Zimmerli, W. 198

JOURNAL FOR THE STUDY OF THE OLD TESTAMENT
Supplement Series

1 I, HE, WE AND THEY:
A LITERARY APPROACH TO ISAIAH 53
D.J.A. Clines

*2 JEWISH EXEGESIS OF THE BOOK OF RUTH
D.R.G. Beattie

*3 THE LITERARY STRUCTURE OF PSALM 2
P. Auffret

4 THANKSGIVING FOR A LIBERATED PROPHET:
AN INTERPRETATION OF ISAIAH CHAPTER 53
R.N. Whybray

5 REDATING THE EXODUS AND CONQUEST
J.J. Bimson

6 THE STORY OF KING DAVID:
GENRE AND INTERPRETATION
D.M. Gunn

7 THE SENSE OF BIBLICAL NARRATIVE I:
STRUCTURAL ANALYSES IN THE HEBREW BIBLE (2nd edition)
D. Jobling

*8 GENESIS 1-11: STUDIES IN STRUCTURE AND THEME
P.D. Miller

*9 YAHWEH AS PROSECUTOR AND JUDGE:
AN INVESTIGATION OF THE PROPHETIC LAWSUIT (RIB PATTERN)
K. Nielsen

10 THE THEME OF THE PENTATEUCH
D.J.A. Clines

*11 STUDIA BIBLICA 1978 I:
PAPERS ON OLD TESTAMENT AND RELATED THEMES
Edited by E.A. Livingstone

12 THE JUST KING:
MONARCHICAL JUDICIAL AUTHORITY IN ANCIENT ISRAEL
K.W. Whitelam

13 ISAIAH AND THE DELIVERANCE OF JERUSALEM:
A STUDY OF THE INTERPRETATION OF PROPHECY
IN THE OLD TESTAMENT
R.E. Clements

14 THE FATE OF KING SAUL:
AN INTERPRETATION OF A BIBLICAL STORY
D.M. Gunn

15 THE DEUTERONOMISTIC HISTORY
M. Noth

16 PROPHECY AND ETHICS:
ISAIAH AND THE ETHICAL TRADITIONS OF ISRAEL
E.W. Davies

17 THE ROLES OF ISRAEL'S PROPHETS
D.L. Petersen

18 THE DOUBLE REDACTION OF THE DEUTERONOMISTIC HISTORY
R.D.Nelson

19 ART AND MEANING: RHETORIC IN BIBLICAL LITERATURE
Edited by D.J.A. Clines, D.M. Gunn, & A.J. Hauser

20 THE PSALMS OF THE SONS OF KORAH
M.D. Goulder

21 COLOUR TERMS IN THE OLD TESTAMENT
A. Brenner

22 AT THE MOUNTAIN OF GOD:
STORY AND THEOLOGY IN EXODUS 32–34
R.W.L. Moberly

23 THE GLORY OF ISRAEL:
THE THEOLOGY AND PROVENIENCE OF THE ISAIAH TARGUM
B.D. Chilton

24 MIDIAN, MOAB AND EDOM:
THE HISTORY AND ARCHAEOLOGY OF LATE BRONZE AND IRON AGE JORDAN AND NORTH-WEST ARABIA
Edited by J.F.A. Sawyer & D.J.A Clines

25 THE DAMASCUS COVENANT:
AN INTERPRETATION OF THE 'DAMASCUS DOCUMENT'
P.R. Davies

26 CLASSICAL HEBREW POETRY:
A GUIDE TO ITS TECHNIQUES
W.G.E. Watson

27 PSALMODY AND PROPHECY
W.H. Bellinger

28 HOSEA: AN ISRAELITE PROPHET IN JUDEAN PERSPECTIVE
G.I. Emmerson

29 EXEGESIS AT QUMRAN:
4QFLORILEGIUM IN ITS JEWISH CONTEXT
G.J. Brooke

30 THE ESTHER SCROLL: THE STORY OF THE STORY
D.J.A. Clines

31 IN THE SHELTER OF ELYON:
ESSAYS IN HONOR OF G.W. AHLSTRÖM
Edited by W.B. Barrick & J.R. Spencer

32 THE PROPHETIC PERSONA:
JEREMIAH AND THE LANGUAGE OF THE SELF
T. Polk

33 LAW AND THEOLOGY IN DEUTERONOMY
J.G. McConville

34 THE TEMPLE SCROLL:
AN INTRODUCTION, TRANSLATION AND COMMENTARY
J. Maier

35 SAGA, LEGEND, TALE, NOVELLA, FABLE:
NARRATIVE FORMS IN OLD TESTAMENT LITERATURE
Edited by G.W. Coats

36 THE SONG OF FOURTEEN SONGS
M.D. Goulder

37 UNDERSTANDING THE WORD:
ESSAYS IN HONOR OF BERNHARD W. ANDERSON
Edited by J.T. Butler, E.W. Conrad & B.C. Ollenburger

38 SLEEP, DIVINE AND HUMAN, IN THE OLD TESTAMENT
T.H. McAlpine

39 THE SENSE OF BIBLICAL NARRATIVE II:
STRUCTURAL ANALYSES IN THE HEBREW BIBLE
D. Jobling

40 DIRECTIONS IN BIBLICAL HEBREW POETRY
Edited by E.R. Follis

41 ZION, THE CITY OF THE GREAT KING:
A THEOLOGICAL SYMBOL OF THE JERUSALEM CULT
B.C. Ollenburger

42 A WORD IN SEASON: ESSAYS IN HONOUR OF WILLIAM McKANE
Edited by J.D. Martin & P.R. Davies

43 THE CULT OF MOLEK:
A REASSESSMENT
G.C. Heider

44 THE IDENTITY OF THE INDIVIDUAL IN THE PSALMS
S.J.L. Croft

45 THE CONFESSIONS OF JEREMIAH IN CONTEXT:
SCENES OF PROPHETIC DRAMA
A.R. Diamond

46 THE BOOK OF THE JUDGES: AN INTEGRATED READING
B.G. Webb

47 THE GREEK TEXT OF JEREMIAH:
A REVISED HYPOTHESIS
S. Soderlund

48 TEXT AND CONTEXT:
OLD TESTAMENT AND SEMITIC STUDIES FOR F.C. FENSHAM
Edited by W. Claassen

49 THEOPHORIC PERSONAL NAMES IN ANCIENT HEBREW
J.D. Fowler

50 THE CHRONICLER'S HISTORY
M. Noth

51 DIVINE INITIATIVE AND HUMAN RESPONSE IN EZEKIEL
P. Joyce

52 THE CONFLICT OF FAITH AND EXPERIENCE IN THE PSALMS:
A FORM-CRITICAL AND THEOLOGICAL STUDY
C.C. Broyles

53 THE MAKING OF THE PENTATEUCH:
A METHODOLOGICAL STUDY
R.N. Whybray

54 FROM REPENTANCE TO REDEMPTION:
JEREMIAH'S THOUGHT IN TRANSITION
J. Unterman

55 THE ORIGIN TRADITION OF ANCIENT ISRAEL:
THE LITERARY FORMATION OF GENESIS AND EXODUS 1–23
T.L. Thompson

56 THE PURIFICATION OFFERING IN THE PRIESTLY LITERATURE:
ITS MEANING AND FUNCTION
N. Kiuchi

57 MOSES: HEROIC MAN, MAN OF GOD
G.W. Coats

58 THE LISTENING HEART: ESSAYS IN WISDOM AND THE PSALMS
IN HONOR OF ROLAND E. MURPHY, O. CARM.
Edited by K.G. Hoglund

59 CREATIVE BIBLICAL EXEGESIS:
CHRISTIAN AND JEWISH HERMENEUTICS THROUGH THE CENTURIES
B. Uffenheimer & H.G. Reventlow

60 HER PRICE IS BEYOND RUBIES:
THE JEWISH WOMAN IN GRAECO-ROMAN PALESTINE
L.J. Archer

* Out of print